The Joy Boy's DAUGHTER

An Honest, True Life Story of Great Triumphs
and Unbearable Heartaches

EDIE LYNCH

ISBN 978-1-967361-86-1 (Paperback)
ISBN 978-1-967361-87-8 (Ebook)

Inquiries and Book Orders should be addressed to:

Leavitt Peak Press
17901 Pioneer Blvd Ste L #298, Artesia, California 90701
Phone #: 2092191548

Letter from reader

Dear Ms. Lynch,

I recently had the profound experience of reading your memoir, The Joy Boy's Daughter, and I felt compelled to reach out and express my deep appreciation for your candid storytelling.

Your narrative, spanning six generations, offers an intimate glimpse into the triumphs and tribulations that have shaped your family's legacy. From the poignant tale of your grandmother Josie, born of a white doctor and his enslaved partner, to you own multifaceted journey as a model, film director, jeweler, and educator, each chapter resonates with authenticity and depth.

The challenges you faced—navigating personal hardships such as your husband's departure, your son's illness, and the heart-wrenching search for your missing grandson—are conveyed with a raw honesty that is both heartrending and inspiring. Your resilience in the face of adversity serves as a testament to the strength of the human spirit.

Moreover, your dedication to teaching homeless and underprivileged children the solace found in the Creative Arts underscores a profound commitment to uplifting others, reflecting the enduring power of compassion and creativity.

Thank you for sharing your life's journey with such openness. Your memoir not only enriches the reader's understanding of personal and collective history but also serves as an inspiration to persevere with grace and determination.

Warm regards,

Alexis Stratton

CONTENTS

DEDICATION

For Marcia, the angel that helps all the homeless and orphan children that I love at the Amar Shelter in Vila Isabel in Rio de Janeiro.

Especially for Georgie, Daniel, Gabriella, David, Reginaldo, and Mateus. For all of the Creative Find Children that are dear to my heart in New York City and to Claudia Fleming. Special thanks to **Ruth Battle**, and **Eileen Wolfe**, who reached out to me in so many real ways to assist me in helping the children.

To the kids I met and taught how to paint and sculpt on the street in Rio de Janeiro, Eduardo, Renan, Wallace, Alexander, Thiago, Joao, Andrea, Rodrigo, Raphael, Maryanna, and so many others. To Moses who so deserves a better life. To Quentin Stovall, a precious life.

To the friends who were gracious to me in my journey to find my footing again, especially Jeri Thomas, Reuben Cannon, Dr. Dominick Bioh, Leslie King, Elisete Alves Pasquale, Irving Burgie, Cobi Narita Ash, Deborah Willis-Ryan, Atty. Ira Cure, Susan and George Grgich.

To Rhunette Terrasson, a treasured life-long friend. To Mike & Helen Barry, Monique Serres, Edwina Meyers, Phillip Petrucci, Elaine Magenheim, Sonja Kemp & Hubby, Eve Rose, Goldie, Dorothy, Brittany's Mom, Mwanza's Parents, Tamilla's Mom, Kameeka Williams, Stacey Glass, Donna DiNucci, Vandre Talita, Joanne Paulsen, Barbara Marsten, LaShonda Katrice Barnett and Rhonda Kendrick who loved Abbey, all the members of Abbey Lincoln's Band: Rodney Kendrick, Kenny Baron, Marc Cary. Michael Bowie, Billy Johnson, Alvester Garnett, Jaz Sawyer and Luke Carlos O'Reilly, Kelly Ewins, Alaina Foster, Marilyn & James Cooper and so many other extraordinary people. To amazing composers and pianists RB Lynch and Jacky Terrasson and to Holly's gifted son, "Kyteman" Colin Benders. To drummer Aaron Walker and trumpeter Kenyatta Beasely. To Lynne Charnay, Tyra, Mary, Laura, and Autumn who sang RB's songs. To Todd Young, for his mother Gail's song. To Jose Serra Vega, who was my bus partner along the tree lined terrain of the South and to Anne-Marie Hibbert who appeared on the cover of my book, With Glory I So Humbly Stand. To Ernest Miller, James, and Jimmie Smith, Harlem artist friends. To friends who helped me in Rio: Suely Kise. Claudio Zatara, Johann Heyess. and Andre Navarro. To Tahir Amin & Priti Radhakrishn whose foundation I-MAK does such important humanitarian work. To Dr Craig Thomas, Wendy Marie Thomas, Xavi Menos, Laura Thies, Beata Szpura, Tom Sullivan, Tokumbo Bodunde, Lauren Cox, Duvall Osteen, Rose Marie Armstrong, Mozella Holder, Andrea Adonis at IUniverse, Regina Huber, Doris McCarthy, Lisa White and Ingrid Nicholas who brought light along the darkened paths. To Al Perlmutter, Fred Barzyk, Donna McKechnie, Sharon Miller, Joy Weber, Leon Morenzie, Edie Cuminale, Susan Smith who made me laugh when I was working with them on enjoyable projects. To my brother Jerry, Melba, Lorraine, Tina, Suzanne, Mitzi, Jill, Jane, Joan, Roonie, Jacques, Pam, Linda, Holly, Jacky, Francois, Natalie, Art, & Suzette. I wish you Peace.

To Dr. Suki Han, Dr. Rosa Lee Smith, Dr. Sergio Levcovitz, Dr. Pedro Rodrigues, and Dr. Italo Marsili who gave me critical spiritual support when I needed it most. To Yasmine Omar, Tracy Johnson, Maria Puglisi, Nancy Wei, Ellen Starr, a great singer. To Viola Wright, Karen Zebulon, and Jason Bennett, a terrific editor. To Ron Carlton, Aunt Helen, Joy & Patty. To Connie & Audrey Lynch & Suzanne. To Aunt Gerry's Sandra. To Rinaldo & Miriam in Muriqui. To Art, Jean & Sybila and all cousins and nieces and nephews. For Dr. & Mrs. DeMaio, Roberta & Michael Wolf, Josh & Rebecca and all my friends on 79th street where I did so much important work. To Bert Childs Jones, Verna Edwards, Daniel Kennedy, James Warden, Dr. R. Davis, Rosamond, Monica from Spain, Sally and Jude from Australia, Thomas from Germany, Zaven from Turkey who gave me warm hearted encouragement. To friends in Rio; Bia Wilcox. Luciane Carneiro, Wilma & Arthur, and Altair & Heloisa. To Tracey Gourdine and to Susan Saandholland who reached out to me in remembrance of Meredith Gourdine and Anne Spencer, amazing creative spirits. To Ryan Robinson and Caroline Jones at Springdale Glen. To my friends Sarabeth Levine, Barbara Lapcek, Cobi Narita Ash, and Arden Shelton who appeared in my video *Well Made Woman and shared with the world the riveting stories of their lives, of starting over minus husbands and money and rising to the top of their professions.*

To Frank Macri and John Carter. To Michael Cohen, Peter Lucas, Richard Wolff, Robert Berkman, William Crow, Shari Goodweather Kessler, Joan Schuman, Michelle Materre, Peter Haratonik at The New School. To Freddy and Mercedes at State Farm, Frank Cantania at Santini Brothers and Justin (a kind roommate) who were compassionate to me when times were hard. To old friends, Al Brown, Irving Burgie, Gino Giglio and Owen Brown, and Adger Cowans. To Tony, Betty, Robin, Greer, Carol, and Peter Gilbert.

To the ones who are always in my heart, Leandro, Daniel, Georgie and Marcie and her family who I pray will stay safe. To all of the kind staff and drivers at Amar. To my beloved son RB Lynch for the beautiful music he composes, and to his beloved Dayan. To my daughter Wendy Lynch for whom I am grateful to be reunited with, and for Cary, her son, for whom I pray for each and every day to embrace the magic he was born with. To the Creative Find Kids, Kayon, Lakeisha, Marquitta, Shaquille, Tamilla, Mwanza, Christina, Asia, Ashina, Brittany, Daryl, Julian, Sterling, Miles, Daphyne, Daphera, Candace, Devon, Shakia, Timmy, Maurice, Omar and so many others, know that though you are now grown, I always wish great success and happiness for you.

My deepest prayers shall always be for those who struggle to find a safe pathway back to a life that has dignity and love.

To my friends Heloisa whose generosity to RB is heartwarming, to Pami whose spiritual knowledge brings much light, and to Gennady Osmerkin, I say *Thank you with all my heart for all that you have done for me.* And to Kathi Wittkamper at IUniverse for encouraging me to continue to write, especially to write books for children.

To those of you that have gone on to your eternal life, know dearest, loving friends, that I miss you so much. You are not forgotten Jan Oberteuffer Holt, Abbey Lincoln, Cristina Fonseca, and Jacqueline Stovall. To those of you that brought real friendship to my life, Steven Macri, Bill Hickey, Steve Richey, Cathryn Damon, Richard Monica, Gordon Parks, Cobi's Paul Ash, Lou Jefferson, Gerald Purcell, Nat King Cole, Calvin Lockhart, Peter Boyle, Dame Margot Fonteyn, Lloyd Richards, George Stoney, Kurt Vonnegut, David Loxton, Jim Lewis, Robert Duncan, Morley Safer, Roger Grimsby, Yvonne Warden, Kirk Kirksey, Shirleen Green, Meredith Gourdine, George Obertynski, Nien Cheng who wrote the poignant, Life and Death in Shanghai, and Sergio Viera de Mello, an unforgettable UN Human Rights Activist. And, heartfelt remembrances for Mr. Arpad Fekete who showed me the beautiful, enduring spirit of the human being despite having suffered unspeakable misfortunes. To my Mama and my Daddy, to Poppa, to Granny, to my siblings; Jackie, Gail, Michael, Reggie, Jerry and to beloved aunts, Geraldine, Sadie, Ruby, Stella, Elizabeth and Julia. To Mike Cimino, a kind and gifted director to work with – To Rina de Firenze's beloved son. To all who lost their lives and dreams in the tragedy of 9/11.

To Toussaint L'Ouverture, Dr. Martin Luther King, Jr., President Barack and Michelle Obama, Dr. Lonnie Bunch, and Oprah Winfrey. Thank you for the wisdom you brought to us. God Bless The National Museum of African American History and Culture.

To dear Wallace, a lovely young homeless Brazilian artist shot by the police, who lost his fight to paint his artwork on the streets of Rio. Know that you and the birds that you painted, Wallace, will always be in my heart. I do hear so many special tweets around me, most likely coming from you and your feathered friends. To all of my dear, dear souls up there, please send rainbows to all of us who struggle to keep our beauty and grace Down Here Below, as Abbey Lincoln sang on her gorgeous CD.

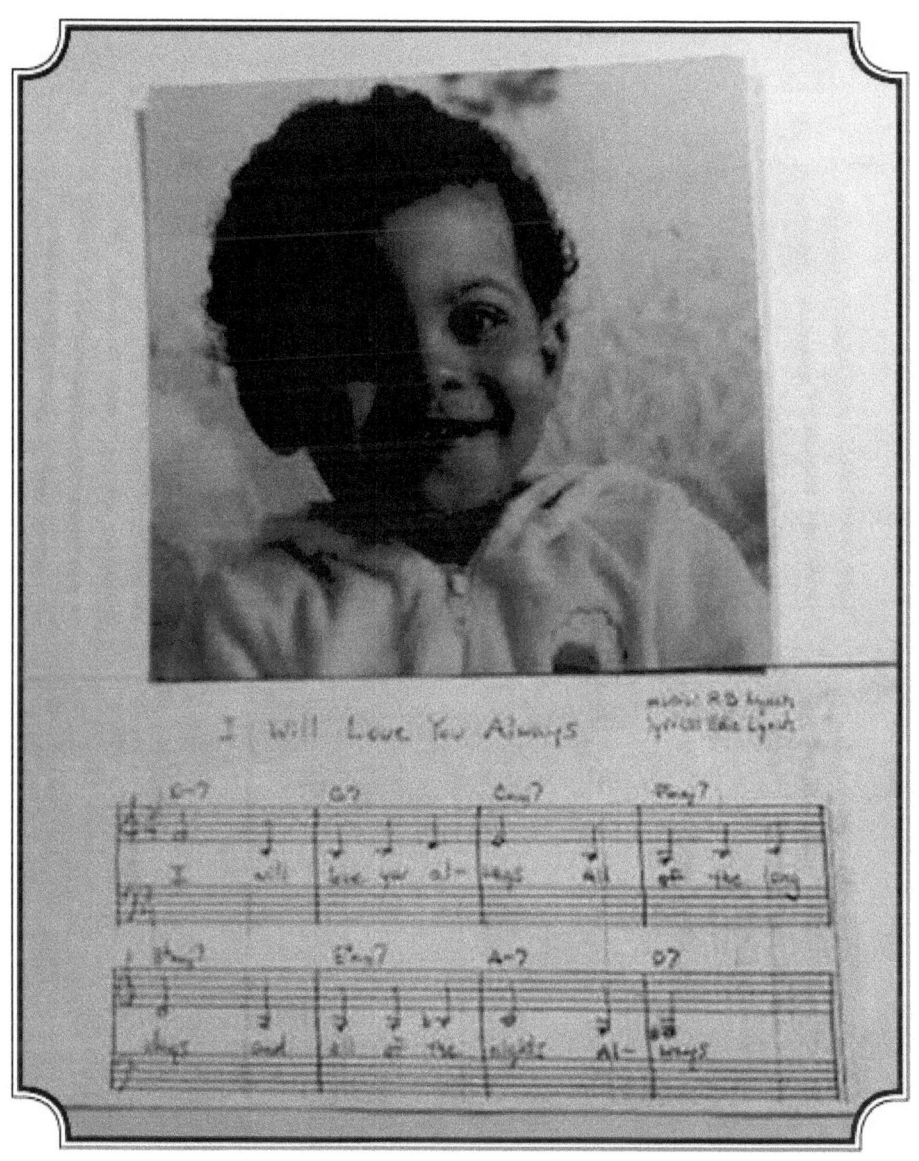

*To Cary, my grandson and to RB, and to Wendy, my
daughter and Dr. Sergio May much joy come to you*

INTRODUCTION

I always felt that I was destined to tell my story. From the time that I was a five-year-old child I was smitten when I met a new person with where that person had been, how they had come to be where they were, and what they would do if they could do anything they wanted to do.

My daddy's mother, my beloved Granny, would allow me on occasion to go deep into her cellar where she stored all of the treasures that she had brought with her from the South. There were big old hoop skirt frames, enormous iron kettles, delicate lace collars, and tiny flat irons that one had to heat up on a bed of hot coals. I was fascinated with these relics and I would take a hoop out of its handmade cloth covering, fasten it around my waist, and dance around that dark and musty cellar.

I imagined that I was in a grand ballroom dress, my visions of grandeur boosted by the fact that I sometimes got to see and hear Duke Ellington, Count Basie, and Cab Calloway rehearse their orchestrations at my daddy's nightclub, the Cosmopolitan Club in Akron, Ohio. It was the only club of its kind in our town and though racism in the early forties was alive and prospering, many Whites would come to see beautiful Lena Horne or Billie Holiday and other elegantly dressed lady singers who appeared with the big bands that were so popular then. Even one of my White teachers who was an alcoholic would come to my Daddy's club and sit in the front row and have dinner and later, at school, she would allow me to skip examinations and even grade other students' papers. Not only did I get the short end of the stick per my studies, but so did my poor classmates who were expecting a fair grade.

I was always enthusiastic about doing something out of the box, so to speak. I wasn't a great team player and it was difficult growing up around seven robust siblings. I remember that on one particular Sunday, all of my brothers and sisters had gone on a drive with my Granny and my Daddy and I had stayed at Granny's house to be with Poppa. I was down in the cellar rummaging through carefully marked cloth wrappings of things Granny had brought with her from Alabama where she spent the first part of her life working in the cotton fields or up in the Big House with her mother Missy.

Poppa called down to me to straighten up everything "right smart" and to come and help him with the dishes. I was drying dishes and Poppa handed me his towel. I told Poppa I had my own towel and Poppa laughed and started to speak, and then he fell out on the kitchen floor. I thought Poppa was playing a game so I threw my towel over his face, but Poppa didn't answer when I took the towel off. I ran over to Mrs. Rose's house:

"Mrs. Rose, Mrs. Rose, Poppa won't get up off the floor to finish the dishes."

Mrs. Rose and her husband were very calm and efficient and managed to get Poppa upstairs. The doctor came and left many times while Granny maintained a vigil beside Poppa's bed for five nights. Despite my Granny Josie's fervent prayers over her bible, Poppa did not make it. Poppa's casket went into the living room and for two days, dozens of important dignitaries and townspeople said their goodbyes to my Poppa, who owned and operated the Brooks Grille on North Howard Street, a hugely popular restaurant frequented by Blacks and Whites.

I sat beside Poppa's polished mahogany casket and though I didn't like all of those strong smelling flowers and Poppa's dark suit (he mostly wore light grey ones with faint pin stripes) I wasn't afraid of him. After all, it was Poppa. When I was sure no one was looking at me I slipped into the lining of Poppa's casket a little picture book he always read to me to keep him company in heaven. I whispered to him:

"One day, Poppa, I'll write my own book and it will be about you." "Young'un, what you doin' disturbing your Poppa's casket?" I hadn't realized that anyone had seen me with the book.

"I am just giving Poppa my book to keep him company in heaven," I said.

"Oh young'un, your Poppa was right smart but he never learned to read, Granny said. *You had best be keeping that book for yourself."*

I was stunned to find out from Granny that Poppa was only pretending that he could read. He was so animated when he told me the stories from the book. Poppa had always worked so hard but he always had time for me. Before Poppa had come North he had once lived on a 200-acre farm in Troy Alabama and raised hogs, mules, and horses. After a while, he had taken his family from the farm to a house on a 3-acre lot and started a grocery business in a little cottage on the side of the house. And then Poppa opened up a restaurant in downtown Troy where his customers were both Black and White, but they ate on different sides of the restaurant.

And so it was, that this grandfather that I had loved so much, was gone in a flash. I was left with this yearning to know so much more about him. He was the one to whom I could tell all of my little secrets, the one that I could count on the most. I began to ask questions of my Granny about her and Poppa's life in the South, about what had prompted them to move up North. I was always storing away events and facts and my own musings about everything in my head. I knew that all that I was seeing and hearing would be important one day even if I didn't realize why.

Late at night Mama would always shout out to me in my attic room that I shared with my three sisters:

"Turn off that flashlight, and put away your writings. Go to sleep right now or you are in trouble young lady."

It didn't matter if I was ten, fourteen, or even a senior in high school, I was always in trouble with Mama. She just felt she ought to police my penchant for writing out my thoughts on scraps of paper, or limit my sculpting time (another piece of junk my Mama would say) or stop me from practicing my ballet. I felt such an urge to get on with my life, to remember the important things but I knew I had to be patient about the things I could not change, namely Mama.

My Daddy used to laugh and call me Raggedy Ann sometimes because if I was engrossed in a project I was drawn to, I would literally forget to comb my hair or take off my ballet slippers.

"Why can't I just wear my pink dancing shoes," I would ask Mama. *"Is it so important what other people think of me?"*

I wanted to read everything I could. I was concerned about the world. The diaries that people kept were intriguing to me. Years later, I realized that the year my grandfather died Anne Frank was hiding out in an attic in Amsterdam and that her very life depended upon so many people keeping her family's secret. Sadly, Anne Frank lost her fight to stay alive during World War II. All I wanted when I was a young teen was to wear a simple pair of ballet shoes, shoes that helped me to feel close to other kindred spirits in the universe. Why did one parent, my Daddy give me free reign to be who I was, while Mama wanted to control every breath I took? I loved my mother but her possessive nature frustrated me. I wanted to shout at her:

"So what if I am reading another story about someone else's life, someone in another country, so what?"

But Mama was concerned about what was happening in her own household. After all, she had eight lives to look after, eight children to route safely through each day, and my Daddy was rarely home. He would come home at four or five in the morning after his Clubs had closed but it was only to sleep for a few hours. I really understood my mother's many tasks but, still, her stern attitude was exasperating. Sometimes, I would count the years I had under my Mama's control and I would force myself to relax and tell myself that I could make it, that Mama only wanted to keep us all safe.

My Daddy, on the other hand, was a free spirit, allowing me to live out my creative urges without any interference on his part. He had an artistic nature and painted his own detailed signs advertising the big bands he featured at his nightclub establishment, The Cosmopolitan Club. I remember distinctly in 1949, I was ten years old, and my Daddy was having a heated dispute with his sister, my Aunt Sadie, over a Louis Jordan Contract. Aunt Sadie handled the booking details for the shows and Jordan had contracted to do a show for $1250.00, claiming 60% of the gross receipts. Aunt Sadie mentioned to my Daddy that if Jordan got called to Hollywood for a movie that the $1250.00 would be lost. Well, my Daddy had a tantrum, grabbed the contract, read its contents feverously, and suddenly the tantrum disappeared. Daddy said:

"It says right here that Jordan must give in writing four weeks prior to the concert notice of such cancellation. We are good because we've only got two weeks until the concert. But it's cash before they play, so drop the price from $1.75 to $1.50 for the ladies if they buy in advance, and run the spot on the radio."

I was very curious about ticket prices because I was always writing little plays for my family, friends, and neighbors to attend and I wanted to know if I could charge for my performances. My Daddy chuckled and told me he would think about me charging for tickets to my productions in the garage and offered to take me with him because he had to go to the printer to order more flyers and more posters for his Louis Jordan dance, featuring a seven-piece band at The East Market Gardens. How I wished then that I had a current play I was planning to put up so I, too, could get a poster to promote it.

I knew that I wanted to be an entrepreneur of some sort when I grew up and despite my penchant for letting myself go when I was busy concocting my junk as my Mama often said about my varied creations, I loved dressing beautifully and keeping an exquisite home environment. I would be the one in the family putting rose petals around each dinner plate or a spray of lilacs near each dessert plate. Never would I let lovely garments be eaten by moths as happened to Mama's clothes or let dust gather on charming evening gowns. Mama gathered things for show and a very rare evening out, and she was quite happy to putter around in an old shirt in her backyard.

Me, I wanted to see the world, live every moment, be as beautiful as I could be. If others appreciate me, good. Looking a certain way for other people's sake was never a priority for me. I wanted to have an "Excelsior" life, and I wanted always to give back to the world community. I cared about the orphans in the world. I cared about the wars raging everywhere. I was conceived at a time when the beginnings and rumblings of the second world war were going on. I seemed always to feel the unrest in the world even though I lived in a relatively sheltered environment.

My Granny's stories of how her grandmother was sold on the auction block for fifty cents affected me deeply and I held that story close to my heart all my life, knowing that someday I would do something with it. When Margaret Mitchell's film, "Gone with the Wind" came out – even though it was a story told from the perspective of White Southerners – I was moved because I could appreciate the shocking losses suffered on both sides of the racial spectrum. After all, I was the grandchild of Granny whose only remembrance of her father was that he was a rich White doctor that had once given her a pair of little red shoes in the cotton fields of Alabama where her mother toiled as a slave and unwilling mistress to this uncaring man.

As a teen I pondered over the Harriet Tubman Underground Railroad stories and spent many a somber hour over those sad and poignant reminiscences. I cried when I read Alexandre Dumas fils, "Camille," about a Parisian courtesan who must choose between the young man who loves her and the callous baron who wants her. Although I was surely not a courtesan, I had to choose between a doctor I loved with all my heart and the corrupt but rich life he chose to embrace or a frugal life where I kept my honor. I chose the frugal life but it came with more heartaches than the life I walked away from.

When I had lost about everything I cared about and was struggling to attain two Masters Degrees in Media Studies and International Affairs at The New School so I could regain some stability in my life, I was introduced by Professor Peter Lucas to Forough Farokhzad's film "The House Is Black." In that film, I saw visions of pain that no human being should ignore. I realized fully why I had chosen to work with at-risk children in Harlem and homeless children in Rio de Janeiro. Human beings feel pain, whether clearly visible on their bodies or hidden with the masks that people wear to try to navigate through society. Pain is so very real and we all need to reach out to others to help them through trying times. It is okay to care.

I have always hated wars and the awful things it does to people all over the world. We must work to change the way society is constructed if there is to be a possibility that human beings everywhere can experience a decent and just life. We must rid the world of nuclear threats. We must stand shoulder to shoulder, human to human, and strive earnestly to be kinder to one another, to change the way we think.

To understand what happened to us all in this out of control world, I have included at the end of this book my son RB Lynch's paper, "The Creation of the Atom Bomb." Though my son is a brilliant composer now, at one time in his life the universe allowed him a profound revelation. RB wrote about it and Daniel Ellsberg who exposed the Pentagon Papers - who was my son's professor at Stanford University - said of RB's paper:

"Outstanding work. You have put very expressive powers of intellect and judgment to work on a profoundly important subject. This deserves publication. I don't know a better paper on the subject. It's very gratifying to have a paper of this quality come out of this session. Good luck. Dan."

The world is even more stressful today than it was in the eighties when my son wrote his paper that garnered such praise. That literally means that we all have to try so much harder to do individually all that we can do to bring about peace. The United States, North Korea, Russia, India, Israel, France, China, The United Kingdom and Pakistan need to shut down all nuclear weapon operations - and all countries that are planning to have nuclear weapons need to close shop, to shut down. Our technological world is anti-human. It must take another course to insure that our children and grandchildren will survive.

We all need to pause, take a breath, and create some quiet time, some real silence so we can think. We need to stop worrying about making our mark in the world instantaneously. We should look at our accomplishments in increments of decades, not months, not individual years. I had so many interests that I could not really appreciate what exactly I did. Gordon Parks, my dear friend, helped me to see that in my young adulthood I had been a model. I had then moved on in the next decade to become a serious photographer.

In the third decade of my work life, I had studied and become a filmmaker and a jeweler. And in the fourth decade I reflected and used all of my previous experience to start a non-profit that helped at-risk children in the U.S. and in Brazil.

Finally, in the past few years I have taken the time to write about my experiences. We are all much too hard on ourselves, but we cannot afford to relax or be derelict in our duties to the world community. We need to incorporate in our daily lives a healthy dose of engaging in activities that touch our neighbors lives whether they are in our own community or afar, in other countries. The world deserves all of the goodness we can put in it. Our children and grandchildren deserve the right to grow up and realize their dreams. It is time for all of us to embrace the Arts. The Arts will help to soothe us, help us grow in the right direction.

THE JOY BOY'S DAUGHTER

BY EDIE LYNCH

My love of storytelling came from sitting on an old swing couch as a five-year-old child on my Granny's shingled porch in Ohio, the thick white banisters lined with her pots of pansies and daffodils, daisies and morning glories, listening to her tell me the heart wrenching stories of her childhood as a slave.

It wasn't until I was nearly thirty, that I asked my Granny about her father. Now, she had never mentioned him and this puzzled me. "Oh youngun,' what you gonna stir up that for," she said. "The only thing I remember about my Daddy is that he gave me one little pair of little red shoes. He was a white man. Dr. Graves was his name. I was in the cotton fields playing with Missy, my mama, and he rode up on his big black horse; a horse that was thumpin' his hooves like crazy, and he said, Missy, bring your youngun' over here." "And Missy, she stuck her plow into the ground and she picked me up and brung me over to him. Now, that horse kept thumpin' his hooves in our faces, swelling up all of that dust, and he leaned down with his big white ruffled shirt, and underneath that shirt he took out a little pair of red shoes and he thrust them into my arms and he said, "those shoes are from your Pa." I told him I didn't hardly have a Pa. "Well, you do now," he said.

I saw him from afar after that but he never paid me no more mind. I could show you youngun,' his marker. He had a right smart marker." Marker, I thought. Marker? And he only gave my Granny one pair of red shoes in his life. Marker! If I go back to any Alabama, I won't be looking up his marker.

1

Well, as I said, I did not want to go back to any hills to see the marker of a man that only gave his child one little pair of little red shoes in her entire life - but I was "hooked" on Granny's stories and her unbelievable magnanimous, beautiful spirit. I began there, on that shingled porch, listening intently to my Granny's stories and writing them down to tell others one day. I am relieved that I have gathered the courage to finally tell these stories.

They are not very pretty stories, some of them. In fact, a few are grim. And the story my Granny told of how her mother Missy brought her over to meet her father in the fields of Alabama made me for years have some really explicit dreams about what poor Missy had to actually endure being the slave/mistress of an uncaring White doctor. I knew that each night, three hundred and sixty five times a year, at precisely seven thirty in the evening, my granny, Josie, opened the big black book that served as her buffer against the inescapable inequities of life, and with a Hershey's Almond bar and a wad of chewing tobacco in on one hand, she directed her frail but firm other hand to deftly turning page after page of her care worn bible until satisfied that she had given sufficient homage to the teachings of the scriptures, psalms, and sonnets, all of which she knew by heart. She would spit out the juice of her tobacco and close her eyes for her cat nap, slipping away into a cotton field of memories of her early life in the plantation fields of Troy, Alabama.

Slowly, her neck would make little snapping noises as her head nodded further and further West, and as it made the last big lurching movement, her eyes would fly open and blink with surprise. She was always surprised that she had fallen asleep. On these Sundays when I was with my Granny I would sit patiently on the stool adjacent to her chair, posed with a calm but expectant look, and treating her nap as a mere pause of breath, I would say "Granny, what were you seeing when you closed your eyes?" Granny would finger her tobacco pail with its little blue and white enameled lid and then dutifully break off two more squares of chocolate, placing one on my tongue and the other on hers. The light from the thin white delicate curtains cast a pale glow on our faces and Granny would say, "Oh young'un, you know that I told you that story already. That is the only thing that I know about my Daddy. He was a doctor and he came to the cotton fields that one day, where I was playin,' that's all young'un."

"Evening Missy," my daddy said as he leaned down and touched my Mama Missy's face. "Just came to bring your young'un a pair of shoes." Missy reached up for the little pair of shoes, and he covered her hand with his, saying, "I've been thinking about you Missy," and then he reached past Missy and handed the little red shoes to me. "Go on Granny," I urged, but my Granny just turned her head to the side and lowered her eyes, and little wrinkles furrowed her brow. "There ain't nothing more I can tell you young'un, that's all I know, excepting Missy sent me back to the fields while she stayed standing there with the Doctor. As I ran, scampering across the fields with the pair of little red shoes tucked under my arms I looked back and saw Missy heading toward the barn, to wash up for the dinner she had to fix in The Great House."

A frightful dream visited me in later years as I puzzled over the writings I had documented in my diary about the day that my Granny met her father in the cotton fields of Alabama. In my dream, Missy is washing up quickly in the barn. Missy's owner, the captain and his missus would be expecting their evening tea. Missy removes her soiled frock and begins to work up a thick layer of suds from the laundry soap bar. As she begins to pour the tin of water over her body, a shadow emerges from one of the horse's stalls. At first, Missy thinks the gate has come unlatched which sometimes happens when one of the field hands is too anxious to get on to their shack after a long day in the field, but too soon it is apparent the shadow is a man's figure, naked from the waist down.

Before Missy can even turn off the trickle of water from the spigot the doctor's voice, thick with desire, is all over her. Missy cries and explains that it is a bad time of the month and that she will likely be with a swollen belly if he doesn't wait. The doctor covers her belly with his mammoth hands and says, "Reckon I can afford another pair of shoes." Missy pleads for him to wait so the last field hands coming in with their horses will not see them and the doctor laughs and holds her buttocks with both hands saying, "Poor Missy, always trying to be the lady." With a playful trot he encircles her thighs from the back and leads her up the small ladder to the hay loft. Missy closes her eyes and tries to imagine that she is in a bed, with freshly ironed linen sheets, in a lovely home, and that the thrusting she feels in between her legs is from the pain of a good and hard loving she is sharing with the father of her children.

Missy has never had sex with anyone other than the doctor and for that she is grateful because the pain and swelling and bruises last for many weeks afterwards. The doctor sucks on her breasts, *"titties"* he calls them, and for a good half hour the discomfort she feels is much worse than when she was wet nursing the captain's child and breastfeeding her own Josie at the same time. The doctor grunts and groans and falls into a fitful sleep after he has spewed out his thick semen. After snoring loudly for a good ten minutes, he is all swollen up, big as a yardstick again. Almost frantic, he pumps away, in and out, in and out, forcing Missy to make little shouts and cries, so unable is she to withstand the pain. He yanks her long cascade of hair up into his fist and bites into her mouth with the most piercing kisses. Missy is sure that her lips are going to be eaten away.

She tries hard not to think about the heaviness of this man's inescapable lust, for what good would it do. She is immersed in a life she has not chosen, and one from which it is impossible to escape. If she could think and reason why she must be ravaged in the dirt and hay, she would never kiss the sweet creases of her children's faces. She, like others before her, would go screaming into the night, thoroughly ready and willing for the other life. That heavenly life that she, too, sometimes longs for. Missy is bone fatigued. Utterly exhausted.

The doctor begins eating away at her insides with his lips, lapping at them like a ravenous dog. She feels like she is being slaughtered, but she knows that she was born to survive, to flourish for her children's sake. Someway, somehow she will figure out how to stay strong. Missy closes her eyes and turns her face from his panting, reddening mouth and raises her eyes to the starlight that is beginning to come in through the uneven logged ceiling. The flickering stars quiet her. Their beams pierce her nerve endings and Missy is able to release her burden and embrace the twinkling flutes of lights. For a few seconds his silhouette and hers will be heaven born. There, nothing can hurt her soul. There, her tear stained face is transformed into a mask of hope and serenity.

The doctor moans softly, almost peacefully, and falls to his side. He pulls her over against his thighs and he snuggles up close, stroking her back very gently. He tells Missy that she is very special, that he likes being with her the most, and that always when he makes love he thinks of her. He says he misses her a lot and does not come around more often as it will be too hard to pull himself away. Missy cries then, for oddly enough she feels a tenderness for him at this moment. She understands too well that his face will be etched forever into the faces of her sons and daughter.

She tries not to think about how much the hay and splinters prick her skin and she knows they will leave behind an ugly rash that everyone will see. She pushes away her thoughts about the airless, tiny shack her children live in. Children who will never know a loving touch from their father, a man who will not give them their rightful name or even a decent meal. She thinks of the greasy fatback they eat when good meat is thrown away by the doctor because his family's bellies are full. But Missy knows that she is one of the lucky ones because the doctor has laid real claims on her. No one else must touch her. She has been allowed to keep her children. So many others have not been so lucky. Missy thanks the Lord each and every night. Three hundred and sixty-five nights a year, Missy opens her Bible and thanks God for her children.

"*Missy,*" the captain's voice bellows from the barn door, "*are you in here?*" Missy blushes under the firm grasp of the doctor's hands, and the doctor says matter of factly:

"*Missy's engaged. Can I help you with something?*"

"*No, certainly not, my friend,*" the captain replies. "*Just be sure to close the barn door when you leave.*"

I wake up with a start. I have forgotten to close the barn door. I realize that I don't have a barn and as bits and pieces of this upsetting dream come into focus, I remember that I was thinking about my Granny and why she didn't want to talk any further about the day she met her father in the cotton fields of Alabama. Though Granny may not have known the details of her mother Missy's private life

5

with my Granny's daddy, the doctor, I can certainly imagine what they had been like. I force myself back to that long ago place, my Granny's bedroom.

Josie half mumbles as my face comes into focus. She is only partially awake and her eyes show a startling uneasiness as she tries to regain her bearings.

"You were talking and then you fell asleep, Granny." I say. "Your daddy rode up on his horse and gave you the little red shoes and then you fell asleep,"

"Young'un, my Granny says, you've done stirred up enough trouble for the night."

"Just tell me again, Granny, what Missy looked like," I say.

"Oh young'un, I done told you a hundred times that Missy had almond eyes and thick brows, with cheek bones so high she looked like a statue out of an ancient Egyptian book. She was a little thing but with a full bosom and no more meat on her than she needed to stay alive. But she was strong, like a man. She looked taller than she was because she had the longest, most perfectly formed legs. I bet she could run as fast as a panther."

I laughed whole heartedly, hoping to keep my Granny talking. "And Missy wore hooped skirts, didn't she Granny?"

"No, young'un, Missy didn't wear no hooped skirts. But she ironed plenty of them. She dreamed of wearing silk dresses with hoop skirts, but she mostly wore faded frocks, darned and patched with scraps from here and yonder." Josie smooths and re-smooths the folds of her dress, answering with a thin, faraway voice.

"Don't you hear that whistling, young'un, out there somewhere. That is someone coming to tell sad stories, and that someone ain't gonna be me."

Josie takes off her strand of pearls and lays it carefully on top of the bible. She turns on the small kerosene lamp which she favors over the electric ones and pulls down the shade to the nighttime closing in at her window.

"Now you best be getting on downstairs as your Daddy will be soon coming to take you home," she says.

Oh, how I wanted to hear another of my Granny's noble stories. They help to validate why I feel I have to document my journey through this troubled world. I want to gain some cohesive meaning out of the many tumultuous experiences I have had. I want to try to understand what happened to me and to my family members, some of whom go all the way back to slavery. I go back and forth, through stream of consciousness memories, to events that shaped me and five generations of my family. Yes, the day is here. I have finally organized these stories with the hope that with their telling I can accept that I learned something important that will put me where I want to be. These stories impacted and changed the direction of my life.

People, young and old, have a real need to hear about how one navigates through this *knock em down, get what you want chaotic, greedy nuclear world.* I want to move on with fondness and love, to not be burdened with negative remembrances. My Granny remembered two different worlds, the world during slavery and the world afterwards, and she always managed to hold on to the things that helped her spirit to feel joy and the other stuff she simply left behind. I believe that is what I want to do, to leave a great many things behind. Others have said it better, that it is not what happens to us that defines us but what we do with what happens to us. I want to rid myself of all that discolors my heart, but for the moment I cannot.

I want to strike down all of the framed photographs on my wall. My once perfect little family does not exist any longer. What is the point in displaying those smiling faces that hold such deep and dark secrets, secrets that led to the destruction of a family? Surely it was more than just folly that did us in. Was it a cruel fate that we could not control or were we all so caught up in ourselves that we could not see what was really happening to those that we loved? I want to take my hands and hurl to the ground the smiles that hide the ugliness of what our lives would become. Photographs of perfect family poses of father, mother, son, daughter, and grandson defy the reality that the lightning has struck already and that lightning has shattered the glass frames and seared the souls of those that it tried to protect. Staring from the bedroom walls in this place called Atlanta that I have been unwilling to love, there are the photographs of the handsome

Doctor husband, the artistic Model wife, the gifted Composer son, the brilliant Producer daughter, the gentle Diplomatic grandson. Photographs that represent the tragedies and the triumphs of a family that once thrived.

The tormented Scarlett O'Hara rage that prompted Scarlett to raise her fist to the Heavens to vow that if she had to lie, steal, or cheat, that she (nor any of her family) would ever be hungry again. That cry has died, has died within me. That ballooning rage has sputtered out with a few gasping whimpers and I sit in my stunned stupor, unbelieving that I can actually be facing a future without the means to care for my gifted composer schizophrenic son, to help or even ever like again my beautiful daughter, to find my gentle, abused and long missing grandson, or to forgive my brilliant, gambling, divorced and dead doctor husband. Can it really be that I fought so tirelessly and endured such pain only to reach this dark and desolate road that provides me with no signal as to which way I must direct myself?

There is not one day that I can erase the memory of seeing the husband I had once so dearly loved lying in that crumpled cardboard box in that empty graveside Chapel ready to be tossed down the chute like a foul piece of trash. True, we were divorced, divorced for many years. True he had turned into a brassy caricature of his former Hollywood-like, brilliant, charming self. But it was also true that he was the man I had married when I was a teen. He was the man who was the father of my son and daughter. Perhaps the most hurtful of all, he was the man I had toiled long hours for during the twelve years I had worked two jobs to put him through medical school.

He was also the man whose reputation and career I had fought to save in two criminal trials that rocked the City of Brotherly Love, Philadelphia. But sullied reputations are quickly forgotten when a charismatic, sophisticated doctor falls and is lifted again by faithful patients and followers. As Presidents of countries and Popes are worshipped, there seemed to be no wrong for which Dr. Richard B. Lynch, Jr. could not be forgiven. So why was he lying in a used, flimsy, pitiful box in an empty Chapel with no one in attendance, with his shoes askew? I still find it hard to believe that this man, this father, this Doctor, could have been so betrayed. Betrayed by someone he put all of his trust in – betrayed by his very own daughter. I close my eyes to fight back the tears that still want to pour out screaming, not flowing but screeching, "Why, why did you do this to your father?" The letter I wrote to our daughter - those muddled thoughts will not stop streaming across my mind – those thoughts are always, always there.

"Daughter, there aren't words to express the shock of seeing your father lying in a crumpled cardboard box in the Cemetery's Chapel all alone, lying in a box that was obviously used many other times to transport other unfortunate people. There your father lay, unattended by any person to whom he had so faithfully given his time and energy. Dr. Lynch was laid out in a box with his shoes untied, with no one who had ever known the sound of his laughter to accompany him to the crematorium.

The father that you said you adored, Daughter, lay in a cardboard box, not in a decent casket that could have been rented for an hour. He lay in a Chapel that had one hundred empty seats, forty- nine on each side of the podium and two additional seats against the wall. And, there were no family members or friends there to mourn his passing, not even you who always pretended to be a devoted daughter.

And that other bunch of people who claim that Dr. Lynch is their father and loved one were not there either to bid their benefactor goodbye. Only the little five-year-old boy, who they say is your father's child, could I forgive as he was not responsible for the circumstances of his birth. There was no service, Daughter, just your "lying words" from earlier emails that the service would be short, one hour, and that your brother RB's song would be played, that his words written to his beloved Dad would be read.

You did not even allow an obituary in the paper to tell the world community that Dr. Richard B. Lynch, who practiced medicine for fifty years in the Philadelphia area, whose patients and friends and adversaries all recognized that he was a brilliant diagnostician, the benefit of knowing that he had passed from this earth.

The EVIL that you did Daughter, conspiring to prevent any of Dr. Lynch's friends and patients and colleagues from coming to the cremation service after RB used his rent money to pay for the announcement of his father's passing in the newspapers.

As long as I live, I will never recover from the shock of seeing no one at all to bid your father goodbye…of seeing not one soul in that chapel to shed tears for a man who gave the last thirty years of his life to people who used him just to make money for them… and who could have cared less that Dr. Lynch lay in a crumpled cardboard box, ready to be thrown out like rubbish. SHAME ON YOU DAUGHTER.

I accompanied Dr. Lynch's body, to the shaft that would burn him to ashes. I cried, really cried for him and for his passionate follies. For it was I who remembered that you, Daughter, were his best buddy, that RB and he played tennis and went to Sergio Mendes concerts together. It was I who put him through medical school and built up the medical center practice with him,

It was I who testified for him in his jury trials that won his freedom, it was I who took a bleeding Dr. Lynch out of that little Hospital where they were going to let him die to Hahnemann Hospital where they could save his life. It was I who raced down that expressway in a speeding police van with a dying Dr. Lynch to take him to a Teaching Hospital where they would clamp his ruptured artery and give him fifty- two pints of rare A Negative blood to save his life.

Yes, Daughter, I cried, really cried for a man who had had such a brilliant career and who lay in a cardboard box to be thrown away like trash. I shall never recover from the saddest day of my life.

I tried, and still try to come to terms with what my daughter did. She does not want to be friends with me or to discuss on any level what happened during that time, but she has moved on from sending me vile Emails and calling me every bad name ever muttered from a human's mouth.

My daughter has moved on with her life and purports to believe that her Dad is in constant touch with her as she blesses the photos of him that are over the Urn with his ashes that after two months of sitting in the funeral home, were finally summoned to California to be placed in a revered spot in her home. The ashes are now in

California, where my daughter now celebrates her Dad and mourns her son, our beloved Cal Boy who ran away from her in 2012.

Though my daughter placed dozens of pleas on Twitter to respected newscasters and the California community to help her find her son, he was not found. Oddly, during this time my daughter wrote many disturbing emails to me pretending that her son was with her and that he wished no contact with me, whatsoever, and that I should just abandon my inquiries about him and leave the two of them alone to live their lives. I knew that if I failed to try to find out about the dear little grandson that I loved that great disaster awaited this dear boy. Once, when he was not quite three years old, I had gone to California to help my daughter move into yet another apartment on the grounds of the Polo Club where she resided. She was forever finding fault with everything and she wanted me to decorate a new apartment that was in a spot that was less noisy.

I had taken a taxi from Los Angeles and was traveling on the highway and was several miles from my daughter's new quarters when I saw a toddler walking alone on a very dangerous stretch of the road. Alarmed, I insisted that the driver stop so I could rescue the child. The driver was annoyed and told me that it was none of my business and that it would be foolish to back up on a highway to pick up a strange child. I insisted. When we reached the spot where the child was, I was overcome as I realized the little boy was my actual grandson. He was crying visibly and clutched me around the neck with all his might as I gathered him into my arms.

When we arrived at the polo grounds my little grandson pointed to his seventeen-year-old babysitter sleeping under a big tree. I knocked furiously at my daughter's door and beckoned her to come and see the sitter she had entrusted to watch her son on what was to have been a fun outing on the pastoral grounds and a visit to the stables where my grandson loved to visit the horses. The sitter was still sleeping under the tree and rather than awaken the girl and reprimand her, my daughter started to scream at me and tell me all the awful things she would do to me if I dared to tell the story of her son walking alone on the highway. Needless to say, the babysitter was fired but I wished with all my heart that I could have gotten away from that awful scene, too, but with my grandchild in tow.

I have tried to move on without my daughter, without my beloved grandson that I remember each day by writing a song, or making a drawing of something I think he would enjoy - or just jotting little scribblings of memories we had together a long, long time ago. Perhaps the Universe grabs some of these elusive reflections and sprinkles them near this dear young man. Perhaps, he perceives he is in my heart in a real way but the realness of life just won't let him respond the way he would like to.

Presently, my daughter wishes me well, I believe, and I wish her the same, now that everything is scattered all over the ground. I always try to get the message to her that I would like to have her back in my life, that I love her still, that together we can try to put the puzzle of our lives back into a cohesive whole pattern that works - but with her brother RB slipping further and further into schizophrenia and her son still missing, it is a formidable hope to hold onto.

I think of the last real letter I wrote to her, and I wish I had not been so harsh. I know that I can't take back the words. I know that. So why didn't I realize that my daughter always had problems coping with real life pressures. She amassed over two thousand dollars in parking tickets, left her brand new Saab vehicle in a corn field for three years, and once did not pay her rent for five months when I went to live in California so I could be near the new man in my life, which she had warned me would not work out. She begged me to take her with her so we would still have each other but I had refused as I was weary of all of my daughter's careless and illogical shenanigans. I paid her costly debts and I loved her dearly but she was well into her twenties, working and making a living, and I felt it was time for her to cease being the "wild child." I simply did not give her the slack I gave to her brother who was ill. Job pressures, amazingly enough, my daughter handled with an iron clad reserve that would make most combat Generals quiver. Those heady "job things" my girl sailed through with ease, but with life's important every day stuff - there she failed tragically, and always has. "Why would I want you in my life, my letter said: Why would I want to stay in touch with you?"

"You bring nothing but hate and venom to my life. When you tried to convince me to get on the plane to go back to Rio before the services for your father had even taken place with your story that "Daddy died penniless and there is no money for RB" - I looked through the window of your soul. You are a lost person who needs someone to hate because you can't live with your own fabricated, dark and devious trickeries. You are not born again."

"There is nothing noble that you do. You are a person enveloped in rage and frankly I am bone weary of being the target, always praying that you will miss the bull's eye and not rip out my heart. You broke my heart a long time ago, Daughter. RB loves you deeply, but that is not the case with me. I have suffered with the degradation that you brought to my life long enough. I am free of your spell. I opt for grace. I am moving on after I figure out the muddle of your father's affairs that always brought me such pain."

My body of work is a testament to the fact that I chose to take the high road and it is interesting to see that Dr. Lynch still brings the spectacle of notoriety to the playing field, even in death. Perhaps that is why you won't bury him. You, too, are addicted to the Fakery of wealth and fame but...Time, Daughter, is truly the storyteller.

"I brought sadness to my dear friend Jeri Thomas and to my eighty-eight-year- old composer friend Irving Burgie. He did not understand, Daughter, the events that transpired that prevented you from wanting to give your Dad a proper burial. He offered to help, but you did not want any help. You said you would take care of everything and one can only suppose that you planned for your Dad to depart this world in the manner that he did, thrown away like rubbish. When I arrived back at Jeri's home after I left the tragic scene at the Crematorium, Jeri said I looked like I had had the blood sucked out of my body, that my skin had turned a dark grey. I felt dead inside, and nothing it seemed would wipe away the memory of that time. Don't you understand the horror of what you did?"

Realizing that venom is pouring out of me as I recall the pain of my daughter's betrayal, I force myself to think of the good things

I have done in life and I allow myself to dwell on the Creative Find children who I befriended in Harlem and worked with for many years.

I founded Creative Find, a non-profit 501 (c) 3 arts organization to help at risk, underserved children unlock repressed anxiety, restore calm and heal the damage caused by sustained, elevated levels of stress. Exposure to a hostile environment triggers a human biological fight or flight response that produces stress as a body's way of protecting itself. Two angels, Yasmine and Maria, helped me define and write down the principles embodied in the Creative Find program. They remarked in our printed brochure that ongoing arts participation provides comfort and healing especially for those coping with unstable home lives, and that the simple process of participating in a hands-on artistic endeavor can actually redirect a child out of a potential nervous breakdown. Creative Find children came from homes where parents were incarcerated, addicted to drugs and alcohol, or were single, even some living in homeless shelters. Creative Find allowed the children to temporarily suspend pain, channel aggression and minimize their rage. What I provided was a surrogate parenting experience that inspired, encouraged and nurtured the children's spirits. My teaching model infused both the visual and performing arts, unearthing the hidden creativity within the children.

I grew up around the Big Bands that my father brought to his Cosmopolitan Club. And, my son's other grandfather was an accomplished jazz pianist. Naturally, with my son being a composer, I wanted to expose the children to some great music. Not only did we listen to fabulous musicians, we got up and danced to their music. One little boy, Sterling, played a really brilliant drum to the Calypso sounds of Day-O, Day-ay-ay-O. Daylight come and me wanna go home.

I asked the children what they thought the song was all about. One child replied:

"Hey, I know that song. Those ladies sing it when they have fruit on their heads, right?"

The children sang another chorus while continuing to hand paint their small clocks. I began to weave in lessons about geography, math, vocabulary and cultural heritage into my storytelling.

Irving Burgie is a famous composer. Listen closely. As the man in the song works, he is also writing and singing about his beautiful home as a way to pass the time and get through a very difficult chore.

I explained how the composer became inspired to write the song because of his mother's storytelling about her homeland. She described how even when a person is stuck in the drudgery of work one still could think and do something creative, for example, write a song. I told the children that was something they could do in their own lives when times became tough. I paused to admire the progress the children had made in decorating their clocks, giving positive reinforcement to each child.

Day-O is a Calypso song that the people sometimes call The Banana Boat Song, and what is the name of the man who wrote it? *"Irving Burgie," the children yelled.*

"That's Right. Irving Burgie wrote hundreds of songs that have sold millions of records. His career has allowed him to travel around the world. He also wrote the lyrics for the National Anthem of Barbados. He was born in 1926."

Irving Burgie was actually born in Brooklyn, New York, not Barbados. But his mother was Barbadian. *She* loved to share stories with him about her homeland. She made the stories seem so real to him that he could imagine exactly what it was like in Barbados. When he wrote that song, he had never actually seen the island, except in his imagination. When he was older, he studied music at Julliard in Manhattan.

"Anyone ever heard of Juilliard?"

Well, I bet you won't forget that elderly man, Irving Burgie, who visited us and who sat at the same table you are now sitting at while working on your clocks. You surely know that just because someone is an elder doesn't mean that he or she won't be interesting.

"Now, let's imagine we have musical instruments and are dancing to Day-O, Day-ay-ay-O. Daylight come and me wanna go home. Yeah. Wow. Day-O, Day-O."

I then told the children, we were going to get all dressed up and go to Carnegie Hall to see Irving's friend, who was also our good friend, Abbey Lincoln. Mr. Burgie was going to see that all the children were dressed like little princes and princesses and then we would allow them all to go backstage to see Ms. Lincoln."

My Creative Find children had endured some difficult experiences and I was only too happy to give them the gift of an uplifting one. The grand evening at Carnegie Hall was a marvelous one.

Abbey Lincoln's Concert sold out. Irving Burgie paid for the kids' evening clothes and dinner afterwards and the excitement the children felt standing outside that famous, ornate hall dressed in their eye-catching clothing was palpable. As they proceeded to their seats all eyes were upon them, a memory worthy of keeping it close to their hearts and mine for the remainder of our lives. Everyone was whispering, *"Who are those beautifully dressed children?"*

Abbey Lincoln walked on stage singing the song, Bird Alone, a song the children had heard a thousand times as *Creative Find Gallery Background Music* while they sculpted, painted and created. The whole audience stood up and cheered when Abbey raised her arms and dedicated the evening to the Creative Find Children in Harlem, and to all at risk children in the world. The children cheered and clapped wildly and were overcome with emotion, some even crying. Afterwards, they were thrilled to visit backstage and to pose for personal photos with the legendary Abbey Lincoln.

Bird Alone was also my grandson's (Cal Boy's) favorite song. When Abbey took this beloved little boy in her limousine to a concert given in Greenwich Village, he requested that Bird Alone be played again on the ride home. When it came up on the radio, he placed his little hand on Abbey's knee and looked up at her with a beautiful smile, saying so preciously, *Cal Boy is an Abbey Boy.*

You see, I have profound memories of a little boy that my daughter does not permit me to see but who *I Will Love Always.* There I go, venturing into an area that is sure to make me lose my bearings, big time.

I take a deep breath. I repeat the number 7 over and over in my mind. The number 7 is my grandson's favorite number. He said to me the last time I was permitted to see him, "Grandmother, Ma'am, when you see the number 7 anywhere, just think of me because when I see that number I think of your pretty face and your golden smile. My smile may be okay but my teeth are bone colored, naturally candlestick beige, but not to my grandson. To him they were golden.

He was nine then. He is twenty-three now and a runaway who is missing. Missing in plain sight somewhere in the U.S., I pray. Missing for three and one-half long, mournfully long years. It is both good and awful those dozen years since I have seen my precious grandson. His distinctive and joyous gargle laugh fills me full up now and then and washes through me like lavender drops sprinkled into a welcoming hot bath – misting and permeating all of the air in the room.

Cal Boy, as I remember him, was the gentlest soul that I was privileged to know on this earth. If only I could close my eyes and break through to that place where he is hiding, or running, or happy even. If only he would come to me for an instant, let me believe that he is okay. I close my eyes. I count backwards, relax every muscle in my body and start to drift away but alas, I fail to conjure up anything except flashbacks of my own childhood. Family was everything to me, even though when I was a teen I often wished to be left alone so I could just dance away in toe shoes to my dream of being a Prima Ballerina. I had gotten a full scholarship to a famous ballet school in New York City and my mother would not even consider my leaving home to attend. She wanted all brothers and sisters in constant contact with one another. Having a brother or sister missing would have been inconceivable to me but having my only grandchild disappear is more painful than anything I have gone through, even more heartbreaking than the unexpected deaths of both my beloved Granny and my Daddy, The Joy Boy, in 1971.

I was busy living every minute of my life in 1971. I spent a great deal of time reading about the many tragic spots on the globe, where there was much unrest and awful warfare, especially in Vietnam, China, and Cambodia. I felt an urgency to see beauty while it still existed as it did seem that the world was unraveling quickly. A friend had come back from Vietnam and he told me he still could not get the smell of blood off of him. He said that his unit had killed about 300 people and he had literally been put on a plane and returned to the States with the dirt from the trenches embedded in his clothes. He remarked that anyone who would think that by lying down on clean sheets at home would wipe away catastrophic Vietnam memories was just a fool. He was overwrought trying to readjust to a normal life and he blamed the armed services for rendering no useful help. He was withdrawn and reluctant to talk about his experience, even to his wife.

I had just come back from Paris, France where the beauty and art of that exquisite city were still very much in my thoughts. How I wished I could have had tea with my Granny on the beautiful **Avenue des Champs-Elysées** *with its stately buildings, fountains, and lush trees lined all the way down the middle, and not a single car allowed. Granny had told me when I left that she would love to hang out with me and the hippies. I had never been a hippie so her remarks made me smile and realize that everything that young people did must have seemed over the top to her. My Granny was sick, but I really looked forward to telling her about my trip abroad. In the U.S., the Vietnam war was very much the topic of concern and discussion. Vietnam student activists after years of proclaiming, "Old enough to fight, old enough to vote" won the right to cast their ballots in the elections. President Nixon signed into law the official voting age as being 18. The My Lai Massacre in Vietnam where thatch roof huts with elders and children residing in them were deliberately burned by US troops brought outrage by irate citizens on all sides of the globe. The ensuing court trial resulted in Lieutenant Calley being found guilty of 22 murders, though he was later pardoned.*

Cigarettes were banned from TV Ads, and this amused me because I had done a Chesterfield Cigarette Commercial but, in reality, I had never even smoked one cigarette. I simply held the pack, and said something like, "Try it, you'll like it." Raquel Welch, Elvis Presley, Dolly Parton, John Lennon's "Imagine," George Harrison's "My Sweet Lord," Duke Ellington's Jazz Grammy, the "New Orleans Suite," and The Temptations "Just My Imagination" were all wildly popular.

The stage was alive with performers; Janis Joplin, Marvin Gaye, Aretha Franklin, and the great Luciano Pavarotti were all revered and celebrated and Pavarotti became the first tenor to hit all nine high C's. I remember because my Daddy's brother-in-law, Uncle Boo, my Aunt Sadie's husband was a tenor and he was always practicing his high C notes, and though he sang in Church and had quite a lovely voice, he did not have the success that Pavarotti had in singing the high notes.

Fans still mourned Jimmy Hendrix's untimely death a year earlier, and Frank Sinatra's retirement dominated entertainment news. My Daddy had closed up all of his clubs and he was always trying to put on a brave face, but anyone who knew him knew he dreamed of being in the Club business again. He just was not the same person without his establishments to run. The USA was just beginning to be in the throes of the "me generation," the Baby Boomers that were famed possessed, convinced of their own greatness, and who more than likely lived with their parents rather than with spouses.

DEAR GRANNY IS GONE, AND THEN UNBELIEVABLY, THE JOY BOY HIMSELF DEPARTS

My Daddy's face and familiar short, stocky frame comes back to me. My daddy is pacing the length of my Granny's tiny porch, stopping every five or six steps to close his eyes and raise his face to the ceiling. For an awful moment his whole body trembles before he returns to the pacing. My Daddy is a handsome man who loves clothes and he wears them with great panache, but he looks pale and thin in his grey funeral suit. Occasionally he interrupts his routine to look at one or another of his eight children with vacant, wet eyes and I sense that he has given up any notion of living without his mother. He begins pacing back and forth again and his face turns a dark gray color and he is literally staring into space though there are dozens of people who speak to him but move on when he does not respond. Every now and then my Daddy stops, drops his head and shakes it slowly as though affirming to himself that "No, it cannot be true." Then, abruptly my Daddy raises his head and begins to pace again.

He looks over the crowd assembling on the porch and the lawn out front and his eyes are so watery that it is clear that he sees very little.

I am very afraid for my Daddy. I have never seen him like this. I want to go to him, to wrap my arms around him, to tell him that he still has his eight Egg Heads – that everything will soon be all right. But I know that nothing I say or do will take away the shock that Granny, my Daddy's beloved mother is gone. He will not permit any to say that she is dead. She is gone and where she has gone is the only thing my Daddy wants to know. He has repeated over and over that we are all aware that he is not a religious person - that he does not want to be a part of any service at the Church and that all he can do is to be with his mother while she remains at home. But as I look at the Pall Bearers carrying my Granny's casket down the front steps to the waiting hearse I know with certainty that my Daddy has given up any notion of living without his mother.

He begins to tremble violently and literally refuses to allow anyone to console him. My Daddy rides in the hearse with my Granny's body and he stands alone in the back of the Church during the service.

When they begin to lower her body into the grave my Daddy flees the cemetery on foot, refusing to be consoled. We finally pick him up a mile down the road and he sits wordless between his brother and me. He will not hear of dining with the many friends and relatives and I am sure that he is sickened that anyone could even think of eating. He climbs the steps to my Granny's room and stands in her doorway shaking his head for a good half an hour before sitting down in her favorite chair by the window.

Certainly, he does not hear a word that is spoken to him by the dozens of people that come upstairs to pay their respects. Finally, when the noisy group has gone, Mrs. Rose, my Granny's neighbor, comes in and sits down on my Granny's bed. She talks and talks, oblivious to my Daddy's pain and silence. "B.T., do you remember how your Mama sat in that same chair when your sister Jevie died, just putting Jevie's ring on one finger after another. And Lord, I thought they was gonna have to put her away when that truck killed poor Fats. Fats was her favorite, you and Fats. My Lord, didn't

Mrs. Charles love you boys? She was a good woman. Loved all her children. Yes, she did. And wasn't she good to them grandchildren? All of them. Loved them as if they were her own. B.T. you ought to be right proud you gave her so many fine children. And Lord, ain't it peculiar that you are the only one of Mrs. Charles' children to have children of your own. The Lord was good to Mrs. Charles, yes he was. Giving her all them fine children by you. God works in mysterious ways. Yes, he does. Mrs. Charles' children gone, one by one, and you replacing them one by one with eight of your own. She had plenty to be thankful for. And you best be thankful too, boy, that you had your Mama so long. Yes, you can thank the Lord for that."

I led Mrs. Rose away, and closed the door softly. I knew that my Daddy would not be thanking the Lord for taking away his Mama. I sat on the top step by the door, thinking that it was indeed true that my Daddy was the only one of his mother's children that had children. My Granny had twelve but four died in infancy and four of her adult children had each died in a tragic accident. And, after each of these misfortunes my mother had given birth to a baby, which my Granny loved as her own. I would miss my beloved Granny, that's for sure but I knew that foremost in our minds should be that my Daddy would need his Egg Heads now but not I, nor any of my siblings, had a clue as to how to help him with his loss. It was simply, insurmountable. Five months later, my Daddy was dead.

I felt the tears streaming down my face and sat up with a start. The feeling of extreme shame visited me again as I remembered that my Daddy had asked to come and live with me and my husband after Granny's death but I had begged him to put it off until after I returned from my Caribbean vacation. I got the telegram on that beautiful, sunny beach in Negril that my Daddy was gone. I never would have the opportunity to tell him that one day I would meet the man who looked exactly like him except that he was White with blue eyes, a man who actually was a grandson of the same Dr. Graves who impregnated my Granny's mother Missy in the cotton fields of Alabama.

Of course, this man's mother was White and when he heard my account of how his grandfather was my Granny's father, he reddened with anger and admonished me to never tell this story again. He wanted no part of having a friendship with me just because he looked like my Daddy and had the same name as my Granny's daddy. He was a Jewish man, Ginsberg was his name, and he was one of the reasons I pushed into the recesses of my mind of knowing anything further about my roots. I wanted to hate this real estate agent who would sell our home, oh how I wanted so to hate him, but I could not because my Granny had not hated her father or anyone in her entire life. She had held close to her heart all of her life where her Daddy's "marker" was located in Alabama. I couldn't escape the impact that this event had on my life.

It tormented me that Missy had lived the way that she did without fulfilling her dreams and that her daughter Josie, my Granny, had instilled in me the notion that I must strive to be kind, to have understanding, even when I was filled with rage. I had wanted to shout to this man who wanted nothing more than a big fat commission for selling our home – "How dare you tell me what I can talk about. This is my story and I will tell it to whomever I want. I will not hold the shameful secrets you want me to hold any longer."

But of course, being my Granny's grandchild I did not shout out my feelings to him. He got his commission and he went his way and I mine. And the truth of the matter was, I did not really want to meet any relatives that might turn out to be like he was. What would be the point? If there would be anything that would make up for the kind of life that Missy and her mother had to endure, it would be me and my children having accomplished the task of having stellar lives and passing the rewards from our lives on to others.

I wanted to leave behind a "roots chain of accomplishments" not grim accounts of suffering. I wanted the adversities to be known but the rewards of those misfortunes to be so apparent that all would see the rainbows that emerged from those turbulent times. Oh, I yearned, I wanted, I fretted, I agonized and still I was far from taking a decisive form of action. How could I see what I needed to see? How could I do what needed to be done? How could I begin?

I had to get out my journals, those diaries that held so many secrets that documented so many undertakings. Surely, in those numerous pages there would be something that would give up the clues as to the direction that must take priority. After some fitful moments I finally sat back with my counting routine and tried again to drift far, far away.

THE EGG HEADS

It seemed My Daddy had been sleeping only minutes when he found himself struggling under thick eyes to capture the face of his eldest daughter Jacqueline. It was as though he were deft, unable to hear as he watched her laugh and talk while she pulled on his arm. His body and senses would not rise from the dark sleep that had swallowed him. "My Daddy, c'mon on, you promised, promised." The words tumbled through the fog of his mind. His tongue stumbled to beg what time it was but peals of laughter bathed his ears and he felt his forehead being stroked as she repeated over and over, "But My Daddy, you promised."

Her skin was still wet with the wash of her bath and as always he was instantly disarmed and incapable of denying her a single wish. His pot belly five foot five-inch flesh, began to pull itself up and was literally enveloped with shoulders, thighs, and soft little faces. His avalanche of children had descended upon him, squealing, "My Daddy, My Daddy." Even the baby had been pressed to his chest, and there was no denying that the promised outing was well on its way to reality, just a scant five hours into his sleep.

He touched each of his children tenderly and gave them implicit instructions to wait in the car without marring the windows with their fingerprints. He would give them ample time to play at the racetrack later but he enjoyed taking them around in his gleaming navy blue Desta that had been especially built to allow each dear boy and girl to have their own seat. There were no more fights about who would sit next to "My Daddy" (a name that they each claimed as though he belonged only to that particular child.) Each one had a special view. They all could reign like little Kings and Queens as the townspeople eagerly waved and reveled in the familiar sight of The Joy Boy with his brood.

Jacqueline insisted upon bringing along the baby and his wife was equally insistent that she could not take the baby. She was ferociously protective of her baby and B.T. averted her eyes as he plucked his little boy from her arms and handed him to his Princess. He felt sickened that he was responsible for bruising her face and wished he had not gone ballistic when she accused him of having an affair with the new barmaid who had phoned him twice, unnecessarily he had to admit. He promised to bring the baby back immediately after buying him a pair of shoes. Delores looked at him through razor sharpened eyes and gave her daughter a deluge of clipped instructions for the baby's care. Jacqueline, wise beyond her years, promised to be the very best care giver and she looked at her mother with a very grown up look of compassion. She was an extremely beautiful and clever girl, well accustomed to the tasks of caring for her younger siblings, all of whom she loved with an astonishing tenderness.

B.T. drove slowly, and as he expected, neighbors waved vigorously from their porches. A few even ran down their front sidewalks and flagged down the car so they could have a firsthand look at the new baby. The neighborhood folk were well accustomed to seeing the older children walking to and from school but they seldom got a look at baby Tony as Delores kept to herself except for her friendship with the Rosemans' and the Browns' on either side of their uncommonly plain wood frame home with its modest bannister railing that boasted two large and lush lilac bushes in front that made the house more important looking than it actually was. The bushes had little rounded heads that spread neckless into full expansive shoulders that drooped generously over their bosoms and enormous lilac bellies and fluttered on windblown hips that seemed to sway in sync with the awesome derriere of Big Nell who would streak by the bushes in a flash to see where B.T. was taking his brood. It looked like Nell was simulating her hips to encourage a comrade dance with her neighbor, our Mama, who loved to let down her full tiara crown of jet black hair and dance spontaneously, in the privacy of her home, with her eight children. When Nell shimmed past these rotund lilac bushes that shook out their scented fragrances our Mama thrust her hands on her hips - a practiced gesture to express her disapproval – and then she dropped them quickly and made wild flapping gestures like a frenzied bird and broke into a grin that radiated with delight across her face as she mimicked Big Nell's lyrical movements.

B.T. knew that his wife enjoyed Nell's friendship and her standoffishness from most of the other neighbors was a form of self-protection, enabling her to avoid confronting the gossip that was in constant circulation about his goings on at his clubs and restaurant. He was sure, in fact, that she was secretive about all of her friendships because the police always arrived at their doorstep before their noisy confrontations had barely begun.

Big Nell came bounding down the street, past B.T.'s sparkling white pebbled driveway and ran alongside the car, pressing her chubby fingers to the windows with great merriment. B.T. bristled with anger at her careless streaking of the windows, but he returned her greeting with his customary wave and, "Hi Ya Jelly Bean," which brought Nell no offense.

But Nell was clearly bent upon getting another point across because she yelled loudly, "The Lord doesn't like ugly," which forced B.T. to abandon his normal routine of just waving jovially and moving on. B.T. stopped abruptly and the rotund figure of Nell soon took up all of the window space on his side.

"Not now Nell," B.T. said through the unopened window, a coldness hardening the look of his jaw. He felt bad enough about the black eye he had given his wife earlier that morning but he was in no mood to hear Nell's sermonizing. "Be careful, B.T. and be good to those children's mother," Nell admonished. Nell was a woman of uncommon good sense and extreme sensitivity but B.T. thought that no good could come of approaching the subject of Nell's concern with all of the children present so after a few seconds of forcing himself to remain silent, he opened the window and spat out.

All of the children said, "Ooh My Daddy, how could you? Ooh, gross." It was a lousy habit of his, spitting, and he honestly couldn't remember when he had started it. It was a kind of reflex action, B.T. thought. Smokers reached for a cigarette during an awkward moment and since he didn't smoke he spit instead. He also suspected that spitting had come from watching his mother chew tobacco. Though she was a demure, fastidious little lady she was known on occasion, when she was under stress, to chew a wad of the southern tobacco that was pressed into big flat bars wrapped like candy. She kept a pail nearby and she would chew and spit, chew and spit.

Jacqueline was peering at B.T. cautiously, and he looked at Nell with irritation and jerked the car into drive. Just thinking briefly of his mother made B.T want to turn the car straight to her door, to the little brown shingled home he and his brothers and Poppa had bought for her. There was nothing about his mother he disliked, including her spewing out the brown juice into her tobacco pail.

Driving along, looking at the neat lawns being carefully attended by their owners B.T. was able to recapture the vision of his mother sprinkling her beloved gardens in the front and backyards, dressed in her printed silk dress with a white starched apron, wearing perfectly polished lace up heels. High tops she called them. Perhaps he would see a pair of white ones for her at the store. Like his wife, his mother had an eye for quality goods.

As they pulled up to the entrance of the handsome and prestigious store on Main Street, onlookers crowded, some silent, some very noisy, around his unusual car and gaped shamelessly as he parked and maneuvered his well-dressed menagerie of happy little faces into an obedient line - the youngest in front with him, and the eldest in back, all arranged chronologically as had long been previously orchestrated to assure maximum security and effect.

Like a locomotive chief looking after his crew on a momentous occasion, he moved from shoulder to shoulder calling out their names. He chatted with each little person he routed safely through the revolving glass door. Little Mike, only two, but forever concerned about the happiness of his siblings, insisted on being allowed to pick out the baby's shoes and asked sweetly, with a whisper, if he might have a pair of red sandals.

Reginald, age three grumbled about Mike holding up the line and assured B.T. he would not wear any sissy sandals. He was intensely bossy and had been fairly much in charge of dictating the sibling agenda since he had begun to walk. Bev, five, B.T.'s little chocolate drop, the rich smooth color of velvet brown gave a glowing shy smile as she glided through the door. Gail, six, and always fighting with one or the other, was B.T.'s angel cake, a name he had arrived at by hoping that she would become sunnier in her disposition. He loved her dearly though, because she had an angel's face and a devil's tongue which often made him weak with laughter. It is important to understand that everybody in the store (and in the whole town in fact) was interested in The Joy Boy's children because a kind remark about one of two of them could earn some desired seats at one his coveted big band performances. As for the kids, they were so used to being fawned over, they were much more interested in what was happening with one or the other of their own siblings.

Bev came running back, her eyes lit up like Christmas lights, chattering about some black patent slippers, with a bow. So excited was she that she skipped along, the shyness literally falling away. Annette, seven, the ballerina of the family, wore an anxious look. She was concerned about pink toe shoes and pressed her graceful hands into a prayerful clasp that she would find them. Of all the children, she loved beautiful things the most, and strangely, was the most forgiving when something she wanted could not be given to her.

Booker Jr., nine, wore an even tempered look, but kept his eyes cast down, the superfluous fanfare being something he could well live without. He was a quiet, studious boy who respected all of his family members. He had a passion for football, a sport that made the family nervous because Junior had suffered with rheumatic fever. But Junior conquered the illness and was determined to make his mark in football. Jacqueline, eleven, dressed in bouffant crinolines and luxurious long black braids, smiled proudly as she carried six month old Charles in her arms. She looked like a real princess as she moved with assurance through the ornate door. The sales people buzzed around them like a pack of mother bees and an enormous selection of shoes began appearing before the children were barely seated.

Boxes upon boxes of school shoes, play shoes, Sunday school shoes, slippers, were opened and tried on. For an hour B.T watched his eggheads rush about excitedly as they tried on pair after pair, laughing and whispering and pointing at each other happily in the mirror. Even the baby, by now contentedly crawling about on the thick carpeting, seemed to understand what the merriment was all about.

Jacqueline tried on the tiniest heel in a gleaming black patent and almost imperceptibly B.T. nodded, allowing her to thoroughly enjoy the moment and exclaim, perfect. Annette found her beloved toe shoes and kept them close to her refusing to allow them to go back into the box. By the time all the selections were made and the children were each in their new shoes with the additional selections and old ones boxed up to go, there were thirty-two boxes. Each had gotten four pairs, shoes for school, play, Sunday school, and of course slippers for padding about at home.

The sales people had asserted that even the little boys needed the proper oxford to assure the healthy alignment of growing bones, bones that wouldn't see the schoolyard for a few more years B.T. had unsuccessfully argued. Even the baby had gotten soft leather high tops in white, brown and patent leather, not to mention the slipper socks, of course. And yes, B.T. found supple while leather lace ups for his much loved mother, Josie. Outwardly though he joked that he'd have to get right back to work as he alone was responsible for keeping the Buster Brown Shoe Company in business, inwardly B. T. was thrilled that he had sired such a fabulous family. Very few families, though, could afford the luxuries that B.T. bestowed on his children and it would be appropriate to say that few families would be so extravagant with youngsters even if they had the money to spend. But, B. T. loved each child and he wanted the best for each one, and nothing but the best. He tucked the bill inside his trousers. He would let the accountant worry about the damage he had done.

B.T. marched his family outside and the sales staff loaded the car trunk and helped guide the obedient brood into Robinson's next door, a one stop, extremely expensive family clothing store. There they would each get two sets of trousers or skirts and shirts or coordinated tops. And all would get a Sunday school outfit and a winter coat.

The girls chose beautiful pleated skirts for school, and pastel, soft woolen sweaters with ruffled Peter Pan collars. In darker shades, they found lovely velvet dresses with long, graceful sleeves and demure ribbons around the wrists. Jacqueline looked handsome in the chic, understated velvet, dressed by choice like her sisters. She was smart, knowing that later she could get away with doing what she wanted to do if she put on the sweet face of being content to go along with the gang, thereby building up important points for more important battles she wanted to win with both Mama and my Daddy.

The boys each got stylish plaid suits for Sunday school and rugged corduroy trousers for daytime wear. Little Mike was ecstatic about his red overcoat and did not want to take it off, though it was still a good four weeks away from any real cold weather. Booker Jr. wanted a bomber jacket, and in a rare display of enthusiasm gave his brothers and sisters a huge grin when an army green wool one was found. Only Annette could not find a Sunday dress, and as expected she could not be persuaded into taking something like her sisters. She was happy to do without she said, amicably.

The packages were wrapped and just as they were about to leave, the owner hurriedly exited and reappeared with a delicate lace blouse that had a velvet sleeveless vest attached. Little gold nail heads were sprinkled along the border of the muted, plaid vest and were elaborately repeated throughout the enormous, circular skirt. Annette gasped when she learned it was her size, and needless to say the toe shoes had just found an outfit ready and willing to be danced in.

It was a very happy group that arrived at the car with their mountainous assortment of parcels in tow. With the packing and arranging at last complete, and little room left for the actual children, B.T.'s Desta headed north for his restaurant, just a few blocks away.

The street was crowded with cars and B.T. was annoyed that his spot in the front of his restaurant was occupied by someone else. Slim and Kenny D were not in sight and he had little choice but to let the kids out and double park until "those ruffians" as he wife called them, could be found to watch the car. He paid top dollar to keep from being aggravated with petty nuisances and he was angry that his men were not at their posts.

As the kids climbed the long staircase to his Grill, B.T. hopped in and out of adjacent businesses looking for his guards. Finally, he pulled into a spot not far away and hurried up to the restaurant to get the meal underway.

It was a cozy restaurant, seating sixty, and the children, well familiar with the surroundings, had placed themselves near the kitchen at four different tables. It was not often that they got away from one another and confidants quickly revealed themselves. Jacqueline had already gotten the cook to give them coca colas and she was engrossed in giving the baby his bottle. Big Benny had wisely taken their orders and hamburgers, french fries, and big slices of B.T.'s mother's famous lemon meringue pie were already being placed on the counter.

Benny was a tall, fat, gay man weighing some three hundred pounds, and was a powerhouse of energy. He could cook better than any cook B.T. had ever had, and was a better waiter than any six put together, but Benny had bouts with depression that would incapacitate him now and then and he would miss a day or two of work. When this happened, the entire operation was thrown into a state of havoc. Everyone on the block would be on the lookout for Big Ben, knowing that a generous reward could be had if Benny's whereabouts were divulged. He could almost always be coaxed into coming back, and B.T. had been known to send in his "eggheads" to bolster Benny's sagging ego. Benny was a kind man who had been born without too many pluses and B.T. tried hard to return the loyalty that Benny had shown him. Already Benny had whisked the food to the various tables and he knew that Benny delighted in pleasing the children and was nonplussed about having four tables to redo.

Slim came running in, saying he needed the keys to park the car in its rightful place. B.T. exploded, like a bag of firecrackers, demanding his whereabouts. Slim was dumbfounded. "Nobody would steal your car, he said, and there isn't anything in it to worry about." B.T. bounded down the steps, half believing that Slim was talking jive.

It was a solemn moment. The car stood there as before but there was not a package to be seen anywhere. He opened the trunk. It, too, was empty. The car did not appear to be tampered with. It was astounding, numbing. Everything in B.T.'s field of vision seem to disappear. He felt weak. Sick.

Big Benny, Slim, and the children were now at his side. The street began to thicken with the curious as the story began to unfold. It seemed as though Slim had really just returned, and knew of no packages. The packages had been removed carefully, and without suspicion, by a man and woman, who had put them into a station wagon.

Jacqueline, Junior and Gail began to cry. They seemed to understand that everything was gone, taken by strangers. Bev wanted to know when they were going to bring back her slippers, and Annette seemed so distraught that she looked like she might perish. She had left her pink toe shoes on her seat. She knew that her Aunt Sadie would be as heartbroken as she was because Sadie paid for her costly ballet lessons and never failed coming to her recitals and performances.

The police came and they tried to help B.T. put the pieces of the puzzle together, to really focus on what facts they could gather from the neighborhood crowd. The man and woman had been seen in the area before, but no one really knew them, or would say that they knew them. It was even harder to pin down who actually had seen B.T. and all of his children go up to the Grill, and why no one had come up to say that his car was being unloaded. Dozens of times in the past, residents and other business owners had reported the slightest odd occurrence to him.

The police seemed to think that the couple had been so efficient and casual about the entire matter, that it appeared to others that they were simply doing what they were supposed to be doing. Of one thing B.T. was certain – that if it was more than just a casual robbery, the thieves would get their just do. If one of his enemies, and he had a few, had set out to harm his family – he would make them pay, and pay good. It wasn't an idle threat. All that knew him knew that B.T.

was well connected with the judges and City officials and that he believed in more than one way to skin a cat.

B.T. was furious with Slim, but he knew that he was innocent. In his gut, he felt that it was a neighborhood theft, executed by people who had begun their lives in those few meager blocks and would certainly end them there, unable to escape the shackles that held fast to their dreams. For a few moments, the newness of leather and the tuck of pleats would bound them and make them forget their own hopelessness.

B.T. wanted to make someone pay for his children's pain. But who? Most of the people in that neighborhood were scarcely able to turn themselves out for their daily ritual of standing on the street corner to watch others have what they could never have. The money and the good times belonged to the outsiders who breezed in with their fine cars and fat wallets to have a meal and take in the entertainment. It would take decades before anything in the neighborhood belonged to the neighborhood folk.

As B.T. drove his woe-begotten crew home, he felt diminished, as though he were not in control of his own destiny. He made the effort of uttering words of comfort to his brood, but the truth was even he didn't believe in his words. His children's happiness had turned into pain and for the moment he was powerless to change it.

With great hardship, B.T. turned into their drive and got the children out of the car and into the house. Delores rushed toward them, hugging each sorrowful face - but looking herself like a wounded animal. Through the mirror, B.T. could see that her eye was hidden under a purple lump and the whole lamentable scene so dragged him that he rushed back to his car, feeling absolutely deformed.

He squinted away his tears, seated himself abruptly and drove off - leaving the pebbled driveway spurting with dust balls. Numbed to his core, he just drove on through traffic and stop lights and streets that he knew like the back of his hand but seemed now as if they had been coated with foggy egg whites, a haze meant to obliterate his memory. Indeed, he had been transformed into a robot who turned and stopped and signaled, but who felt nothing. Losing the contents of his car after a wild spending spree would not even begin to measure up to what My Daddy was going to lose.

Fall turned into winter and My Daddy's long wiener looking Navy Blue Desoto was the only car that could make it up the hill in the three-foot-high snow drifts. Imagine this polished blue contraption pulling up in front of our house that has blankets of snow spread across the roof with glittery streamers of ice hanging all along the edges – twinkling daggers ready to attack the eight Egg Heads bounding out the door. We, of course, are delighted to engage in the game of dodging these spectacular ice daggers. Picking up the groceries spilling out of My Daddy's arms as the bags break apart, we Egg Heads screech with laughter as My Daddy's chunky little frame falls into the snow. Unhurt, My Daddy is literally propelled to his feet by our eager hands that are pushing and hoisting him upwards. We move spritely with laughter and merriment as the ice daggers crackle here and there on ground or shoulder.

Now, picture our Mama in the midst of this scene -without the benefit of a coat or scarf - as she arrives to survey our frolicking in the snow. She is not amused. Her frosty Ice Queen murmurs to my Daddy do not attempt to hide her contempt for him. I have to face that though each of my seven siblings has always called our father "My Daddy"– Our Daddy is in deep trouble with Mama.

Days and weeks pass by. The police cars in front of our house became less of a common sight confronting us when we arrived home from school - not at all like before when my schoolmates would see the red sirens whirling and the neighbors staring from their porches and me walking right past the house pretending it was not mine - so why did I sense on that particular frigid, snowy day, that an eerie foreboding was written on Mama's face - that something - something was going to happen. I keep asking myself when did I know that my parents were in trouble but as I look back to that telling day, that look on Mama's face clearly reflected that My Daddy had already melted away from Mama's mind.

Mama was surprisingly calm and cheerful for days on end. We made fudge, were allowed to play outside longer than usual, and even permitted to skip a few chores. The brooding indignation that seemed to penetrate her mood disappeared. Our mama was laughing, and fixing herself up prettily and spending time with our neighbors. It wasn't hard to see that something was making our Mama walk with a definite spring to her step. She greeted us gaily when we arrived home from school and tried to make our meals more enjoyable. Mama hated cooking and it was unusual for her to fix more than the compulsory meat, frozen vegetable, and some form of potato but we were experiencing new casseroles, even picnic type arrangements at the dinner table. It became an adventure, wondering what Mama would concoct to present to us next.

THE MOVERS COME FOR THE CHILDREN, NOT THE FURNITURE

We were carted off under the cloak of darkness to various neighbors' homes and -unbelievably true - a moving van truck picked each child up. Secreted in the back of this padded van we siblings huddled together until we arrived many hours later at our Mama's parents' home, some two hundred miles away. There, amongst hushed whispers per out grandfather's persistent drinking and a flurry of phone calls about the location of various living quarters, our lives were scurried here and there and somehow we moved through the tedious hours. I can only say we lived.

We had only seen this grandfather a few scant times and Mama's mother, Nana, was always hiding behind nervous laughter and an uneasy smile. I personally remember very little about the whole experience of being pirated away. I have brief flashbacks of the truck pulling up near train tracks, and then waiting a long time before the bumpy journey deposited us in an alleyway of darkened houses where we went through a mass of tangled weeds and up some uneven wooden steps and through a back door that led to some strange beds and more whispers in the dark of this unholy odyssey.

It wasn't long before we were stolen back by My Daddy. My parents' fights intensified. I became so nervous by their violent arguments that my skin would break out into huge hives. Sometimes, I would even faint. Once, when I thought one or the other would be killed, I fell to the floor with giant, pancake like hives all over my body. I couldn't breathe and I had to be taken to the hospital.

Mama blamed my Daddy, and of course he blamed her. The doctor told my parents how dangerous my condition could become if I didn't get immediate medical help. For a short time, things improved but then the shouts, accusations, and terrible rumblings in our little shaky family home began again. Sometimes it felt like a war zone. I vowed that if I ever had children that I would never allow them to grow up in an environment like ours. Brothers and sisters found a sibling to empathize with and my little brother, Tony, always clung to my side. Our house was ripe with tension. Things could not stay the way they were. A Court date was rumored, and then scheduled. A date that would forever change the history of The Egg Heads.

THE JOY BOY FIGHTS FOR CUSTODY OF HIS EGG HEADS

"My Daddy" was at the lowest ebb of his life at this point and nothing hurt him more than when all eight of us Egg Heads had to go to Court to choose what parent we wanted to live with. We sat in that awful courtroom and heard our Daddy fight passionately for custody of us. The thought of being taken from one or the other of our parents was unthinkable.

The Court ruled that the seven youngest children should remain under the custody of Mama and that My Daddy should be given custody of Jacqueline, the eldest daughter. It was a ruling that defied logic and to this day I find the ruling to be absurd. It seemed so strange to have our sister Jacqueline cut short her visits became it was a school night and she had to return to Granny's house where she lived with my Daddy. Though Jacqueline seemed to adjust to the change, it wasn't long before she began to miss school and get into trouble. The real trouble was that my parents were fighting over her and she simply wanted away from the eye of the storm.

Jacqueline continued, however, to miss school. Someone made the decision to put my sister into a hospital and unbelievably – she was given highly controversial shock therapy treatments. Mama finally got permission to bring Jacqueline back home and my sister told her that all of the family trouble really depressed her and that she planned to run away and get married to a nice man that was five years her senior. Mama agreed that anything would be better than the hospital and she turned her cheek and pretended to know nothing of Jacqueline's secret plans. For a short time, my seventeen-year-old sister had some peace in her life but she soon determined that she was not happy and that marriage did not suit her. Jacqueline had always regretted that Mama had not permitted her to date the football captain at her high school that she had an enduring crush on. Other suitors never quite measured up. My sister was depressed and had many flights of escape, and in between two other marriages, she would return to Mama's house several more times. Jacqueline tried to be a good mother to her two children, a daughter and a son - who did not share the same father – and always she remained friends with her former spouses.

AN AWAKENING BRINGS CLARITY

I came out of my deep reverie into my past and was both troubled and relieved by my recalled memories. It feels like so much has happened that it is remarkable that these experiences come back into my memory bank at all. I am really surprised that I am able to still recall that awful day in Court when my siblings and I had to choose a parent to live with. And, to still be mourning that childhood dress that had escaped me ever wearing it - is truly crazy, but honestly, I have never found a dress that was perfect for me like that one was. I am relieved though that I have survived many more awful things than the robbery of a carload of clothes belonging to me and my siblings.

I have survived a forced incarceration that was more terrifying than anything that I have ever experienced. I do not need a dream episode to bring it to the forefront of my mind. I am happy to get it pushed to the backburner straight away so I can move on to more important memories - memories that can help me to put together the puzzle of my life, or at least to let a portion of that puzzle rest in a secure spot so that it is not easily uprooted. I do want to be able to put all of the pieces into a perspective that will enable me to live an Excelsior Life. I have always been interested in excelling, in being my best self, and I often wonder why it is so hard to deal with the changes that come on a regular basis when living one's life. Why am I not able to get back so easily to that high road that will really enable me to give back to the World Community in the way that my mind envisions it? What I want to put to rest is the following memory. Perhaps you will understand why.

THE GOOD DOCTOR

"I wanted to stop his breath, to see him hurting like I was hurting. I wanted to prevent him from ever telling another lie that could have the awful consequence of having someone end up in an insane asylum, an asylum they didn't belong in.

It was hard to believe, but there I was, in a mental ward with crazy people - and I had gotten there because my husband had uttered outrageous lies to high powered police officials and judges that he was friends with. He wanted my controlling stock, fifty-one percent, in our medical center and he committed a bastardly deed to get it – he put me away.

I had built the medical center with him, with the wages from my twelve, long and hard years of working two jobs while he was in medical school. Yes, he was the doctor, a damn good doctor, but I was the working mule that had made our dream possible. I put that medical center together with my sheer determination that brick by brick, contractor by contractor, it could and would go up. Everyone would get paid and they all would rejoice in our victory. And that is just what happened. We opened our beautiful Medical Center amidst words of astonishment and praise. It had an attractive and welcoming environment thanks to my gift of successfully coordinating lots of plants, books, and paintings with interesting antiques and comfortable modern furniture. The Center was well staffed with doctors and medical personnel and featured the most up to date technology in all of its treatment rooms. It set an example, blessed the neighborhood. I was the President and Dr. Lynch was the Head Doctor and Chief. We had made our dream come true.

He grumbled about my controlling stock but I had only to mention his penchant for gambling money we did not have on boxing matches and tennis games and he let out the air in his wounded, puffed up cheeks and headed for his favorite bar. Everyone knew the good Doctor - and his outings over the years always served to increase his business. There were new patients waiting to see him first thing in the morning and at the very end of each long evening. It was hard not to understand that he needed a drink and a game of poker with his friends after a tedious day at the Center.

The months rolled by, turning into years. I managed to go back to school and enter into a film course at New York University. I even managed to get nominated for an Academy Award for my first venture into feature documentaries. I produced and directed a film, Lost Control, about the patients my husband was detoxing at the North Central Mental Health/Mental Retardation Center where he worked part of each day.

He was one of the most successful detox doctors in the City and it was fascinating to see him interact with patients. I followed some of the patients from their maximum security prison environment to North Central's Rehabilitation Center where my husband helped them get off of drugs.

There was a big film screening at the MGM Theatre in Manhattan and the invited crowd brought other important guests and it was necessary to hold two screenings back to back. Fortunately, I had planned for a big celebration and there was plenty of wine, champagne and tasty appetizers to please the overflow crowd of friends, family, and colleagues that had come to wish me well with my first film endeavor. There were also several noteworthy male filmmakers who were not invited that crashed the screening to make sure, I guess, that they were apprised of their female competition. There were few people of color making films then and it was sobering to think that the road to success would not be paved with well-wishers but with those that had hidden agendas that would certainly bring angst.

I was happy with my success, and was the beneficiary of interesting social invitations all over the United States. I was becoming known and admired. I even entertained the notion of building our own hospital but I could not let go my fascination with film. I invested in a new cable television project that promised to be a winner and my husband, the good doctor, was so furious that I would spend my money in such a reckless way that I lost my nerve and asked for my $17,000 back. The investors honored my request and it was I who was the loser as that project turned out to be one of the biggest ventures in Cable TV and paid handsomely in million dollar profits to the original investors.

Each season promised that with just a little more patience on my part the work schedule at our Medical Center would calm down, that by Spring or Fall, all would be favorable for us to start to enjoy our lives. Sometime soon we would go away on vacation, if not by ourselves, at least with our children – but until then it was work, work, work - day and night, weekend after weekend.

It was a tumultuous year, 1974. I remember seeing Chet Huntley, a bigger than life figure, on the elevator on one of my New York City appointments. I smiled and spoke a friendly greeting but he did not smile back or utter a word to me. It startled me that he did not acknowledge me and I instantly realized how foolish it was to have expected an acknowledgment from him. He did not know that I looked forward to his newscasts, that he was an important part of my daily routine, that his accounts of what was happening in the world I believed.

I stopped believing in the news that was reported by celebrity figures after that and opened my world to many other sources of information. I wanted to know from all perspectives what was happening, and I started to have a deeper respect for the people without big names that were doing good things - things that helped to make the world better. When I read that Chet Huntley died, I realized that none of us gets to choose our moment of departure from this earth. Though you may be big and important in the world - in an instant you may not have another chance to do or say what you want. The hurt I felt when Mr. Huntly did not return my greeting revisited me and I was grateful that this memory brought to me the realization of the importance of living in the moment – of not failing to return a greeting or kindness if at all possible.

Then Duke Ellington died. He was my Daddy's friend who used to play at his entertainment club in Akron, Ohio. I recalled that a few years earlier, Duke had felt sad that our family did not notify him where he was playing in Germany of my Daddy's untimely death in Ohio. He said he would have never been too busy to remember "The Joy Boy," the pet name that people called my Daddy because of his enormous joy for living in the moment. I learned a lesson from The Duke. He taught me that all people deserve a moment of recognition, even from bigger than life figures.

On my birthday in July, my sister Jacqueline was driving her new Pontiac home from the showroom in Ohio. The wheel came off on the highway and she lost control of her car and catapulted over the divider and tumbled down a cliff to her death. I had experienced the death of my grandfather when I was five and then over two decades later the death of my grandmother and father in the same year, but the business of being confronted with death was a rare occurrence in my life. So now, in the same year, I had experienced the deaths of one of the greatest jazz composers of all time, Duke Ellington, and my beloved sister. Few people would ever know that my sister Jacqueline had been Ohio's first Black Homecoming Queen.

I would do my book a great disservice if I did not tell Jacqueline's story. I called her Annie Babe. Annie Babe was more than just a beautiful young woman – she was a force - a force so strong that she took up all the breath in the room. When she walked into a room, all eyes were on her – everyone breathed a breath of astonishment. She was delight and devilment, magic and mystery. There was a vulnerability about her that you couldn't miss but there was also an amazing self confidence that was readily apparent.

She had presence without artificiality. She was an old soul that still retained her sense of wonder. She delighted in meeting people and people felt that they were in the midst of someone that would change their life. She was simply, unforgettable - but bear with me and I shall shortly tell you her story.

The year that Annie Babe died was also the year marking the deaths of Ed Sullivan and Jack Benny, two enormously popular TV Stars. It seemed impossible to imagine that I would never see them on television again. Death was something I shoved far away from my thoughts as I had learned when President Kennedy was assassinated, and then Reverend Martin Luther King Jr. that I had a tendency to hold on to the sadness. I did eventually learn to document the losses I felt in my diaries and even to compose songs that would help me keep the memories of those I loved - alive.

Unbelievably, that year our own President, President Richard Nixon was forced to resign the Presidency due to the Watergate scandal. When India announced that it had created the Atomic Bomb, it became clear that other countries had caught up to America and were capable, too, of dropping an Atomic bomb like the U.S.A. had dropped on Hiroshima during the Second World War. The world was speeding up, changing, and becoming very dangerous.

I was forced to realize how naive and uninformed I was. It was sobering to think that the negligence of someone not tightening a screw on a car wheel had caused the death of my beautiful sister – and that misguided hatred could trigger an atomic button to be pushed that could cause the demise of millions of countrymen across many different borders. I thought of my son's term paper that he had written on "The Creation of the Atomic Bomb" while he was at Stanford University and how his Professor Daniel Ellsberg had commented that he had put "very expressive powers of intellect and judgment to work on a profound subject."

My son R.B. wrote "How could such a bombing have taken place – how could it happen. We are reminded of the causes – the legacy of W.W.II, the assumptions of policymakers, the German threat, but still, we feel unsatisfied. Our questions then become more penetrating: How could scientists consciously devoted years of their lives for such an evil end? How could our leaders have thought in such power oriented terms? Why were moral considerations involving matters of life and death of innocent people given such little attention? Why did the scientists continue work on the bomb although they knew the German threat had been dispelled by intelligence reports? Why didn't they refuse to continue work on this instrument of mass murder when it became plainly obvious the bomb would not be needed to deter the Germans or end the War?

In short, how could real human beings have done all of those things with a good conscious? Here lies the origin of disaster; society as we understand it must be changed if we are to survive the creation of genocidal weapons." My son goes on to say in his brilliant paper which I will include in its entirety at the end of this book, that "if the bomb had not been developed during World War II it would have been developed later on. The will to build the bomb was always there from the very beginning of the war. All the decisions during the war – the decision to bomb cities as a matter of official policy, the decision to build the bomb, the decision to complete construction as quickly as possible, the decision to continue the project, and the decision to drop the bomb on Hiroshima – all of them, all were morally compromised before they were reached. For this we must blame the principles on which modern society, culture and civilization are organized, and our leaders who embody the perversity of their authoritarian logic."

I was forced to think of how one's world could literally explode at any moment. Forced to accept that bad things happened not only to other people, but in my own little comfort zone as well. I wanted earnestly to take a closer look at my little family to see if I could tighten the loose screws, make it all make more sense.

The good Doctor was never home. Everything began to be crazy. On the surface, all appeared normal, but underneath the appearances I sensed a dark cloud that was ever so slowly approaching that threatened to envelop our whole little world. My husband would come home each morning visibly tired, and change into fresh clothes for the office, telling me that he had had a rough night at the hospital, had gone to a bar for a couple of drinks and then back to the hospital.

I accepted these sad, pathetic lies, and hoped that soon the lies would stop and that he would return to normal - but in my heart I knew that everyone was drinking his drinks and he was bragging in some seedy gambling Casino about what great kids he had that soon would be going off to college. I didn't want to be a shrew, and I didn't want to make scenes so I resisted these negative urges but there was real fear in my heart about whether there would be any money for college.

Month after month the good Doctor would crash his car, the new Cadillac or Mercedes, and I fully expected I would get the call that he was killed on the highway, straight out of the Casino. The bars were just a lie. He was always gambling at the Casino. I tried making witty jokes about his behavior hoping that he would see his own folly and seek help.

Then I called his doctor friends and urged them to talk to him, to somehow find a way to help him. But no one seemed willing to interfere. Instead of getting the help that I begged him to get my husband just smiled his conceited smile and gathered new friends. Disheveled and exhausted he would show up at home and I would go with him to see his patients so he wouldn't make a fool of himself. Everyone loved the good Doctor and nightly he still met his friends in those fake gambling halls, in those red carpeted, black tabled bars where everyone wanted something from him. He gave them what they wanted - a drink, or some valium to relax, perhaps a few diet pills to lose some weight, and a sleeping pill or two to help them sleep. And he took plenty for himself as well. But soon he became depressed. Everyone at home had to attend to him, to feed him aspirin for his headache or Maalox for his stomach ache, or to get his sleeping pill so he could sleep. He had to have his bath drawn for him or the water turned off for the bath he had drawn for himself or the whole house would have been flooded. And no one could speak about the state he was in because it depressed him. And if you depressed him too much he wouldn't come home at all. And he needed my stock shares. "Why did I need the controlling stock in a medical center," he would ask.

An Alfa Romeo and a Datsun ended up on the Corporation books, in the names of his secretary and a barmaid he was friends with. I tried to suppress my suspicions. I told myself that he would not be foolish enough to buy cars for women friends when his own family needed money. The mortgage payment for the house went unpaid and the bank cancelled the loan we intended to get for our son and daughter's colleges. Things were bad, but the good Doc still showed up for work. The patients still came.

I beat myself up constantly for not returning home to Philadelphia, permanently. If only, I think, if only I had let go of the housekeepers, sold my New York apartment and returned to the Medical Center full time, all unpleasantness might have been avoided. But of course, I was in New York as a result of my husband not wanting to do things correctly, and it was a way to keep our marriage together without causing any major rumbles.

I loved my husband and my children and I still held out hope that somehow our little family would weather the stormy patches we were traveling through. After all, I had out of necessity worked two jobs for nearly twelve years to get my husband through school and our children seemed well adjusted. My daughter had been attending a wonderful school, Calhoun in New York and living with me as I no longer dared to leave her care to the whimsy of the housekeepers. I had hoped to enroll our son in a New York High School as well but he was determined to graduate from Penn Charter, the school he had entered when he was in kindergarten. I was certain that with my daughter and I returning home each weekend that all would settle down and return to normal.

CHAINS, TEARS, AND
THE UNIMAGINED

And then one day the unimaginable happened. The good Doctor gambled away our home in a poker game. After frantic calls, and great maneuvers to gather all of my personal monies, the debt was paid and our home was again secured. But soon, there was more and more talk about needing that stock, the controlling stock of the Medical Center. The good Doc's lies came tumbling out, one after the other. I believed nothing.

That awful night before I was taken away - I screamed and thrashed out at my husband like a madwoman and then I went into the spare bedroom to cry and cry. Like a limp old worn out rag doll, I cried about what I couldn't fix. And he politely said that he had an appointment with Harvey to play tennis and he left quietly without ever admonishing me for my tantrum.

Liar. Terrible, disgusting liar. You knew you weren't going to play tennis with Harvey. You were going to some crooked judge to pay for some horrible policemen to burst into my home to chain me and drag me off to a mental institution so you could steal the stock I owned in the Medical Center."

Oh, how I hated him the moments that these memories flashed over me - how I loathed the good Doctor. His false papers that had me committed for observation were signed by four psychiatrists. I had never been to a psychiatrist in my life. I thought of how the wood had splintered everywhere as the police officers broke down my bedroom door and ripped the phone out of my hands. They hit me in my knees with their night sticks and crippled me with pain while they handcuffed my hands and tied chains around my legs, and threw me on a stretcher.

As they lowered me down the narrow front staircase - just as we neared the bottom the two officers that held my shoulders lost their footing and I spun forward and was spilled into an icy puddle. Choking, I was lifted from the water and carried to a van in the driveway. I was literally thrown into the van by the officers with my stretcher hitting the side. My body shook. My teeth felt loose as they made a loud rattling noise. I caught the last glimpse of my house as we turned the corner. I would have rather been in a hearse than to leave my home in such disgrace.

I fell from one side of the bench to the other as we weaved in and out of traffic. Everything seemed to buzz and it was some time before I realized that the buzzing I heard was actually the sound of the siren. Through the grated window divider, I could see the back of two of the police officers' heads in the front and I wondered how they could go home and sleep on nice clean pillows after beating up someone's wife and carting her off to a mental institution.

The reflection of lights from the traffic and the revolving van light cast shadows on the van's walls, and as the lights bounced crazily around it looked as if a witch moved about. I realized with horror that the witch was actually my tumbled body, with disheveled hair, inching its way to a sitting position. I felt like a sewage rat as leaking water oozed around my shoulders and I had to repel my urge to vomit. Near a grayish stone wall I was hoisted up onto a cot and carried through a large revolving door and down a dimly lit corridor to a tiny cement cubicle where two orderlies, two white uniformed doctors and a single nurse had gathered. I was removed from the cot and placed on a narrow steel bed and the nurse yelled to the occupants, "Clear out, I've got my work to do."

"Spread your legs I'm going to do a vaginal search for weapons." I couldn't believe what I had heard. She thrust her hand into a rubber glove, shoved her fingers around in my vagina and tossed her soiled glove onto the floor. A sweaty looking doctor came in and peered down at me. "Don't get yourself all worked up, he said, try to relax," and he left the room.

"Nurse, I said, please help me to call my attorney, my husband has done a terrible thing to me." "Shut up," she said, and called for an orderly to come. "Put those restraints back on her." I was dressed in chains and handcuffs again and my gown lay at my side. "I have the right call my attorney," I said, raising my voice. "Lady I told you once already to shut up. The next time I'll show you. Keep her quiet while I get my needle."

"Don't worry ma'am, the orderly said, we take good care of the folks here." He smiled at me broadly. I closed my eyes. Only seconds passed before I felt a hand on my breast. I gasped and opened my eyes. He stood holding his naked penis. "This thing here is going to make you feel really good," he said. I screamed. The man growled and shoved one whole hand up into my insides and put his dripping penis across my mouth. "Keep your trap shut, cunt, or I'll mess you up good," he said, as he hurriedly zippered his pants. I was unable to use my hands to wipe the filth from my mouth.

The nurse returned to the room and thrust me harshly over on my side and stuck a needle into my buttocks. "Please don't leave me alone nurse," I begged. She looked at the orderly and then looked at me. She gave me a harsh smile. "Okay, the party is over," she snapped and shooed the orderly out of the room. How I hated this crude woman, but not as much as I hated my husband. I wanted to do something really awful to him. I wanted him to hurt like I was hurting. Yes, I wanted to cut off his penis. I wanted to cause him as much humiliation as he had caused me.

"Shhh, don't move, don't. If you take my "S" away again they will take my scalp off." I opened my eyes. Long blond hair touched the edge of my chin and foul breath filled my nostrils. I tried to bring my arms up to cover my face but they would not move. My head was clearing now. I was not in a dream. My arms would not move so that meant the restraints were still on me but I could no longer feel the cold steel slab I had been chained to. And, I was no longer cold. So I must not be naked I thought. When had I been moved?

"It's coming. The "S" is at the second bend. The "S" is going around the corner – no, no, - look what you've done. It's gone. My "S" is gone. You moved. You bitch, you horrible bitch. You moved

51

and now my "S" is gone." Through the tears flooding my face I watched the tall, pale woman standing over me rip away from the top of her head, her hair. The woman was bald now, completely bald. She was holding her wig, standing over me and she repeatedly shouted that I had "moved, moved." The woman flailed her arms and screamed, "They have taken my scalp because I did not finish the "S." My face twitched and I was powerless to do anything but watch. I felt my body turning into sponge. I realized I was numb. Was the light coming in the early morning dawn or the evening dusk?

The bald woman moved away to a bed that I could now see alongside a far wall. The woman kept crying and saying, "Oh mama, I am so sorry that they have taken my scalp because I did not finish the "S."

I wondered then if this was the way my life would end, in a mental ward that I had, unbelievably, ended up in. Had I been raped? How many hours had I been unconscious? Would that crying, bald woman try to kill me the next time I let her "S" get away? "Oh God, Dear God," I cried out, and then I suddenly stopped. "No, I said, I will not call out to God, again. If there is a God, he has not heard my pleas. I must think of another way to save myself. I must not let my life end in this awful room. I have to think of a way to help myself, I kept thinking. I shall go crazy if I do not think of how to get out of this mess. I shall be as loony as the woman making the "s" sign.

Dear God, is she making those "s" signs because of the drugs they have given her? No. She is baldheaded and crying about her scalp being taken. Surely she is crazy. She is not like me. Could she have been like me when she came in here? I must get a hold of myself. I must not let the good Doctor get away with this. This cruel game of his has gone too far. I must find a way to convince them that I am not sick.

I must tell them…th-thh - that, th- thh that…ooooh, God, nooooooo, no, no.

"Shut up immediately," the nurse said.

"It is five o'clock in the morning, shut up."

"Pp- pp- please, hel- hel- help me, I cried." The words would not come out of my mouth. I did not even realize it was me screaming until I heard myself stuttering. I closed my eyes. I could not face another terror. I could not speak simple words, and without eyes or words, how could I defend myself? It didn't matter. Neither had done me any good up to that point.

After a long time, the nurse came back into the room and got me out of bed and told me I must go out and have breakfast with the other patients. I put paper slippers on my wobbly feet and walked out of my room into the dayroom. There were a dozen patients seated at an oblong table sipping carbonated fruit drinks and eating packaged cupcakes.

A brown skin man with an Apache strip of hair across his otherwise bare head barked at me to stop staring and to sit down. A greasy haired blond man clothed in a spotted, shiny, blue satin robe ordered me to sit next to him, saying "You can stay where you are lady, Aristotle is not the boss of us." I looked at the man with the Apache strip, who I realized was Aristotle, but I said nothing. I closed my eyes and, with tears streaming down my face, I sat down. I made no attempt to wipe the tears away. "We are your family, a voice said. Look at us, we are all you have." My mind screamed, "no, you are not my family" but I managed to remain silent. I opened my eyes and looked slowly, deliberately, at each and every one. I said, "Forgive me. I do not mean to cry but I am frightened."

"You've got reason to cry in this crummy joint," Aristotle said. "How long are you here for?" I told him I did not even know how long I had been there. "Your husband is a doctor, isn't he?" Yes, I replied, how do you know? "I heard you screaming when they brought you in, and I heard the nurses talking about you," he said.

"Did you see my husband," I asked. "No, he didn't come, but a young girl came – but they wouldn't let her in - they said you weren't allowed to have visitors." Aristotle looked at me with red rimmed eyes that darted back and forth - and then settled into tiny, piercing daggers. Energy drained from my body. I closed my eyes to pray.

After a long moment, a very nervous sounding voice announced, "I don't want anybody to take my seat while I make a phone call." I almost laughed out loud. "Who is he kidding," I thought as I opened my eyes. "He wishes he could make a phone call." A little, wiry man with an uncontrollable mound of unkempt dark hair rose and fished around in his pocket and came up with something that sounded like change. My heart raced. I sat on the edge of my seat as I watched the little man move away from the table. Could it be true? Was it possible that he was going to use a phone?

I looked around the large dismal room with its ill fitted plastic furniture and tried to see where he was going. He passed two open doorways and stopped. He looked back at the nurse's station, which was empty, and sort of slid around a large gray cabinet and then just disappeared. I got up out of my seat but was too nervous to make a step. I imagined myself walking to the gray cabinet and finally forced my feet to move. I was halfway to the cabinet when double doors, which I had failed to notice behind the nurse's station, swung open. Two nurses walked hurriedly past me, paying me no mind.

I started to walk quickly now, not looking back over my shoulders. My paper slippers made far too much noise so I slipped out of them and raced to the cabinet, barefoot. Just to the far left of the cabinet, the little wiry man stood gesturing wildly with one hand while holding a phone receiver in the other. He was standing beneath a pay phone that was almost too tall for him to reach. My heartbeat quickened and then nearly stopped. I was so excited about the phone that I failed to appreciate that the little man did not want me near him.

"Shhhh, shhh," the little man said, jumping up and down with both feet as he swung the receiver around with one arm while he kept me away with his other arm. I stepped back. "Shhh, shhh, I'm from the FBI and I've got to call the CIA," the man said.

I could not believe my ears. The change was right there in his palm but the man was too crazy to even put the coins in the slot. "Shhh, I'm from the CIA, and now I must call the FBI." The man was confused, really confused as he had now decided he was with the CIA.

I will call for you, I told the little man and I beseeched him to give me the money. The man held out his change and I took the phone. I put the coins in and dialed my attorney. My coins came back. I had dialed the wrong number. I could not remember my attorney's number. Shaking, I put the coins back in and dialed my home number. "Oh, please, please, answer," I prayed. The little man was gesturing wildly and ranting about the CIA, the FBI - and my number just rang and rang.

Then, suddenly my daughter answered the phone, saying, "I'm very sleepy Mommy, please call me back later." I couldn't fathom what was happening. "But I can't call you back," I stammered. The phone went dead. There was no one on the other end. There was only the little man yelling, "Did you tell them I am from the CIA?"

"Put the phone down, immediately," a harsh voice shouted. I turned around and stared into the face of an unsmiling nurse. "You are not permitted to use the phone. You will not be given any more dayroom privileges."

I thrust the little man's remaining change back into his hand and put my head into my hands, weeping, in utter despair. The nurse accompanied me back and just as we were about to enter the dayroom, I saw my friend Rita at the nurse's station. My impulse was to pick up my feet and run, run as fast as I could to my friend but I could not risk doing anything that would make me seem out of control.

"You have no privileges presently," the nurse said. "You must go back to your room." I did not look at the nurse but instead spoke to Rita who was staring at one of the patients. "Hello Ri-ri-ri-ta," I said. Rita looked at me but with unknowing eyes. She did not recognize me. She was fascinated with looking at Gilda who was seated nearby rocking her blond wig in her arms as though the wig were her own little baby.

I touched my friends arm and called her name once more. I thought she would break apart when she finally realized who I was. I have never seen such pain on another human being's face. Pain and rage and disbelief. It had been sometime since I had showered or set my hair or even brushed my teeth. Without the benefit of good speech, or makeup, or proper clothing, I was a sorry sight indeed.

Though I stuttered, I was able to briefly tell Rita how I had ended up in the insane asylum. She held fast to my hand and refused to leave. She pulled out all the stops in my defense and told the staff that she herself was a doctor and would be going to Court to obtain my release. Rita held me tightly, assured me that she would not abandon me and cautioned me to remain calm, to be brave. She told me that she was going to immediately call my attorney and private doctors and that she would be back to get me out.

Tearfully, I had to watch Rita walk away from me, but she kept her word. She went to Court and got a Habeas Corpus Decree from Judge Juanita Stout and hours later I was released from the worst nightmare of my life to a private hospital.

My mind is still a fog about the days I spent in the private hospital, but one day those memories are bound to come back. They can't be any worse than the ones I have recounted here, but why, why have I blocked them out? It remains a puzzle to me."

What I remember clearly, and wish I could forget, is my ride from Philly to New York just hours after getting out of the hospital. I called a Car Service to have a driver take me to my home at 74th and Madison in NYC. A Limousine picked me up and I was surprised that it was not a Sedan. I had used a Limo several times in the past for big film events but the circumstances under which I was presently getting out of hardly warranted the use of a Limousine. I tried to act as though I deserved the fawning, elaborate posturing the driver made as he closed down all of the middle seats that made up the long space between the driver and the rear seat where I was to be seated. As I was helped in, I fought to think of the hand on my elbow as a friendly one but my mind wouldn't let go of the fact that very unfriendly hands had only a week earlier grabbed my elbows and chained me down to an unwelcomed police stretcher.

The trip got underway and I was grateful that I did not have to talk to the Driver as his few attempts to converse with me were thwarted by the fact that I could not hear what he was saying. After some moments of imagining the many festive occasions that must have taken place in such a Limousine, I fell asleep somewhere near the number 10 Exit on the New Jersey Turnpike.

"Get out of the car. Put your hands up and get out of the car." I awakened to rifles pointed at the Limo windows, extreme shouting, uniforms, and a barrage of badges, none of which I could comprehend. Doors were opened, I was ordered out – to stand at the rear- and the driver was ordered to stand at the front driver's door. He was frisked and had numerous obscenities screamed at him.

Then, some uniformed madmen came and threw open the trunk, and tore up the matting on the Limo's floor, attempting to find something. When nothing could be found, I was ordered back into car, and after many more terrifying minutes where the shouting continued, the madmen suddenly got back into their vehicles and sped away. The driver returned to our vehicle, shrugged his shoulders like, "Boy that was something, wasn't it," and proceeded with our trip.

My shoulders were quivering and my hands shaking when I arrived at my building, but I managed to sign the driver's invoice and propelled myself through the doorman's greeting to the elevator. Trying to smile away inquiries about where I had been by pretending to be expecting an important call, I stumbled through my door after several unsuccessful attempts to use my key. Immediately, I succumbed to a floodgate of tears and finally managed to call my elderly neighbor Mr. Fekete and his girlfriend Donna, and they came downstairs to assist me. I told them about my life's sad events of the past few weeks and the shocking incident with the Limousine in which I had just traveled. My friends listened with horror. Mr. Fekete had lost his entire family, excepting one sister, in the Nazi Concentration Camps in Poland, and said he understood too fully the cruelty of mankind. He sent Donna to get some fresh fruit, and then very patiently after I confessed I had been unable to eat for days - fed me, spoon by spoon, tiny slices of oranges that Donna had cut up.

For weeks I lay in a vegetative state but encouraged by the dearest friend I have ever had in this world, Mr. Fekete, I gathered my courage and began to think about having a life again. During this very somber period of my life, I remember nothing about my interactions with my children or my husband, but I do recall lying across one or other of the beds in my beautiful apartment and thinking deliberately about everything that I could that would coerce my memory bank back to many precious interactions with Poppa, my grandfather who had always brought me such joy and sound advice.

My apartment was actually two apartments where I had been given permission to break through the walls when I purchased them and construct a stained glass door that separated my Film Studio and Editing Rooms from my Living Quarters. I would walk through this beloved place imagining my Poppa saying, "You did right good young'un, right good." How I wanted Poppa to look down upon me and say, "You will pull yourself out of the abyss, young'un, and the Lord will put you on the right road." Over and over again, I imagined Poppa's voice talking to me. I would fall asleep tormented by that "Road from Hell" I had been on and then hours later I'd wake up feeling that I had been in Poppa's presence. I could definitely feel something had changed and there was a spirit awakening in me – a spirit that said, "Yes, you will have a sighting of rainbows."

POPPA

With the dreadful tale of my incarceration out of the way I am now free to remember the truly interesting and tumultuous multi- generational life stories that stretch from my chic 74th and Madison Avenue neighborhood of New York City all the way back to the red clay hills of Troy, Alabama where my grandfather Charles Brooks was born. During the Post Civil War Years, slavery was abolished technically, but the harsh daily reality for slaves searching for work was definitely not like following a recipe for making peach cobbler where you first did this and then did that and you could be guaranteed a finished pie. You could do everything right and still not know if you would ever see the pie. In other words, some sturdy souls survived the hardships they faced after slavery and became great mentors for their families and for society as a whole. I was fortunate that I had two powerful mentors in my life, my father's parents, Poppa and Granny.

My grandfather, who I called Poppa, was a wonderful storyteller and a great mentor. I knew that he was very special because he always took that extra moment to consider my needs before he gave his heartfelt response. Poppa always seemed to put his thoughts on a "balancing scale," weighing them carefully to measure what the outcome would be if he tipped the scale in favor of my urgent "please, Poppa, please can we go to the park now" or should he let that scale measure out the weight of giving in to his grandchild's too many indulgent whims and thereby affect the rest of my life adversely.

In the instance of my wanting to go to the park "now" - Poppa took me to the park as it was one of the rare times that I had Poppa to myself without my seven siblings. Poppa packed a quick lunch of fried chicken and two containers of my Granny's peach cobbler which he put in the wicker basket with the rounded wicker handles that he had brought from his restaurant in the South, the first integrated one in Troy, Alabama.

Poppa was oak colored with a shock of wavy white hair. He was very tall and distinguished looking. He was a man who always wore gold rimmed eye spectacles, a three-piece suit, bow tie and a long gold watch chain on his vest. I cannot remember ever seeing him when he was not formally dressed, even this day as we walked up the street past all of the little frame and brick homes, their trimmings painted in varying soft colors of blue, beige, or pale celery green. Poppa, even on this casual day, was in his smart, pin striped suit.

In my grandfather's neighborhood, there was only one bannister wrap around porch and that belonged to Poppa. It was a spanking clean porch that had Poppa's big old metal swing couch in the corner and pots and pots of my Granny's pansies and morning glories all over the scrubbed surfaces of the ledges securing the bannisters into place. All of the homes had manicured lawns with plump white and lavender lilac bushes on either sides of the porch steps and Poppa's lawn boasted not only the beautiful lilac bushes but a giant apple tree as well.

As we made our way up the winding hill and found ourselves in the park near that ancient oak tree where a weathered leather strap swing hung on rough chains under it, I suddenly bolted ahead and ran to the top of the sliding board, barely giving Poppa a chance to catch me as I slid to the bottom. With a chuckle, Poppa gathered me in his arms and we began to swing. Poppa squinted his eyes and smiled and said, "young'un,' before you get all tuckered out we will have a taste of this lunch. It is just the kind of lunch that folks were crazy about in my restaurant in Troy. And Poppa took a bite of the crusty chicken, smiled wryly, and I knew the storytelling would begin."

"O Youngun," Poppa said, I kept aplenty, kept a big old barrel of fresh chickens to fry and a woman standing by the stove all day doing all the frying. Fried a piece brown and she'd put it up on the warmer shelf along with the mullet and steak - so when they had an order, all you had to do was reach up on the warmer, take down that big ol'piece of meat, put gravy over it and folks was ready to enjoy my cookin.'"

"One day, the day of the big circus show, the overflow crowd growed so thick that I took down the rope that separated the white tables from the colored tables and the whites spilled over to the colored side. It wasn't long for the old sheriff stopped in for his usual meal, and he was taken back seeing the Whites and Blackers eating side by side. That sheriff was coughing and choking and he brung a hush to that room with his booming, raspy voice - "What the hell do you think you are doing, boy?"

I reached upon the warmer and took down a big ol' piece of steak, poured gravy over it youngun,' and put it on a plate with the other fixins. We always served greens and skillet bread, and I put the plate on the table in front of that puffin ol' red faced sheriff. I pulled out his chair, and said n'er a word to him, just motioned for him to SIT DOWN. Well, he purpled all up but he sat down after a bit and I paid him no more mind."

Imagine, that's how Poppa integrated his restaurant.

Everything was going great in Poppa's fine Southern Eatery. His four boys and four girls worked like clock -work together but one sunny afternoon everything fell apart. Poppa and Josie were preparing supper for their family in their cottage that Josie tendered so lovingly. The boys were in the driveway playing ball - and suddenly Poppa heard a commotion in the driveway. The neighbor was screaming and carrying on something awful.

"I don't want no niggers playin' in the driveway," the woman hollered.

Poppa stormed out of the cottage and confronted the old White woman. He argued, "my boys was in the driveway playin' ball. They wasn't keepin' no noise, not a bit."

That poor White woman was adamant. She kept shouting, "I don't want no niggers' playin' in the driveway."

Poppa got mad, real mad. He had always been respectful to the neighbors, even giving them food during their hard times. But Poppa knew right then and there that he would not stay in a place where his children would be called "niggers." Poppa closed up his restaurant and packed up all of the family's belongings. On the morning that Poppa and Josie left their home, Poppa said Josie was cryin' her heart out standing in the yard under that big Apple tree she planted in memory of Gus, the little youngun' she lost to pneumonia.

"My Angel boy's spirit is here. How can I leave my boy under this tree, Poppa? Little Gus helped us grow the sweetest apples in the South, you know that Poppa." Poppa took Josie in his arms and held her and said, "Little Gus Will help you grow the sweetest apples in the North."

And, so it was - against the backdrop of the red clay hills of Alabama, and the mighty cornfields that Josie ran barefoot through when she was a child - and with the hurt of things left behind that are stuck in his mind - Poppa boards the restless train with Josie and her numerous bags and bunches, her pansies and her pots, her morning glories and cartons, her tulips and rolled carpets, and her children.

Eight children running, eight children rushing and scrambling to stack bags, find seats. Beloved children, each one of them. All were aboard and Poppa had not left behind a single member of his family to suffer being called a "nigger" again.

STRIVING TO BE ONE'S BEST SELF

Our ideas of who we are come from the stories we digest. I reheard this old philosophy from my Media and Ethics Professor, Robert Berkman at The New School and it served to remind me of why my Poppa knew in his gut that he had to remove his children from an environment ripe with prejudice and put them into one that would help foster positive thoughts and noble goals. There is a wonderfully inspiring story that people young and old can profit from. It is the life story of Dr. Ben Carson who went from the inner city streets of Detroit to the halls of Yale to becoming one of the most famous and respected neurosurgeons in the world for his dramatic and ground breaking work in separating conjoined twins. Dr. Carson, now retired but active in politics, and in fact ran for the President of the United States on the Republican 2016 ticket, was for many years the Director of the Pediatric Neurosurgery Department at John Hopkins Medical Center.

Dr. Carson in his book, "Think Big"[1] said he was headed for jail, reform school or the grave before he realized he had to take a different course. Carson's father abandoned him and his brother and his mother and by sheer will Carson's mother found the strength to institute procedures into the daily routine of Carson's life that enabled him to turn his life around. Carson's mother insisted that he go to Detroit's Public Library and read two books each and every week. He could only watch two TV programs per week and with the time that he would have spent watching mindless TV he was encouraged to listen to music, engage in his imagination and visit museums. Just imagine going from dire poverty, poor grades, a horrible temper, and low self- esteem, to becoming Director of Neurosurgery at a major hospital. Ben Carson's mother was one of twenty-four children, raised in rural Tennessee, who got married at just thirteen to try to escape her environment only to discover that she had married a bigamist. Determined to do good, she raised her two sons by herself with only a third grade education. Carson's mother told him "If anybody can do something, you can do it too, except that you can do it better."

Carson encourages one and all to "Think Big,"[1] the title of one of his books. "If your life is a series of shattered dreams, if you have no dreams at all, or if you bought the lie that you'll never amount to anything, don't believe it," Carson says. Carson believes that each individual can choose another pathway by developing another mindset that will lead them to success "It doesn't matter where you are; you can make something out of any situation. You must develop that mindset."

It is difficult for many people in this modern world to find a niche for themselves, and particularly for the many thousands of children in the inner cities. Wynton Marsalis says "our culture has experienced a decline of intellectual rigor along with an unchecked decadence. When there's a greater degree of decadence, a higher level of heroism is required to combat it because there's much less reward. More stress lies on the people who want to be serious, and if you are serious, you run the risk of falling apart and crumbling because of the stress. In this New America the absurd reigns and we cling to commercial integrity; the right to put whatever we want into the marketplace and charge as much as possible for as little as possible." He points to the omission of plots in films, the killing of each other, left and right, and getting naked for no reason at all as proof of the absurdity that abounds. The degree of conformity to the absurd is what shocks him the most he says as he travels the world. He says African Americans, White folk. Liberal, Conservative are all holding a script like a machine stamped them on the forehead right off the conveyor belt.

To have integrity in a time when you are in a time with no standard of integrity - demands hard choices - and one has to be able to understand that only he or she can make those choices. Marsalis asks us to consider how do you sift integrity from corruption and absurdity if no one takes the responsibility to tell you, to show you? Teachers. mentors, leaders, just plain good people have a responsibility to step up to these dire challenges that those who are temporarily misguided or lost are facing and I earnestly believe that in some definitive way we each can help guide the way, not only for schoolchildren but for all in society who feel a weariness of heart.

Marsalis said in one of his appearances at a school a little boy "grabbed his johnson"[2] while singing and Marsalis asked the teacher if indeed he had seen what he thought he saw and the teacher assured him "that's what they do nowadays." Marsalis replied, "Well, who's teaching them?"

Marsalis cautions us to remember that excellence reigns when one gives their best effort to their work. He believes that people study all great disciplines and art forms with such intensity because the individual "channels the spirit of the nation. It not only reflects the values, it embodies them, it ennobles them, it emboldens them."

"The arts survive, Marsalis says, when whole civilizations perish and they remain useful because they point to the excellence that reigned when one gave their best effort to their work. In art, there is only one generation, the generation of man," Marsalis affirms.

Students must be warned about the depression that can come when they can feel successful only if his or her work rivals the best work of the greatest artist ever. Those goals will kill you, Marsalis says. " Instead of feeling bad because you can't rival one of the six great innovators, instead of being consumed with matching the legacy and likes of the Louis Armstrongs of the world, why not redirect your priorities and strive to be your personal best by becoming one of the best trained musicians. Marsalis tells the musicians to "Invest in your discipline, your practice, and your personal growth. Develop your soul by participating in the lives of other people in a positive way, through giving." Like Barack Obama, Marsalis believes that "activities must also have an objective of the soul." Your work must have something in it that will benefit the world. "We need soul objectives on a high level, a level higher than the pursuit of money, and one-upmanship over another person."

Wynton Marsalis reminds us that Art Blakey said, "you never see an armored car following a hearse." This is exactly the sort of thing the inner city kids across America need to hear and hold close to their hearts. I certainly have examined, and am still thinking very seriously about the reasons I wanted to document the deeply personal story of my life. I was offered money from a Hollywood film producer for my story and once was given a publishing opportunity from a noted publisher but I turned both down because I wasn't ready. I needed to try to understand my journey, to write the experiences down and to reflect, even brood over them. In reliving the dramas, I endured, I hoped to gain valuable insight - to answer the big life question of "Why Am I Here?"

THE DEATH OF A HOMECOMING QUEEN

A truly life changing experience for me was realizing that I would not see my beautiful older sister again. Jacqueline had visited me for a week in NYC and had just returned to her town in Akron, Ohio. On her way home from picking up her new car at the Pontiac Dealers Showroom, she was on the highway and, unbelievably, one of the wheels of the car came off and she careened across the divider and plummeted down a cliff and was killed instantly. A nurse and her husband, who were in the car behind my sister, said they had witnessed the woman in the car ahead frantically trying to control her car and suddenly the car was toppling down the cliff. The couple painstakingly climbed down this treacherous terrain only to find that there was nothing they could do for Jacqueline. She had not survived the crash.

This was unreal as only hours earlier she had said goodbye to me in New York City. It was my birthday and she was anxious to get home to her children, despite my protestations that she stay longer and have dinner with me. What was really bittersweet was the fact that Jacqueline had been given an opportunity to do some modeling assignments which was what she really wanted to do and I had worked hard to get her interviews with the right agencies. But after agonizing over her age - she was thirty-nine – she had decided that leaving her two teenage children for such uncertain work was a fool hearty notion and she left me with the offhanded quip, "I can always tell my grandchildren that I was singled out to be a model in New York City but I turned it down because there I would have been just a little fish in a big sea and in Ohio, I am the Queen, a really big fish in a tiny little pond."

She laughed at herself but I knew that she was terrified of getting old and did not want to face the rejection I regularly had to face in the tough competitive pool of models and actresses in New York. It had helped her greatly that I was regularly working in commercials and that my agencies took to my sister's timeless beauty and irreverent and friendly humor, but Jacqueline wanted a sure story that she could always tell - one of acceptance. Jacqueline wanted fantasy, not frustration. What she knew she could achieve was regular fashion gigs at local Charity Events, with her being the Star. The hardest thing I ever did was to make up my sister's face to cover the wounds from the crash. Our mother was certain I could repair the Funeral Home's botched efforts, and I did, but it cost me much emotional distress and to this day is something I cannot wipe from my memory bank. Jacqueline's story deserves so much more than the accounting of her funeral and I strive to honor her always as she was so human - so brave, and yet so very vulnerable, too.

JACQUELINE, THE ONE AND ONLY "ANNIE BABE"

My sister Jacqueline had extraordinary looks and was one of the most uniquely giving and mysterious characters I have ever known. She couldn't imagine growing old and being ignored, and she was obsessed with the meaning of life and how and why one was remembered when they died. She loved dramatizing about what her funeral would be like. She imagined that everyone that she had ever known would be there and that the multitudes of red roses would make her departure seem more the celebration of her homecoming where she was crowned the Queen at the football game. She never tired talking about how she would never be forgotten and I have long felt that indeed she did have a foretelling of her early death. The entire town was moved by the tragic turn in Jacqueline's life and the Church could not hold the enormous crowd that came to the funeral to bid her goodbye. For sure, our Granny knew why she stored Jacqueline's story in a sacred place.

I was always storing Granny's stories in my head, and when I wasn't doing that, I was rummaging through her old Southern wicker basket filled with scraps of paper, photographs and memories from her life. One day, I brought that basket out to the porch and I was immersed in studying the births and deaths of family members dating far back. They were written on a piece of paper which was clearly fading away but it was carefully tucked into the family bible. I noticed a curious envelope near the bible marked "private" but the envelope was unsealed so I looked inside. I was surprised to find the diary of Jacqueline, my sister.

Jacqueline, who I called Annie Babe, was a bigger than life character - beautiful like a Hollywood Star, bold like an adventuresome cowgirl - she favored western boots, sweeping skirts, and colorful, bold language. Oddly, she was childlike, too, and could be easily hurt. In an instant her feelings could be wounded and she'd turn into a limp "Raggedy Ann Doll." Hence, my pet name for her was Annie Babe, which depicted her innocence and her brashness. It was impossible not to curl up on that old swing couch and memorize every word of that diary. Jacqueline took her yearnings and her pain all the way back to the cotton fields of Troy, Alabama. This was the riveting tale from Annie Babe's Diary.

"Certainly, everybody at the school wasn't happy that she was chosen. Maybe some were even a little jealous. Perhaps even one of the parents had put the person up to the heinous call. Still, she wasn't going to stay away from the game. She had won her place fairly in a school wide vote, and she was going to walk onto that field tomorrow night and take her place right alongside the girls whose parents were in the social register's Blue Book. She would stand proud along with these young women who lived up "on the hill" in their stately mansions with tennis courts and swimming pools."

Her granny who had worked in the cotton fields and who had ironed barrels of pretty frocks for her mistress in The Great House would finally see one of her own in one of those grand party dresses. Layers of white tulle were already fastened to a glorious hoop her granny had brought with her from that beautiful big old plantation house she had worked in all of her young life in Troy, Alabama.

For a half a century Granny had saved that hoop and her collection of hand molded black flat irons on one of the hand- made shelves her husband, Poppa, had fashioned out of dirt walls, deep down in the cellar of the little frame shingled home that would be the repository of not only Granny's canned peaches and pickled beets, asparagus, onions, and just about every vegetable you could name but those shelves were layered with years of soft and tender touches by Granny that the future would be bountiful and bright for all of her children and grand young'uns.

For two weeks now, she had tried the dress on. Each and every day she would practice walking in it with her new high heels. The books she had placed on her head to help her keep her balance were finally gathering dust on the attic floor. At last, she could walk naturally in its long sweeping skirt. No nigger calling mean spirited person was going to ruin the best night of her life. When the school marching band stood still on that big field and played the beautiful refrain she was prepared to walk to when her name was called - she would walk proud. And she would walk tall. Down that long football field, she would go, as graceful and perfect as anyone could ever hope to be. All of the rotten eggs in the world could not spoil the honor that was beating in her heart. If she was a "nigger," then she was a blessed one, because one little colored girl was going to make her granny proud.

"Ladies and Gentlemen, West High School is proud to present its 1953 Homecoming Court." It was hard to believe, but here she was, listening to that big booming voice and waiting to walk on the arm of the football captain, right out to the middle of the field. The frantic day and missed lunch and dinner, even the fraught moments of the run for the bus that would take her and the homecoming members to the stadium was a blur of sketches now. The royal black night sky and the little iced puffs of air she made with her breath seemed to validate that indeed she must be on schedule.

It was all happening so fast. "Oh God, please walk with me," she thought. "Look for the North Star, take a deep breath, say your prayers again," the wise little voice in her head said. Finally, she focused. She wanted to take it all in. She wanted to remember everything. "Jacqueline Sonja Brooks." That was her. Her name had been called. Slowly, on the arm of her handsome football Captain, she walked. Walked tall and perfectly. There was no head spinning like a top or legs moving like limp spaghetti. "All of these people are applauding and cheering me," she thought, and they will never forget how tall I walked."

She reached the center of the field and took her place with the other homecoming girls. At last, all of the names had been called and the perfumed line of starch and crinoline bowed and sang their

Alma Mater. The commentator began calling names again. The girl whose name he called would step out in front and stand to the left or the right, leaving a space in the middle for the Homecoming Queen. Only two names were left to be called, and she realized that hers was one of them. "Oh, good," she thought, "I get to put the crown on the Queen's head."

There was a thunderous roar, and then blue eyed Sue, very much a member of the titled Blue Book, stepped out. She tripped, regained her footing and walked timidly to join the line of waiting attendants. Jacqueline stood alone. There was no one waiting with her. She was completely alone, waiting.

"Our Homecoming Queen is Miss Jacqueline Brooks," the voice said.

She looked about. She smiled. But, she just stood there. She couldn't move. She couldn't believe it. They had called her name, "Jacqueline. Jacqueline Sonja Brooks. Or had they said Sonja?" She couldn't remember. But they had said Jacqueline. She knew that. They definitely had said that she, Jacqueline, was the Queen.

They began to place a red velvet robe around her shoulders, and a jeweled crown on her head. They pulled her out front, and the stadium went wild. Sixty thousand people stood and cheered. Cheered a fifteen-year-old little colored girl. She just couldn't believe it. The football Captain placed a dozen red roses in her arms and the football team lifted her high up as she fixed her gaze on her North Star. They brought her down gently and placed her atop the back seat of a shiny open white Cadillac convertible. She was the Queen, the first Negro Homecoming Queen in the history of the city of Akron. With its fabled *No Negroes or Jews in the Firestone Country Club*, Akron, Ohio now had a Negro Homecoming Queen.

She rode around that big stadium and waved to one and all as the school band played, Hail The Queen. "I am so happy," she thought, but her mind kept wandering and coming back to the words her grandmother had burned into her heart, "Young'un, there ain't n'er a pretty dress in the world worth losing your dignity over."

Though she imagined she must indeed look beautiful with her white tulle and red roses and crown, she knew only too well that someone out there, a very hateful, perhaps even dangerous someone was not smiling about her crowning. To that person, she was just a "nigger" and not a lovely young Queen, not yet sixteen.

She looked up again at her North Star. "Thank you, my shining light," she said, "for keeping me composed tonight, and, for protecting me from harm's way so another colored child will wear my dress one day."

She made a little cross on her heart with the little "white poofs of magic air" she had captured from her own breath - and with more than a little heave and sigh from deep within her bare and frigid shoulders - she stood and waved triumphantly for her Granny and all who had come before. She knew her ancestors had paid a heavy price of enslavement and servitude to make one little colored girl's dream come true

DEAR GRANNY, JOSEPHINE
AMANDA BROOKS

I always feel empowered when I tell my sister Jacqueline's story but without our dear Granny's sacrifices there would have been no Jacqueline Homecoming Queen Story. My grandmother was such a proud woman and I realize now the pain I must have caused her by my constant urging as a child that she tell me about her memories of how the slaves were treated when she was a youngster in the South. She would always say "Oh young'un what you gonna stir up that trouble for," and then she would settle down in her glider swing couch on her shingled porch with all its little pots of flowers sitting on the banisters and she would beckon me to come and sit by her side.

She would furrow her brow slightly but her eyes would be steady and very gentle looking as she gazed at me, and she would begin to tell me the stories that were in her mind and heart.

She would speak with a quiet, but determined voice and her face would reflect the things she seemed to be seeing right in front of her, things from a very different world than the one I was familiar with. I would be cemented to my seat, hanging on to her every word. I would conjure up these images of the people and places that she described and I prayed that my imagination was as rich as my Granny's descriptions.

One Sunday afternoon, after Church and dinner with all my siblings - and the mountainous dishes were all washed and put away, my Granny was indulging me in my usual "Story Quest." With my five-year-old legs crossed eagerly and snuggled against my Granny's petite frame on her old porch glider swing, I learned that my grandmother's mother's name was Missy. "Oh young'un, Missy was a looker, she was, with her long braid spilling down the back of her frock - she could turn a head, she could. Even with her arms full up with bushels, Missy was a sight to reckon with." I was fascinated by this name, Missy. Surely, that couldn't have been her real name, but Granny insists that it was.

Missy, as it turns out, was a beautiful slave on Captain Knowles plantation, who divided her time between cooking and caring for the Captain's family in The Big House, and working in the fields with her own three children, all fathered by a wealthy but uncaring Caucasian man, Dr. Graves.

The Captain learns that he has lost all of his money and is going to have to let go most of his slaves. The Captain has kept a tight rein on all of his free labor and despite the Civil War's end, for more than a few years, has managed to keep his unpaid laborers away from the growing number of slaves moving about in hopes of finding salaried work. Missy has heard talk about shares of the plantation being divided up and sold off but she doesn't know what to make of it. She feels beholding to the Captain in an odd way. When he was heading up his regiment in the Civil War she had wet nursed the Captain's baby, offering one "tit" to the Knowles baby and the other one to her own son.

Missy had benefitted by being in The Big House. The Captain's wife had taught the Knowles children how to count and read and she had watched and listened intently. Little by little Missy had learned to count and read a bit and she had passed this learning on to her own. When the Captain came back with his whole arm shot off from fighting in the war, Missy did all that she could do to help the Captain regain his health. And now he has come to tell her, "Missy, you are free, free as the day is long." Missy is overcome with emotion. She realizes she must decide whether she will leave with the other slaves or stay on with the Captain.

Missy knows that everything depends on her making the right decision. She alone is responsible for her Aunt Mary and sons, Jack and Johnson, and daughter Josie. Aunt Mary needs not to lose her home; the one room shack in the woods where she lived since her sister was stolen from that dark cottage with its lone window. The cottage, situated at the far end of the blackened corn fields, was a stone's throw into the woods. Missy, too, needed to be close to those woods. Amanda was Aunt Mary's sister, but she was also Missy's own mother. It was hard thinking about Amanda being put up on the auction block and sold for fifty cents and it was something that Missy could still not accept.

Missy stays on with the Captain in the tiny cottage and for years her two sons Jack and Johnson work as porters at the big hotel in Troy, Alabama. Missy puts aside half of their salaries each month, a sum of ten dollars, to save for the plot of land on which her little cottage shack sits. Missy, herself, has begun cooking large trays of chicken and pies for her boys to sell to the hotel's restaurant. Missy's cooking is such a success that she hires out her daughter Josie and the two boys to cater large parties.

Just as Missy learns that she finally has enough money to buy the little plot of land on which they live, Aunt Mary dies. Missy is devastated. She buries Aunt Mary in the spot where Amanda was put up on the auction block and sold but stops short of putting up a marker – promising her beloved Aunty that someday she will put her and her mother in a "Right Smart" place and that everyone will know her name and her story.

Jack and Johnson move away to better their lives and Missy is heartbroken. She struggles to regain her spirit and rallies a bit when Josie meets a beautiful chocolate colored man at the New Troy Hotel in Troy Alabama. Charles Brooks, a chef, is no ordinary man - working a second job running his own cotton gin in Smut Eye, near Troy.

Charles diligently saves his money, and dreams hard of opening his own restaurant.

Just off the Square in Troy, at 408 East Academy Street, near the H. Sacks Department Store, Charles makes his dream happen and opens his new business. Charles' feet are firmly grounded with hard working soles that propel him to cook and cater seven, brutally long days - but he saves plenty enough spirit to gather his beloved Josie into his arms to plant his seeds for a large family.

Missy will not live to see Josie's children and she dies quietly with Josie at her side. But before she goes, Missy begs Josie to get a plot of land for all of them - with space enough for the entire family's markers so one day they all can be together again.

All of the years that I knew Granny she expressed herself in the plural - our House, our Sunday Clothes, our Pastor, our Garden, our Playtime, our Naptime, our Poppa, our Storytime. Everything was about family, for family, with family. I marveled at the bigness of her heart and her utter inability to consider that I was asking selfishly to hear another tale of her days in the South when she had so many other important things to do - pies to make for Poppa's Grille, jars upon jars of canned goods to get onto the cold dirt shelves in the basement, stacks of Poppa's shirts to spray and starch and wrap tightly so they would not dry out before they were ironed. But when I summoned her to that old glider swing to beg the telling of another one of her tales of the South, Granny seemed as unwilling to disappoint me as I was unwilling to "simmer down" as she would say when I would cling to her side, begging to know "how the family came to be."

THE BROOKS'- POPPA AND GRANNY - AND THEIR YOUNGUNS

'Fats Eugene was the firstborn son of Charles and Josie - followed by daughter, Ruby. And when Charles looked at Fats Eugene's worried face and daughter Ruby's tearful eyes as the family disembarked from their long train ride from their home down South, Poppa knew that he had to make good the promise he had made to his children that great fortune awaited them in a town called Akron.

My Poppa was a truly a gentle, strong willed man of uncommon strength and determination. He used his immense resolve that he could and would make things right when he moved his large brood up North, knowing nothing about the town where they would settle but believing in his heart that it was the correct thing to do. Poppa always felt that if he remained calm and cool and balanced, that all would balance out correctly on "life's balancing scale."

Believe, that Poppa and his large brood traveled a full day and night on that fateful day that he left the South and they certainly did arrive in the thriving city of Akron, Ohio. Akron was the home to the largest rubber factory in the United States, the Firestone Tire and Rubber Company. Poppa knew that there must be a lot of people in that big factory that would welcome a good Southern cooked meal and he found the spot, 107 North Main Street, where he would make his Brooks Grille.

Josie considered that it was a good sign that Poppa discovered the restaurant site before he found their home because if Poppa's instincts were right all of their children would soon be working too

78

hard to have the time to miss Alabama. My imagination takes hold as I recall my Granny's vivid storytelling:

"You have a handsome family there," the realtor tells Poppa as he prepares the lease. Poppa nods and replies, "They are all right smart, my young-uns, and they are blessed to have a smart Mama." Poppa hands the fountain pen to Josie. She is the one that will sign the lease. That is the way that Poppa wants it and the realtor does not argue as Poppa and Josie pay for the whole year in advance, in cash.

Poppa has spent his life working hard for others and he is happy the Lord has blessed him with a large family, all with fine entrepreneurial sensibilities. It is no one's business that Poppa has yet to learn to read. Poppa is pleased with the respectable, brown shingled home he finds at 650 Rhodes Avenue. It is not big, but it is adequate. What pleases Poppa the most is the garden out back and the excellent soil for Josie's apple tree in front that has a perfect dose of sun and shade. Already it seems as if Little Gus' spirit is ready to take root in their new home.

There are four bedrooms on the top floor with another tiny bedroom on the ground floor. Poppa and Josie have taken the bedroom in the front so that Josie can have her morning sun, and Ruby and Caleb have taken the large one across the hall that has its own adjoining kitchen. Caleb is a fisherman and needs a large area to clean and prepare his fish that the family has grown accustomed to enjoying each weekend. In Poppa's Grille in Troy they would always have a barrel of the red snapper and a barrel of the mullets. If anyone can find the good fish in the Ohio Rivers, it will be Caleb.

Sadie gets the other front bedroom which is larger than the room that Jevie and Mildred will share. Poppa teases Sadie, saying "Young-un, you will need a bunch of room to sit and count all that money you are going to make." The truth is, Sadie really misses the beau she has left behind. Poppa knows the sunny room will brighten her spirits. It helps, too, that Sadie is a light sleeper as Poppa needs a light sleeper so that he can rest at night – assured that everyone has returned home safely, whatever their schedule might be. Poppa knows that Sadie will keep everyone in line.

B.T., The Joy Boy, gets the downstairs bedroom as he is the least likely to come home at a reasonable hour. The large attic has been converted into a cheerful bedroom with two double sized beds where Fred, Fats, and Grover sleep. The first one home for the designated attic beds gets to sleep alone but soon it is clear that the last one home has some confusion as to what bed he belongs in. Poppa is confident, though, that his boys would work it out.

The cellar is comfortably cramped with Josie's treasured mementos from Missy's life in The Great House. Her ornate flat irons, handmade quilts, a bundle of high top lace up shoes, iron soup pots and cradles, even a big old hoop for a ballroom skirt are carefully stored in neat, marked crates with see through lids. In the back of the cellar, Poppa builds a little cold storage room, made out of the black, earth walls where Josie put all of her "fixings" in jars on those dirt shelves – pickled beets, sweet peaches, and candied apples, plums, and pears – something good for the house or Grille. Yes, it seems that Poppa's move up North is working out just fine.

There is a flurry of activity preparing for opening night of The Brooks Grille. The Joy Boy has carefully made a hand painted sign with coat after coat of a lustrous midnight blue lacquer applied behind the fine lettering. With the dozens of handsome little lights placed all around the sign, Poppa has himself a marquee that stands out like no other on the street. Josie hugs B.T. when the lights are turned on. "You've made your Poppa right proud," she says and the enthusiastic gathering of brothers and sisters let forth a grand hoorah. They all know The Joy Boy and Fats Eugene are the movers and shakers of the family, next to Poppa, that is.

Mildred has placed two large urns in the window of the Grille filled with long white roses and carefully snipped branches of their neighbor's apple tree. Mrs. Rose confesses that her apple tree has never before produced such plump white blooms. Josie's apple tree is barely in the ground, but Josie knows that Little Gus' spirit is nearby and producing his magic with the neighbors until he can hang around in his own backyard again. Mildred has decorated the tables beautifully with smart white starched tablecloths with a little checkered border. On each table she has placed little pots of white tulips and apple blossoms. Sadie sits carefully counting the change in her change box and Jevie stands poised by the front door, all dressed up and smiling, willing to let loose her charm on the large crowd outside that is already lined up and eager to come in.

Ruby and Grover are busy organizing the table china and the menus and Fred is immersed in arranging his golden fried chicken while he keeps an eye on his greens. Josie is taking out the last of her peach cobblers and rhubarb pies and Poppa is stacking his famous skillet breads that are ready to go into the fryers.

The Joy Boy and Fats Eugene are on the street corner dressed in their Sunday Best handing out the handsome flyers The Joy Boy designed. The first twenty-five customers will get a pass that entitles them to a free meal in the coming weeks and the second twenty-five will get dessert and coffee. Prohibition laws will prohibit the use of alcohol, even in Josie's acclaimed punch.

Caleb's scaled fish is plumped up and sitting on ice. No one knows if fish is popular in Ohio despite Caleb's assurance that no one can resist the fine fish he has reeled in. Grover has been to Chicago, and he says that to insure that they have success like the popular eateries enjoy in Chicago, there should be music in the background – so it is Grover's job to keep the Victrola busy with the likes of Fats Waller, Louis Armstrong, Jelly Roll Morton, and Bessie Smith.

When Jevie opens the doors and lets in the well-groomed crowd, it is clear that Poppa's young'uns have done their job. The restaurant is a hit. Everything that Poppa had planned to serve quickly vanishes, including all of Caleb's fish. Ruby saves the night by fashioning up some fancy looking corn fritters and ham stew that only she could imagine from the staples left. Too soon these staples are history as well.

The Joy Boy, realizing that they will run out of desserts, improvises and runs out to buy gallons of vanilla ice cream which he serves with carefully arranged slivers of Josie's pies. Josie's pies will be the talk of the town and Josie will soon realize that people will drive many miles for them. When Poppa's clan finally sits down before tackling the big clean up, they are joined by two eager suitors, Bratcher, smitten with Sadie, and William, helplessly infatuated with

Jevie. Poppa gives both a long and hard glance but it is clear that for now he thinks it is safe to take Josie home.

Jevie says coyly, "Poppa, may William bring me home, and will you leave the porch light on for us." "Sadie will leave the light on young- un as she always does and your brothers will see to it that William gets home first," Poppa replies. Surely Jevie knew that one night would not change the rules. Poppa, beaming with pride, takes Josie by the arm, saying, "Y'all were right smart tonight, right smart."

Poppa's restaurant continues to thrive and it is clear that one business will not contain the bountiful energy with which the family is endowed. Fats is encouraged to start a little club and soon he like Poppa, will not let anything deter him from success. Fats calls his club The Cosmo Club and everyone in town is determined to check it out. Many Whites, just as they did at Poppa's restaurant in the South, patronize the Brooks Grille and The Cosmo Club for food and entertainment.

Grover is away frequently now in Chicago and Poppa worries about this. He knows that Grover is ambitious but he does not want any member of the family to be far from his watchful eye. Too much trouble can happen elsewhere and Poppa knows that strangers will not look upon his boys in the same way their own community looks upon them. Poppa prefers having all his boys together, looking out for one another.

One late evening, while Jevie is sitting in the restaurant with her faithful companion, William, she is startled to hear Poppa and Grover raising their voices with one another. "I cannot arrive at your home at the hour that you wish Poppa. I am a grown man with a life to live," Grover says angrily. "That's no excuse, young-un to worry your Mama like that. You can do better, Poppa replies. You had a fine upbringing."

Jevie departs from the coziness of her little table with William and goes to join Grover. Touching Poppa's shoulder, she says softly, "Poppa, Grover is trying to open a little club in Chicago. He was hoping to wait a little longer before telling you so you could get used to him being away." Poppa steps back a few paces to study Grover's face intently. "I never raised you to tell no lies young-un. Are you trying to tell me you have moved away from your family?"

"I love my family, and you and Mama the same as always, Grover says, but I want to live in Chicago."

"This is going to break your Mama's heart. There is a right way, and a wrong way to go about things, and you are wrong, young-un, you are wrong," Poppa admonishes.

Jevie intercedes, "Grover has been feeling bad, Poppa. He just didn't know what to do."

Poppa looks from Jevie to Grover and says somberly, "Actions have consequences young-uns. We'll break this news gently to your Mama. Trouble comes when families don't stick together. I'm telling you, y'all belong together, in the same town, so you can help one another." Grover begins to laugh nervously, asserting, "You've got more children to run things than you've got places to run. Poppa. Things will work out, you'll see." A dark, worried look crosses Poppa's face and he walks away, moving with heavy, wooden feet.

JEVIE

It is Friday evening, one of the two busiest nights of the week. Charles and Josie are not at their thriving restaurant on North Howard Street. Neither are their children, who are all very dedicated to helping to run "Poppa's Place."

Jevie, just twenty-five, the brightest star of the many bright stars in the family, the only one to have graduated from Tuskegee Institute is gravely ill with peritonitis. A surgeon has punctured her appendix and Jevie fights for her life.

It is nearing the fifth anniversary of that fateful day that Poppa packed up his family and moved up North. Grover is on his way from Chicago, on a train like his entire family was on just five years ago – his brain exploding with all of the various scenarios that could happen, hurrying to his little pal Jevie.

Fred, too, is hurrying. Hysterically, he tries to move his arm to put the phone receiver down. But he will not make it to the hospital to sit with his brothers and sisters and Poppa and Mama. He finds his hidden cache of liquor and drinks himself into forgetfulness. Fred had a premonition about Jevie. He begged Jevie to get an older, more serious looking doctor to look after her. Jevie just laughed and said, "Oh you just want to get out of your walks trying to push me off on some old stodgy that will keep me bedridden for a month."

Of all the family members, Fred and Jevie are the closest. Jevie is the one that always would wait after the long weekend nights, to take a walk with Fred after he had finished with all of his cooking. Even when her boyfriend William was with her, Jevie did not fail to look out for the wellbeing of her brother. Even in his stupor, Fred could not help but think of the sound of Jevie's gay laughter, laughter so captivating that it felt like a great wash of sunshine – sunshine that wiped away the memory and fatigue of the long hours spent over the hot and busy grille.

The whole family, unhinged, prays shamelessly in the hospital waiting room. But that vigil is to be in vain. Jevie will not pull through. The surgeon sneaks out of town unable to face the grieving parents and Charles and Josie are left to mourn their beloved daughter. Hundreds upon hundreds of community people and regulars at the Grille come to visit Poppa and Josie in their home. Josie sits erect by the casket and looks on steadily at the stream of mourners. Her face is frozen in a faint smile, an acknowledgment of sorts to all who have come with their condolences, but ever so often she stares into the casket and looks over at Poppa. She shakes her head back and forth - in utter disbelief that Jevie is dead.

Jevie Elizabeth Brooks, born Sept. 2, 1903 in Troy Alabama is dead on Friday evening August 24, 1928 at 10:45 p.m. She is just a week and two days' shy of celebrating her birthday with her scores of friends who waited patiently in line at Poppa's popular restaurant so that Jevie, herself, could seat them at their tables. Jevie, who made the family proud when she graduated from Tuskegee Institute, Jevie who taught school in the South, Jevie who was President of the Tuskegee Club, Jevie who proudly helped to build Poppa's business in the North on that neon lit brimming with life Akron street is forever gone.

Mildred holds in her lap some of the dozens of telegrams that have arrived – and one from William, Jevie's beau, is particularly heart rendering. He writes, "It is near the greatest shock of my life, second only to the death of my own mother, to learn of Jevie's passing. She was the most pure and dearest girl of all my life's experience and the only girl whom I have truly loved." But no words are able to soften the sad experience of Jevie's tragic misfortune.

As Jevie's casket is lifted into the hearse, Mildred places a beautiful spray of white flowers from Josie's garden over it. In the center of the spray, with little twigs and tiny green leaves, Mildred has inscribed the words, "Our Angel." Josie, who has been standing by Mildred, says in a barely audible voice, "Goodbye young-un, angel, you brought 'sparkle aplenty' to our lives." Josie and Poppa look at the solemn faces of Jevie's Pall Bearers - James Green, Roosevelt Mitchell, Eddie Walker, Willie Rhodes. They see the visible pain of Clyde Hawkins, Roosevelt Glenn, Richard Felton, Willie McReynolds, and Horace Stokes, Jevie's friends, as they all bear the weight of her not long ago vibrant presence that is forced into a bronze and wood encasement without the benefit of bidding even a single farewell. And so it is - with broken hearts - that Poppa and Josie take their once healthy, carefree, and vivacious daughter to the Chapel Services at the Cemetery.

Charles and Josie move through the fog of the depression without complaint. The Cosmo Club, defying the times, is doing brisk business thanks to The Joy Boy and Fats selling Prohibition liquor they get from Chicago to their customers. Poppa does not know about the liquor shenanigans and more than once when he has stopped by their Club he has raised his eyebrows to the envelopes that his boys slip to various inspectors that drop by to ensure that everything remains legal. Poppa wants no trouble with law enforcement and believes that most friends are content with the homemade Pot Liquor they are able to get on occasion. Poppa is grateful for his brisk business at the Brooks Grille and is happy to feed dozens of workers who have lost their jobs. Every Saturday, Poppa gives each worker a paper bag special tied with a string. The bags are lined at the bottom with thick skillet bread that is topped with heaping portions of greens, rice, and black eye peas mixed with chunks of ham- enough food to feed a family.

Since Jevie's death, Fred has been drinking "big time" and when the prohibition ban was lifted, Fred made no attempt to hide his alcohol. Poppa had given up talking about Fred's drinking problem and was just grateful to see him come home at night.

Something on the radio captured Fred's imagination and he yelled to his sister, "Sadie, come and listen to this. Here is a man crippled with polio, in a wheelchair, addressing an entire nation, well that's enough to impress me. The President is talking about reopening the banks and I've decided to invest all of the money I've saved. I never put my money in a bank to lose in the depression, but I figure I can gamble with a man like Roosevelt."

"Go to bed, Fred, that's old news, a replay of last year's Presidential Radio Chat. They call it a Fireside Chat, Sadie retorted.

"Why Sadie, you know we have a coal furnace, what are we going to do with a "Fireside Chat" Fred replied. Sadie just looks at her brother and laughs. "Go on to bed, Fred, she says patiently so you can get straight before Poppa comes home."

Fred does not go to bed but leaves the house instead. He walks out into the bitter cold without a coat or hat. For many months after his walk in the cold, Fred hangs on to a ferocious cough. Josie tries to fortify him with steaming cups of hand grown teas laced with honey and her special herbs but Fred will drink only a sip or two. On April 18, 1934, Fred will die too quickly of pneumonia. He is gone and no one can believe it. Everyone knows that Fred has died of a broken heart. He just never learned to live without Jevie.

LOVE LAMENT

I understand one's inability to fathom living without the person they are deeply attached to. Like Fred, I fall into the abyss when I imagine life without my son, RB. I simply cannot imagine living without him. I am trying so hard to save him from Schizophrenia. This monster of an illness is altering his brilliant mind. It is challenging our own real love for each other.

I look into the mirror and I don't recognize myself any longer. I look strange. I dress strange. I don't know whose life I am living anymore.

My son says, "Mommy, don't stand there. They can steal your voice over there."

"Who can steal my voice," I say? I look at my son and cry, really cry. I know that he can't help that he hears the voices, but I want the voices to go away, to leave us alone. I want us to be able to go back to the life we used to have. "Don't call me Mommy anymore, I say angrily, you are too old to call me Mommy."

"Mom, sit down, he says, I will play my new songs for you." He begins to play his beautiful songs, "Love Lament," and then "When Autumn Sings." Looking up from the piano keys to me he gently says, "I know you want me to call you Mom, but in my heart you will always be Mommy."

In my mind, I see him as a dear little boy again, making faces and blowing bubbles as he takes his bath. I see him with his crayons at his school desk in the first grade. I see him walking his beloved Irish Setter, 'Dayan' through the autumn leaves, through all of the many pathways that he loved so much in the park, through the change of seasons, from autumn into fall, from fall into winter - and always, always he is with Dayan.

My son had a complete and irreversible emotional breakdown after the death of Dayan. And, even though Dayan had lived a long and tender life until the age of sixteen, which is very old for a dog, RB could not accept his death and he began to act irrationally. He began to write music eighteen hours at a stretch, eating only hardened loaves of bread that he kept on top of his piano.

His every thought was for Dayan; he wrote sonatas and preludes for Dayan, and wept during the night for him. He burned candles for him and began to believe that God had chosen him, RB, to hear all of the evil voices in the world so that God could spend his time doing more important things, helping out the "Good People" on earth.

The Doctors call my son's condition, Paranoid Schizophrenia, and say it was caused by an acute traumatic episode in his life. They feel that he will never recover and will have to listen to "these terrible voices" for the rest of his life.

I cannot accept this doom and gloom proclamation and spend all of my time researching new medications and treatments.

Sometimes, I feel that it is all just too hard, and that there is just no way we can continue to live in this altered world, and then I hear the beautiful melodies and lyrics that my son writes and I realize that though his illness dramatically changed his life in one respect, it also gave him the ability to write hauntingly beautiful music that he had not previously written. His music now comes from deep within his soul, and when he does something that I find particularly "nerve wracking," I force myself to think of the gifts that came with the Schizophrenia.

It is so hard to think of my beautiful son as incapacitated. How could this happen? My son has four degrees. Degrees in International Relations and French Literature from Stanford University, a Masters in Journalism from Columbia and another degree from the Berklee School of Music in Big Band Arranging. My son speaks three languages fluently. Surely his brain is just tired, not unrepairable.

How can my son be beyond repair? What started his inappropriate laughing, I ask? Did he always do that, and I just failed to see it. Did he always listen to the TV without any sound? Did he hide from me that he preferred a cold shower to a hot one? Why didn't I think it was strange when as a teenager he preferred eating his food cold rather than warming it on the stove?

"Was it the breakup of my twenty-three-year marriage to Dr. Lynch," I ask? RB loved his Dad so much even though his father did not see him for fifteen of the schizophrenia years. It was hard for my Ex to see his "Golden Child" disabled.

In my heart, I believe that it was my son's unrealistic attachment to a woman that he loved desperately but who did not love him in return. I think about Virginia saying, "Oh, you artists, you think that having smoked cheese, is having a swell life."

When Virginia just picked up and went back to Spain, my son said he felt as though the breath had been knocked out of him. He went deeper and deeper into this dark abyss, and then he just closed down. He began to walk like an old man. He couldn't pull himself up from the bed except to compose music. The doctors said that the breakup with his girlfriend came too fast on the heels of the death of his dog.

Love Lament was a turning point in RB's life. He wrote it in remembrance of Virginia and he just forever closed down about having another meaningful relationship after that. He had only dated a few other women in his entire life but when he met Virginia he was certain that she was the one for him. Virginia just considered my son a sweet, gentle soul and I believe the relationship was ill advised from the beginning. She was a good ten years older than my son.

Schizophrenia, the doctors say, is here to stay. Only three percent of people ever recover from it. "Move on," the doctors say. "Just make sure he takes his medicine," they warn, and then, as if purposefully to disarm me they say. "The medicine will prove ineffective over time." "It is God's will," the doctors say. "What can you do?"

I try hard to keep up my courage, to give out love, and all, but inside, I feel that little snippets of pain are burrowing into my every flawed bone, puffing up the joints like a trumpet ballooning one's cheeks. *How I hate my son's illness,* I scream silently to myself, and then I quietly give up the rage and begin to meditate or begin a new piece of artwork.

I thought that maybe if I wrote a screenplay about RB's Life, that it would help to heal me, to accept what I cannot change and to think of my son's new life as a Gift from God, a beautiful and rare gift that we normal people just don't understand. I don't think there is a more spiritual person on this earth than my son. I have never heard him gossip or say anything unkind about anyone, not "Ever." My daughter, who I know loves her brother deeply, is reluctant to visit with him, though every few years she will call him at his little humble apartment, where he lives in Brazil. There was a school yard beneath RB's bedroom window, and I marveled at the whimsical and gay composition, "Children at Play" that RB wrote while listening to the children play outside.

I want relief from the drudgery of it all. I want some imaginary person to just drop from the sky and save me, save RB, from this horrible illness that robs us, mother and child, of our much needed sanity, not to mention our DIGNITY. Sometimes, when RB is dressed as humbly as the most impoverished beggar, as that is the way he prefers to dress, I want to just shake some sense into him, but he always disarms me by saying, "Mom, you care far too much about Dirt; a third of all of the people in the world live like I do. It is the spirit that counts."

"Yes, but the spirit can use a good scrubbing once daily," I say.

I remember vividly one day, when the voices, nagged at him, he threw plates, and ropes, and an odd assortment of records into an old, battered suitcase and fled the house. He was missing and homeless, for three days. When I found him finally on an old park bench he was so relieved to be back at his Piano again, composing happily. He said later, "Mom I just couldn't take your nagging about taking a hot shower anymore."

"But, weren't you afraid that you would be robbed or harmed" I asked.

"Yes, but I was more afraid of the hot water." I looked at him in amazement and we both had a good laugh. "I try to smile and cherish the humor in these little offbeat moments of memory - but secretly I want so desperately to be out of this mess, to be in my old, lovely apartment at 74th and Madison in New York City. Oh, why can't I just be happily making films and dressing beautifully again I ask myself?

When will I not have the worry of facing each day desperately poor – not knowing how I will raise the money to secure my son's expensive medicine? I own nothing, not even one piece of the exquisite gold jewelry I worked so hard to make. Everything is in hock or has been sold. I don't have a decent pair of shoes. Our three amazing homes are all gone, gobbled up by creditors to pay taxes, and lawyers and hospital expenses.

I am left being a Tennessee Williams character, a battered soul with shattered dreams, an aging woman still trying to save her schizophrenic son while grappling to preserve some semblance of grace. Grace was always at the top of my list of concerns. I can easily remember my head and heart being infatuated with beautiful, white layered net crinoline skirts with satin cording all around the waistband – and that this concoction spilled over pink ballerina slippers. I can assure you that I nor my precious pink ballet slippers had no premonition that one day they would be tucked away for more sturdy shoes that could travel into the nightmarish worlds of asylums and schizophrenia.

I was always a graceful young woman as a young teen because I had followed my passion for ballet and had through the graciousness of my Aunt Sadie - who paid for my lessons - taken years of Ballet and performed in many recitals and dance groups and even once was offered a ballet scholarship to a famous Ballet School in New York but my mother refused to let me go so I turned my interests elsewhere.

Once, during an enormous snow blizzard in the 1970's in New York City I was on Central Park South trying frantically to hail a taxi. I was in snow drifts well up to my knees, waving my arms and suddenly I saw the much sought out yellow car coming through the blustery mist and I propelled myself with a giant leap into the car's path, managing to get the driver to stop.

Out of nowhere a woman in white, wet and dripping with sleet begged to go with me – wherever that might be. During the ride she asked me several times if I was a dancer. I said no and the mysterious woman replied that I ought to be. She offered to take me to London with her where she knew some great dancers. With amusement, I leaned forward so I could see her face better and I realized I was staring at the greatest ballerina in the world, Dame Margot Fonteyn. We exchanged numbers and I promised to be in touch if I ever considered going back to dancing, which was really as far- fetched as taking a trip to the Planet Venus. I often wish I had taken Margot Fonteyn up on her offer to visit her on her farm in Panama. While Fonteyn took care of her ill husband, her life was anything but the glamorous lifestyle I had imagined in my mind's eye. I never got the chance to tell her how touched and grateful I was that she had reaffirmed for me that my grace had not totally abandoned me. And to think, it took a blizzard to bring it to the forefront.

I was frantically busy at that time, rehearsing the lead role of Catherine Holly in Tennessee William's Suddenly Last Summer which was opening at Henry Street Settlement's New Federal Theatre, a new Off Broadway venue in the lower East Village of New York City.

On opening night, the producer made crude sexual advances just fifteen minutes prior to the curtain going up and panic stricken - I fled from the Theatre, leaving my husband and children and friends sitting in the audience. I did finally return to the stage, taking with me the rattled and turbulent emotions I was experiencing from the aborted sexual assault. Though I got wonderful reviews for my electrically charged performance, I lost heart for the Theatre after that – I was sick of being confronted with the Casting Couch Scene – and I entered New York University to study filmmaking. I never lost my penchant for the Theatre though, and still feel privileged that I had the great fortune of studying for so many years with some of the great Masters, Lee Strasberg of the Actor's Studio, Lloyd Richards, Herbert Berghof, Stella Adler, Bill Hickey, and Philip Burton.

DREAMING BIG AND DIRECTING
A FILM IN MEXICO

I have always been able to dream big, to initiate and complete projects that no one in their right mind would have started in the first place. My Mama constantly nagged at me when I was a teenager because I started on a hook rug that grew by inches over a year but failed to multiply into anything other than a foot-long pile of yarn stored in a bag in the attic. Then there was a strapless pinstripe dress that I cut out meticulously from a pattern book but it too suffered the same fate as the hook rug, relegated to a storage bag with its seams half sewn. As an adult, I was always searching in antique shops for things that I could make over with little effort. Hunting through flea markets became a favorite hobby of mine as well and I was forever rearranging an old dress to make it look new and boldly different. I did manage to master these projects and become a trendsetter.

I traveled with my daughter to Mexico and became enthralled with the colorful Mexican shawls that I was sure I could fashion into a beautiful garment. While perusing the many stalls on market day, I contemplated my next film project. My first film, Lost Control, had unexpectedly gotten an Academy Nomination for my producing and directing efforts. I envisioned doing a film about Children's Dreams and thought I would find some children with riveting life stories in New York and document their stories in an hour long Documentary. As fate would have it, I encountered some Mexican children who had compelling stories and I decided to learn Spanish and do the film in San Miguel de Allende, a historic town two hour's drive from Mexico City. I spent the rest of my vacation learning the language, getting familiar with the children I had chosen to participate in the film, and scouting locations. I chose children ages 10-17 and to portray these children's real dreams it was necessary to transform a schoolroom into a magic show. Like young people everywhere, the children wanted to reach out to enjoy the things they did not have in their everyday lives. The goal was to gain insight about the ways in which wealth, non-wealth, and social rank (both high and low) affect the adolescent. A young wealthy girl from a socially prominent family wanted to live in a remote Indian village where the people judge one by what is in their hearts and minds and not one's social position or one's monetary worth. I actually made a costume skirt for her from a hand embroidered Indian shawl I had found on one of my forays into the market place.

Another girl who had had been a maid since she was twelve wanted the good life. She dreamed of being the "Senora de la Casa," of wearing beautiful dresses, of walking through sumptuous gardens, of taking a leisurely bubble bath in a huge sunken tub. A young boy, whose family had little money dreamed of owning a big blue truck. He imagined that as he drove through the town square everybody would recognize him as a famous and important person. This little boy reminisced of his fondness for bargaining with his friends in the market place and dreamed of eating in a fancy restaurant. I planned to utilize a bilingual (English and Spanish) sound track to effectively show how languages create a bridge to promoting the understanding and appreciation of another's feelings.

I returned to NYC to find a film crew and to gain permission from my daughter's school so she could accompany me back to Mexico. I took my mother as well, and she was constantly admonishing me for wasting my money on a foolish film but it was an exciting time for me. And though we encountered difficulties in getting permits, securing the locations, and in the actual filming process (mostly with the children encountering stage fright while reenacting scenes from their lives) the film managed to get finished. John Carter - a noted Hollywood Film Editor who had been the editor on my first film and who graciously edited most of Mister Magic, the film of which I speak - had worked tirelessly on perfecting the editing in sequences where I had shot far too little footage. He created miracles to cover scenes that needed a close up or to find some feasible shot that could suffice as a fade away transition – in other words, he covered my errors with strokes of genius.

We had a very interesting opening in NYC where I asked all of the guests to come to the screening dressed in costumes reminiscent of their childhood dreams. I have always found that people want a bit of fantasy in their lives and colleagues and friends were happy to oblige me and show up in some wonderfully imaginative clothing – dressed as sports heroes, princesses, kings, circus performers and such. Having worked in fashion for so many years, doing Mister Magic allowed me to escape again into the world where fantasy meets reality. In one scene a child became nervous and quit - and not only did I have to worry about losing that important story component - I had to jump in as the moderator (with a quick costume put together by my daughter fashioned from a towel covered with giant paper flowers) and I kept the story moving onward in our schoolroom that had been cleverly transposed into a Magic Show with John Carter's editing tricks. We were on the strictest of budgets and one mishap could have closed the filming down entirely. I had put half the production costs on my American Express Card, not something that I would recommend to young filmmakers. The film had many screenings across the Country, as well as the 2nd Annual Jamaican Film Festival where I met famed Director Sergio Giral from Cuba. We enjoyed a long friendship and I was instrumental in finding this gifted filmmaker's son who he had not seen for eighteen years but our friendship suffered when his son died tragically. He gave me many helpful tips on my film Mister Magic which became particularly popular in school settings where children engaged in critical analysis of why having wealth or not so impacted one's self esteem. I had always admired the educator, Maxine Greene, who said, "Without the ability to think about yourself, to reflect on your life, there's really no awareness, no consciousness. Consciousness doesn't come automatically – it comes through being alive, awake, curious, and often furious." I was glad that I had opened up an important avenue of dialogue for young people where they could discuss their lives, even though, in the many screenings I sat through, I mourned the many technical imperfections in my film.

A CHANCE MEETING

I was always blessed to have many friends and when I wasn't working at the Medical Center or as a model and commercial actress I would take my children to all of the local haunts on the Upper West Side, especially to Lincoln Center with its beautiful Arts Center that included the New York Ballet Theatre and the Metropolitan Opera. We would eat across from Lincoln Center at the Ginger Man, a cozy restaurant frequented by many stars. I was friendly with Mike, the owner, and always delighted in his warm welcome. On this particular day I was alone, waiting to have lunch with a musician friend who was bringing his friends with him, a couple soon to be married. My friend was tardy and a famous band leader, Quincy Jones, came to my table and asked if I was the party intending to meet with Al Brown, a talented viola player who played in the orchestras of many Broadway shows. "Indeed, that's me," I replied. Quincy seated himself and we commenced.to have a fascinating conversation that lasted nearly an hour.

Quincy and I chatted as though we had known each other a lifetime and he said at one point, "I think I might be marrying the wrong woman." It seemed a startling thing to say but I understood instantly what he meant. There was no posturing and artifice to our heart to heart talk and frankly I had never had the occasion to talk to my husband or anyone in such an open and honest way. Too soon a gorgeous, tall, blond European woman joined Quincy and my friend showed up at just about the same time so the conversation took another course. Years later, I was spending the night at a friend's home, prior to a very early call for an important runway show in New York. My friend tried to encourage me to stay up late as she was having some guests over for drinks. I begged out of the get together and went to bed early as I had a 6 a.m. call - and right after my modeling assignment I had to head home to Pennsylvania as I had not yet found a permanent apartment in New York City.

It must have been around three in the morning when I heard a soft tap at my door. Before I could fully arouse myself I felt a gentle hug and I sat up and stared into the face of none other than Quincy Jones. It was a wonderfully warm moment, one that I have cherished. Always I wish I could remember what we said, but my sleepiness did not want to abandon me. Strangely, Quincy and I have never met again – though I divorced and he married and divorced several more times. I have always followed his tumultuous and accomplished life. I prayed for him when he suffered his two tragic and nearly fatal brain aneurysms and in many ways I always felt we were kindred spirits – probably due to the fact that he so loves big band music and he attended the Berklee School of Music as did my son, RB. Both my Daddy and my son were hooked on that sound that can only come from a big band and none composes in that genre better than Quincy Jones. Quincy's mother suffered from schizophrenia during most of his childhood. Like my son, Quincy's mother spoke several languages and held advanced College degrees. I always keep a place in my heart for him and wish him and his many children the best that life has to offer.

Edie Lynch

I was the first Black model in the history of the Philadelphia Models Guild and I was shown the back door when the owners realized that I was not the suntanned, pampered wife of a doctor but a Black person. Never mind that I had won my spot legitimately, going through the arduous elimination of three thousand hopeful models who were cast out, one by one, leaving five winners that included myself. There were Black models in New York, but not in Philadelphia, and Philadelphia wanted it to stay that way.

No, I did not walk out the back door but went instead to the town's big newspapers to protest the Guild's not so subtle attempt to block me out of the rightful spot I had won in the competition. Not wanting a big Civil Rights Suit the Guild relented and sent me on my first assignment, to model for Saks Fifth Avenue. I arrived for a fitting and was beckoned into a room that had ankle deep plush carpeting and glittering chandeliers. After hurriedly trying on several gorgeous gowns, I set out running with the Fashion Coordinator, Libby Hyman, for the actual Hotel venue where the big wedding show was about to hit the runway. I was introduced to a bevy of beautiful blondes but not one returned my greeting excepting Adrienne Toth, a stunning Moore Design student who was pinch hitting as a model.

Adrienne and I hit it off right away and became long- time friends. I gave her a ride home in my beat up Volkswagen and had to stop on the highway to maneuver the butterfly cap in my carburetor to get the car moving again. Adrienne was startled that I took such things in my stride and I learned later that she too was possessed of a tenacious spirit for willing things to go her way. She had actually fought with soldiers in her native country, Hungary, to keep from being put on a truck to be taken away with other unfortunate residents who were being rounded up like fugitives during the Second World War. Adrienne and her family escaped and fled the Country for the USA with just a few paintings hurriedly snatched from their frames. She later would finish her studies and establish her beautiful knitted designs and then marry a wealthy Italian and become Adrienne Vittadini of the 350-million-dollar Fashion Empire. We traveled to Hong Kong, Paris, and London together and shared many interesting, and a few rather heady experiences.

Whenever I walked the famous designer runways of the world wearing the creations of Oscar de la Renta, Emilio Pucci, Princess

Galitzine or some other notable designer, I always remembered that the real princesses in my life were my Granny and her mother Missy. I shall always love telling their stories because they are the ones that endured slavery, the ones that made the sacrifices that enabled my many walks on the runway and changes of hats possible.

One series of hats I almost did not endure wearing - the ones that belonged to the famous Ebony Fashion Fair. Ebony Fashion Fair was a very big deal in just about every major City. John H. Johnson, the publisher of Ebony Magazine and his wife Eunice created this Bigger Than Life Spectacle – literally a bevy of long legged models traveling from City to City all over the United States on a bus that let the women out hours before the Fashion Show at an often mediocre Hotel to nap, bathe, and scramble to the Glitzy Halls and Hotels that usually had the town's most prominent citizens - doctors, lawyers, and socialites waiting in line to see the Ebony Fashion Fair models.

Spectators were as eye catching as the many outrageous offerings we wore on the runway. Though the women may not have had on original Parisian $10,000 Haute Couture Gowns, the anxious ticket holders were at the Stage Doors decked out in stunning Italian suits, French Evening Dresses, and the most extravagant coats and shawls from New York's Famous Fur Salons. The many men who came paid fastidious attention to their attire, knowing that the show was about what the audience was wearing as well as what the Ebony Fashion Fair Models wore.

We models often looked like a bunch of bleary eye nomads, arriving with wig boxes in tow and hair tied up in *Do Rags,* but once inside, all knew how to Make Magic with hair, hat, and wig to compliment the often opulent attire we were showing off. We were in some City, somewhere, in the North or South – I don't remember – and if it seems that I am being derisive, I'm not, it's just that it was a really hectic time and I needed the money that the tour could give me so I could get my soon to be doctor husband out of medical school. I was tired and homesick, and wanted away from the endless traveling, the constant partying, the fact that I just did not fit in – anywhere.

There was a small, jubilant, almost aggressive crowd at the Backstage Door. We were all just disembarking from the bus, struggling to move through the crowd as we balanced our many shoe and wig boxes, make-up cases, clothes hung over our arms - and I suddenly remembered that Elizabeth had not returned my wig, and that I could not afford to lend it to her any longer because I had been called aside and told not to come out again on the runway in my assigned bathing suit without the appropriate hair piece. Well, I couldn't wear the wig I was supposed to wear because Elizabeth had failed to return it to me. I had loaned it to her during a real fashion emergency that she had but she seemed not to care that I got it back.

"Elizabeth, I said, I have to have my wig back before the show starts because you have had it for three weeks, and Mrs. Johnson is annoyed with me for not wearing the correct hair piece for the bathing suit segment." There was no answer from Elizabeth. After a bit of having to stop here or there to talk briefly with the spectators, we all got through the crowd and inside to our dressing quarters to begin the task of making sure all our "clothing changes" were in place on the racks, that we knew who our dressers were, and that we had mapped out our own personal make-up area.

There was the rumble of the crowd up front - restless, talkative, excited. Then, a hushed silence, a speech, wild clapping, a drum roll, music – and we were on. A blur of faces, a dozen bodies thrusting this hat to you, or those shoes, "those." "Don't let your shawl drag too long on the floor, keep it clean, now go, go, go." I jumped in and out of outfits. Raced down the runway. I liked to walk fast and do a lot of intricate pivots – learned from my ballet training - and I always got an approving hand of applause from the enthusiastic crowd.

Now it was my fifth change. I needed my wig. I walked over to Elizabeth and said, "Please, give me my wig as I need it for my bathing suit entry. Elizabeth said nothing. "Elizabeth, I said, I insist you give me my wig. You have had it for three weeks." Elizabeth said, "Yes, I have it and what can you do about it?" Without raising my voice, and with a steel calm that came over me, I looked Elizabeth in the eyes and said, "I know this my dear, you have thirty seconds to give me back my wig or I will beat the Holy Shit out of you." It didn't take Elizabeth but ten of those thirty seconds to give me back my wig. I had had enough of nonsense. I wanted out from the idiotic pressures that depressed me and I was more than ready to let it all spill out.

I was called Miss Goody Good Shoes on the tour as I was the one guilty of not having an affair with one of the Higher Ups or someone closely associated with the Top Management. Actually, another model and I spent many evenings playing cards silently in a darkened hotel room with a towel across the bottom of the door so no one would think we were in. We did not want to go to another cocktail party to watch the senseless drinking and carousing. Some models shared boyfriends and one newly married model was clearly involved with a very powerful man that it was actually amazing it was not disclosed in the press. Not only was there the risk of her husband finding out but the whole nation would have known as well.

I always thought that it would be nice if all parties involved in affairs would just be honest so that their partners could exercise their own wise options. When my husband moved away to attend Medical School, there was a Judge who would stop by on his way home to see how me and the kids were doing. He was the only male friend I had and I realized that I was venturing into a cloudy area when his wife called and accused me of having an affair with her husband, and warned me that she was going to tell my husband.

I was relieved that things could not stay the way they were. I was lonely and tired of working long hours with no husband of my own to wrap my arms around and though I did not want another woman's husband – I certainly was not wise enough to tell the handsome judge that his friendly and unexpected visits were unwelcomed. He was a friend who seemed happy to greet me and who worried about how I was faring all by myself. My aunt was living right next door and she was always in and out with my son and daughter – and though she understood my friendship with the Judge I realized how foolish it was to expect the world to understand why we were meeting without the knowledge of our spouses. I don't remember if the Judge's wife called my husband or not but I know that I did.

I told my husband I was lonely and afraid in Columbus, Ohio - working two jobs to keep us afloat and that perhaps the Judge had done us both a favor by stopping by because I knew for certain that

I did not need or want to live alone. Was I attracted to the Judge? He was very good looking but I definitely was not desirous of an affair with another woman's husband. I just wanted to be around an interesting and vibrant life. I knew that I loved my own handsome husband.

The Judge and I remained friends from afar for over thirty years and he wrote a recommendation for me when I applied for a luxury apartment in a landmark building on Manhattan's Upper Eastside.

He called me one day when he was in New York and wanted to take me to dinner. I had not seen him since my husband and I had moved from Ohio decades before that. When he arrived at my beautiful apartment he was sick and said he felt faint. Before long, he had a bout of vomiting and was too weak to leave. He lay down in the guest room and for two days while he checked in with his wife and his doctor, I was relegated to cleaning up the after effects of his mysterious malady that caused much vomiting.

It was not a fun time for me and I was unhappy that he did not want his wife to know where he was so she could come to claim him. He lamented over and over what a wonderful woman his wife was and how he wished he could buy for her even one of the lovely pieces of fine jewelry that I owned. I found myself being angry at him and wishing him to soon be gone for he did not seem fond of the fact that I was fortunate to have a few beautiful things, many that I made for myself after tedious years of learning the art of jewelry making in school at F.I.T. I knew in my heart that my friend wished me nothing but good will, but it seemed ridiculous that I had to defend why I had my small, but lovely little jewelry chest while his wife had nothing.

Getting back to my story of being the young, forgotten wife of a medical student – my husband did come to pick our little family up and we drove to Philadelphia in our little Volkswagen to begin the odyssey that would end with this book. I never expected Philadelphia to be the City that would bring my fashion interests into focus and I definitely did not expect to leave my young children to travel three long months with The Ebony Fashion Fair. So many young, beautiful women longed to be on the runway showing off the incredible clothes Eunice Johnson, the Publisher's wife and her staff found in the Couturier Houses of Europe. Just wearing some of those luxurious outfits for a few minutes could be quite a sumptuous, thrilling treat. Floating down the Cat Walk in Ostrich Feathers, or velvet trimmed with thousands of hand sewn beads could make you definitely appreciate that it was a moment to be savored.

During one of the biggest shows in California, Nancy Wilson, the well- known jazz singer stopped back stage and told me she had wanted to model at one time. She invited me to visit her home, and though I was reluctant to go because I knew my husband had dated her before we were married and she had not been the friendliest to me. Nevertheless, I went and spent several hours with her as she showed me her collection of evening gowns and mink coats. That was the last thing I wanted to see - more clothes - after making the dozens of hectic changes from Fashion Fair's extravagant "Gilded Racks."

Nancy told me that she had her chance with my husband and that she was happy with her choices. I was not so rude to say, "When I met my husband I heard he was dating you, but he broke that off and married me." I knew that he and Nancy were friends and I wisely just did my duty of witnessing the contents of her closet. I never, in all my years, believe I was guilty of deliberately being hateful or mean spirited towards another woman - but looking back, I remember being very happy to return to my little rented Ebony Fashion Fair Room.

There were sometimes downsides to sharing a room with a model. One of my Ebony Fashion Fair roommates was dating a huge NFL Football Star and he returned with her one night expecting to make out in the same room in which I was intending in a very short time to go to sleep. I protested and asked if he could not afford to get his own room, which at that time was only about $15 to $30. Evidently, he did not want to pay the money because I was forced to sit outside of the room for a good hour or more. The model later turned up with a badly bruised face and I heard that he was known for abusive behavior and had thrown her down the steps.

I moved into my own room thereafter and was content for a moment until another model was assigned to share with me. We got along quite fine until I balked at being pushed to engage in a lesbian affair. I was not at all homophobic, having many gay friends that I adored that worked in the performing arts, but my vocal protestations of being in love with my husband and happily married fell on deft ears. So, one night while my roommate jumped up and down on the bed, completely nude, I quietly walked out and checked into another room. I came back for my things later.

I ran into this woman many years later in Bloomingdale's in NYC and she told me she had married a very important and powerful man in government and that she was now based in Washington. I read many interesting stories about her connections and glittering social life at The White House and always hoped that she would continue to prosper. She is a very beautiful woman who was always extremely intelligent and certainly she had the right and the opportunity to live the life that suited her best.

What I was best at doing during those very exciting but often troubling days on the road with the Ebony Fashion Fair was visiting all of the Southern Colleges that I could take in on our rare days off - and seeing some of the Great Halls of Learning at the Universities and, of course, visiting Museums so I could indulge myself in my love of the Arts. My mother said that when she sneaked my diary out of its secreted place and stole off to read its contents – that she was never "so bored" in all her life. I wonder now what my mother would have thought of me writing this book.

Clearly, my mother was hoping to digest some really "juicy" stories from my travels as a model. She said she thought my life then was interesting, burden-free. It was startling that my mother thought about my fashion career because she was truly beautiful and had many extraordinary clothes, but rarely seemed to want to wear them. In fact, I had never known she was even remotely fascinated with modeling as she had so often talked about her yearnings to become a Senator. Mama loved politics and fancied that she would have followed the many political links that would have ultimately led to her becoming a Senator. "If only, I had not married so young,"

Mama had said more than once. Actually, I can imagine my mother in politics but there is no way that I can see her without her eight children. Her life was always concerned with raising her generous brood. We weren't just children. We were her possessions. Mama dictated when we could study, when we could play, when we could talk on the phone. There were very few moments in our lives that were not fashioned by Mama. It was not possible to sit down and drift off into one's own world. Mama had to know what we were thinking, what we were doing at all times. I couldn't practice my ballet without Mama putting a time limit on it. It was not that she did not want me to dance, it was just that in her mind she had had enough - for the moment - of my dancing, even though I was dancing in another room far away from her sight.

One evening, it was eight o'clock, and I was seated at the kitchen table working on my term paper for my high school senior finals and Mama came in and told me it was time to go to bed. I told Mama that I couldn't go to bed as I had to finish my paper because it was due the next morning. A few minutes later, Mama returned and told me again that it was time to go to bed. I explained I could not go to bed until my paper was finished. Mama left the room and I returned to my work. I heard Mama come back but I did not look up. Suddenly, I was doused with a bucket of cold water and all of my papers were ruined, soaked with water. That was Mama. There was only one way of doing things, Mama's way.

I had to find a way to hold onto my spirit and I just kept pouring out the contents of my heart on random pieces of paper that I would put into the pockets of my clothing or in between the pages of my school books. I graduated to documenting my thoughts in journals and diaries over the years but it was always a task to keep things away from Mama's ever watchful eye. I would read and re-read the many letters I saved and I was forever dumping out the contents of old purses to find scraps of paper where I jotted down something that I never wanted to forget. But isn't that life, the constant challenge of maintaining hope and finding meaning?

I agonized for months, years actually, about "Dare I write the story of The Joy Boy's Daughter?" I did not, do not want my life's story to be thought of as a sensational account of a woman who moved up the ranks from model, to actress, to a wealthy doctor's wife who was publicly shamed by her husband's illicit activities. I always wanted honor in my life, and there was for a long while. I like to think about that long spell when there was honor in my husband's life, too.

He was an extremely hard working doctor. He arose at five in the morning, at the very latest, six a.m., and was always at the hospital doing rounds before going on to his medical practice. There was an unforgettable day when he had come home early on a Thursday evening as he was not feeling all that good and for reasons I can't explain I ran for the train to come home early from my work in New York, a whole day early in fact, and I found my husband that evening sitting on the edge of the bed. He said as he got up, "I'm glad you're home because something strange is going on."

Before he could utter another word he had fallen unconscious onto the floor. As I was calling an ambulance my husband awakened, stood up, and said, "Come, you are going to drive me to the hospital as I need to have some tests done." Though I protested loudly, we got into the car and I drove him to a small community hospital near our home where he had many colleagues and friends.

CALM, CHAOS AND A MIGHTY FIGHT TO SAVE THE DOCOR'S LIFE

We were only in the emergency room a scant five minutes where his medical buddies had begun assembling when my husband, Dick, suddenly started to vomit blood. It was only minutes later that I stared blindly through the operating room window at my big strapping husband's bare feet and asked myself how, how did this happen, and why, especially now. He was midway in his second year of practice and the bills and frustrations from all those years of struggling through medical school were just starting to ease up. I had finally been relieved of working at jobs I hated and was happily engrossed in an acting and film career I had long awaited and prepared for.

I crept into the patient's bathroom and knelt on my knees and looked up at the ceiling as if I expected to see God there. Too stunned to cry I simply began to talk in a low whisper about all the things that were going on inside me. I talked about the things Dick loved doing, making homemade chili, taking our children to the supermarket and racing down the aisles with his cart as the kids threw in the items he had sent them scurrying for. I talked about the little jazz club of his own that he hoped to buy one day, but mostly I just murmured out loud all the things we never did together, the times we could have spent together but didn't.

There was a beautiful little park down the street from the very first tiny, three room apartment we shared together. We never got there. We never sat on one of those benches holding hands, awaiting the arrival of dusk, just the two of us, alone. We never took off for a fun weekend with other couples, those marvelous, nameless couples

109

we never had the time to find. I searched for a meaning of our life together and realized that most of it had been spent saving it for a more convenient time, a more promising future. I asked God what the future held for me now, and it occurred to me that too few times had God been an important part of my life.

I heard the door creak open and felt the presence of another. "Mrs. Lynch, Dr. Lynch will have to have round the clock nurses when he comes out of surgery." I arose, looked at the doctor with a flood of tears running down my cheeks, and returned to the hallway to watch through the window the frantic activity taking place around my husband's operating stretcher.

"We ordinarily would be able to handle the arrangements of private duty nurses for you but due to this being Easter weekend, you'll have to make most of the arrangements yourself." I had trouble listening to this voice that droned on and on about what I must do while the only thing I wanted desperately to do was to pray and to keep my vigil near my husband's defenseless feet.

"Get the orderlies, never mind, let's go." There was a great deal of yelling and suddenly the operating doors flung open and doctors and nurses were moving down the corridor with my husband in tow. I ran alongside, trying to understand what was happening. "Mrs. Lynch, we're taking him to recovery where he will receive many blood transfusions. He has A Negative Blood that we don't have here so we must put out an "All State Alert" to get all of the blood we can get. Do you know anyone in the family who has A Negative Blood?" It was all surreal.

Did I know anyone in the family who had A Negative Blood? Yes, I did. My husband's mother had A Negative blood but would she be able to come from Ohio to Philadelphia to give blood? I was led into a room where I had access to phones. I had to call my husband's sisters to track down their mother's number, which I knew would not be easy to locate. I was most unsure of the welcome I would get when I got her on the phone.

Finally, I got through. I explained to my husband's mother, Bella Bloomberg, that her son was out of surgery but he was still bleeding actively, that the doctors had cut off the Vagus Nerve to the stomach and given him seventeen pints of blood but they had failed to stopped the bleeding. I told her that I had just been given a note that the Red Cross was standing by and were ready to fly her from Youngstown, Ohio to Philadelphia to donate the critical blood that her son needed. Bella's response took my breath away. "I am sorry my dear, but I am working this week-end and unable to come." I did not argue with Bella. I knew her heart ran cold. She had walked away from her two daughters and son when my husband was only ten years old.

Unable to face the bigotry of racism in Youngstown after her gifted musician husband, who was Black, had returned from playing with the Big Bands in Harlem following the Great Depression, Bella had succumbed to the racial bigotry and walked out on her family. For twenty years my husband did not know if his Jewish mother was alive or dead, but a patient had remarked how similar he looked to her good friend. That friend turned out to be Bella and she agreed to meet my husband and me in front of a dilapidated train station at midnight – but she would not meet with our children or her daughters.

That fateful and reserved meeting - where Bella had surveyed me like a piece of real estate and asked how big our house was, what kind of car did I drive - lasted for one hour and my husband never saw his mother another time, nor did she ever agree to meet up with our children or her daughters. My husband often talked to her when she would call and reverse the charges but I never spoke to Bella again and was greatly pained that she would not come to give blood to save her son's life.

Jolted back to a harsh reality, I faced two of my husband's doctor friends, Stanley and Sydney. "Edie, Dick is a very sick man. He is still bleeding actively and we're going to stay with him every minute but we may have to take him to Hahnemann Hospital to meet the supply of his blood demand. You should call your children and perhaps have them come to the hospital, immediately." I sat in stunned silence and thought of how bowl after plastic bowl had been filled with the blood my husband had vomited prior to his frantic exit to surgery and wondered why I had waited so long to call my children. Amazingly,

Dick had even said to one of the doctors attending him, "Sydney, this looks like arterial bleeding." Why hadn't I realized how critical he was, for surely my husband Dick had known.

I watched my children bounce up the front walk of the hospital. My son's gaze caught me standing in front of the huge picture window on the second floor and he waved gaily. I barely brought my arm over my head to return his greeting and then turned abruptly to survey the room. Cool, impersonal thin, wipe clean leather-like cushioned divans, massive low single slab tables, cold bare linoleum floors, everything defying any leftover remnants of human disorderliness. Such an insensitive room I thought in which to tell a daddy's dear nine-year old boy and adored eight-year old daughter that at any moment that much loved daddy might die.

I hoped to find the words to explain to my children what I, myself, did not understand. My husband had never been sick, never had his tonsils taken out, never had a bad cold or even a noteworthy headache and now we were forced to consider that he could surely die in the precarious moments that lay ahead.

"Daddy loves each of you preciously and would change what's happening to you now if he could, but he can't so we three must go on together if it comes to that. Wherever we are, whatever we're doing we can carry with us his memory. We'll always have that memory along with a deep understanding of his worth. There's still a chance, there's always a chance, but the bleeding has not stopped and the cause is not known."

"Mommy, give me a crumpled piece of paper," my son said. Everything seemed unreal, us being in this room, my talking this way, my son asking for a piece of paper at a time like this. No, he said a crumpled piece of paper. I searched the room – saw those same divans, those same tables. No, it wasn't a dream. I pulled out a piece of paper from the bottom of my purse.

"When my school won their first football game I noticed afterwards that all the time they were playing I had had a piece of paper crumpled in my hand. So, before the start of every game, I crumpled a piece of paper and put it in my hand and we never lost a game. If I do this for Daddy, he'll win too." I looked at my son in disbelief, and realized a little nine-year-old had found a way to have faith, more faith or hope than I, twice his age. I learned later that he kept this paper in his hand, slept with this paper for three days without ever once taking it out.

As I was comforting my children, a doctor came and pulled me aside. He whispered, "Edie, there is no time – we will not make it to Hahnemann Hospital in time." I hurried my children into our housekeeper's hands and watched them walk away with my daughter begging me for her Daddy's watch. I raced to my husband's recovery room, found his watch in his belongings and ran back and slipped it over my daughter's wrist. As my children were getting onto the elevator, two orderlies disembarked with a stretcher and sensing an urgency in their step, I quickened mine and followed them right back to where I had just come from, my husband's recovery room. They placed him on this roll away stretcher and began attaching his bottles of saline and blood. Not fully realizing what was happening, I was jolted to my senses when the hospital administrator came in and told the doctors they were not authorized to take my husband to another hospital; that procedures had to be followed.

I looked at my critically ill husband and started pushing his stretcher myself, out of the room, down the hall toward the elevator. I was not going to follow any procedures. I was not going to let Dick die in that little hospital where they did not know how to help him. Amidst much yelling, as I struggled to keep bottles and stretcher all going in the same direction, Stanley Schiff jumped into the elevator with me to help and we all landed somehow near the big folding doors by the emergency room ambulance exit.

It was very cold and my husband had nothing but a sheet over him but the hospital personnel would have no part in allowing me to use the ambulance or the emergency room's phones so I pushed my husband out onto the parking lot where I saw an emergency phone. I yelled into the receiver that I was in the Hospital's Parking lot with a critically ill doctor just out of surgery and that he needed to get to Hahnemann Hospital, STAT.

Unreal as it was, a police van showed up and my husband was placed on a flimsy stretcher with me holding on to the two bottles attached to his veins. "Hang onto your husband and forget the bottles if you have to," I heard a voice scream at me. I realized then that the van had lurched into motion and that Stanley had jumped in and was seated at the other end of Dick's stretcher, desperately holding on to the stretcher as he steadied himself on the wobbly bench. I became acutely aware that I had a definite job to perform other than stroking my husband's forehead and holding onto precious bottles.

Stanley's presence, despite the deafening sound of the blaring sirens, had a quieting effect on me as he repeated calmly over and over, in between being thrust from one side of our speeding vehicle to the other, "we would soon be there, we would soon be there." Dick was motionless and I found myself watching the blood drip, drop by drop, from the bottle into the attached plastic tube in his arm, wondering from whom this blood had come, and also wondering if my husband was still alive. I looked out the steel grated window as we sped by all the cars we passed on the expressway and said over and over, shamelessly, "Pray for us, oh do pray for us." I placed my fingers on my husband's mouth and said loudly, "Hang on tiger, Hang on."

"I need that blood, are we at the end of Vine Street?" I could not believe my ears. "We're almost at the end of the expressway, Dick, just a few more minutes." Stanley and Dick were talking. Finally, I realized the van had slowed down and it was becoming quieter inside. Dick seemed strangely quiet too after that outburst and I searched Stanley's face as he took his pulse. We were making a turn. No, we weren't stopping, just going very slowly. Stanley was extremely busy organizing Dick and himself.

The doors opened but I never remembered the ambulance stopping. Stanley thrust my bottle at a policeman, grabbed his, ordered me out, yelled at a policeman who was already struggling to get on the van to grab the far end of the stretcher but the policeman tripped over the cord of the bottle attached to my husband's arm and the bottle went crashing to the ground. I became hysterical, and Stanley yelled, "it doesn't matter, we're here now," and somehow we all ended up in an elevator where it became necessary for the doctors to do CPR to keep my husband alive.

Dick went immediately into surgery where they had to give him 52 pints of the rare A Negative blood that they had gathered in an All State Alert. His major artery had burst and it was a matter of clamping it and replacing his blood as quickly as he lost it. For four days I sat in the Intensive Care Unit watching my husband fight for his life. He never closed his eyes and the day that the needle on his heart monitor started to jump up and down erratically, he whispered to me that I could go home now, that he was safe. I had not realized that the straight line I had been witnessing was a proclamation of doom, and that the quivering one that rose like a steady stream of little mountains, lined up one after the other, actually meant that his heart was returning to its customary, steady beat.

Dick remained in the hospital another month and came home to a heartwarming celebration. It seemed as though everyone in town wanted to wish him well, none more than the pretty Korean nurse that had been his faithful care giver in the intensive care unit. Months later, I realized that my husband and she were having an affair, but so grateful was I that he had been given the gift of continuing on with his life that I decided not to put any more strain onto our marriage. I actually felt grateful for the sensitive and kind care she had rendered to my husband in his month long hospital stay, and began to accept that such a relationship could occur when two people are put together in extraordinary circumstances. I did, however, send the woman scampering from my beautiful New York City apartment that I had graciously lent to her on weekends so that she could enjoy the many exciting cultural events of NYC.

I made it clear that if I ever heard of her around my husband or family again, that she would lose her job. Her only remark was, "Now why would you want to be so selfish? You had him for a dozen years, so why not give another woman a chance for some happiness." I learned to be more careful after that, about inviting those that I did not really know into my home. The comforting words that this woman, Grace, recited to me during the sorrowful times that my husband was so ill were difficult to erase from my mind. "Know that I am praying so hard and working with all my strength to save your husband," she had repeated to me daily. I had counted on her, and considered her our guardian angel. Though I came to realize that she had a personal agenda to achieve that ultimately could have caused me and my family great harm, I found it hard to hate her. She had gotten my husband through some very rough days and I was truly thankful that he was still on this earth.

I threw myself into my fashion work, and did my very best to put on a happy face. As I began to get more and more commercial work and acting jobs I found that I regained my confidence and returned to genuinely being a person who enjoyed life. I started volunteering my time with the orphanages and brought children home to teach them my skills in photography, especially developing in the dark room. I took a few children regularly on field trips with my children, to the theatre, out to eat, and I helped them to fashion special treasure boxes to store important memories. Our comfortable, spacious home was the center of much activity. There were many sleep overs with my kids friends, and always underfoot would be the kids beloved Irish Setters and little fuzzy black, mix breed Maximillian. The dogs would be romping and playing and racing around the house. My husband would go stomping after them, pretending to be upset, saying he was going to "get rid of you dogs." Then my husband would grab their faces and kiss them each on the nose. It was hard not to be happy.

LOU JEFFERSON

I was twenty-nine, a model, and I didn't spend much time thinking about the future. My husband was back into his busy practice and I was grateful we had weathered the storms we had been through. One day, I was taken by a respected literary agent up to Harlem to visit one of his clients. We walked into the apartment of Louise E. Jefferson. I could not believe the meticulous manner in which her dozens of beautifully illustrated books were displayed amongst her hand carved statues, all done by herself - and on the walls hung the portraits of the imminent artists, celebrities, educators, and intellectuals that she had personally photographed. Her hand painted and detailed maps of the world were everywhere and a testament to her knowledge and travels. I remember becoming very quiet and thinking, "now here is a life that has been lived with discipline, integrity, and passion." I was never the same afterwards. I had found a role model and we would remain friends for the rest of her life.

Lou sitting at her cluttered   Jefferson's Photo, Alabama Boy
but very neat desk

"Imagine a dynamo of human energy so quick, so bright, that it electrifies the space that it is in. That was Louise E. Jefferson. I called her Lou and though she was a petite woman with calm but mischievous eyes, her powerfully gay laughter and sharp tongue would grab and hold your attention for the full time you were in her presence. Lou lived in an impeccable little house that she called "The Cottage," framed by a picket fence.

But, I want you to get a good clear picture - so just imagine that you are following the map from New York City to Litchfield, Connecticut - turning off of the Interstate Highway and moving through little sleepy, lush towns dripping with the greens, golds, and reds, of the fall foliage. As you approach Litchfield, you roll down your windows and breathe in the fragrances of the wild flowers that grow thick by the roadside and you drive past all of the neat and proper white frame homes as you glide by what the locals call the Green on historic West Street. Now, you go just two houses west of the Town Office Building and you see a courtyard which looks like an inverted U Shaped Compound. Drive slowly and proceed to the center of the courtyard and stop in front of the little frame house. That is "The Cottage."

Oops, slow down, because here she comes, bounding out of her tiny doorway with the combustion of a big Mack Truck. "Hang on, I'll call the Fire Department and the Police and tell them to call off their search. Did you stop at some lover's hideaway?" There was Lou, right in my face, practically bowling me over with her energy. She was very sharp witted and with her one did not talk about the mundane unless it was of her own choosing. In this instance, I had not seen her in a couple of years and what mattered to her the most was that our connection should be spontaneous, interesting, and real. So, I simply climbed out of the car and pretended to coax the invisible lover out of the back seat and immediately we broke into gales of laughter.

She took my breath away with her rapid fire retort. "Spit it out or I will have to come over and resuscitate you." I laughed and thanked her for giving me detailed instructions of how to bypass the hurriedness of the highway traffic and bask instead in the loveliness of the many small towns I would pass through. I indeed had followed the advice of the "master of minute observances," Jefferson herself. Lou was famous for her world maps, all detailed by hand and many bearing her gorgeous pen and ink drawings, so I knew that no map offered by another would be as clear, logical, and outstanding as the instructions given by Jefferson.

Lou was a world renowned cartographer, and had traveled numerous times to Africa under Ford Foundation Grants to lay out - with her fine eye for detail and her brilliant hand for illustration, painting, and calligraphy - The Decorative Arts of Africa. In a book by the same title, "The Decorative Arts of Africa," she offered scholars and artisans a brilliant visual sampling of African works of Art; showing the costumes, metal works, wood carvings, weavings, hair designs, tribal markings, things from Uganda, Kenya, Tanzania, Senegal, Zaire, Rhodesia, and Morocco, all very important in the documentation of Africa's Art History. Lou's book became the "Bible" for any serious student wishing to learn about the history of art and artifacts in Africa. Lou's genius resonated around the Art World as countless Museums and Universities across the globe reached out to her and benefited from the meticulous research she had done. Jefferson had lived her life with passion, strict discipline, and patience. She often remarked that photography takes a lot of patience because "you sometimes have to wait for hours to get the clouds you want, or a particular movement from an animal." What Lou loved was the joy of discovery, of finding new ways to look at things and how to incorporate them into her ever growing body of work. She often joked that she had photographed every stone in Litchfield. Lou did not go anywhere without a camera, not even to her own backyard. She would spend long hours getting the photograph that she wanted and then spend more tedious hours after the prints were developed choosing and cutting her own mats out of delicate color hues. Often she would make the frame herself.

Lou was a perfectionist. She could muster up a great deal of emotion if someone used the word "Snapshot" in her presence. She hated that word - and what she hated most was "snap part." Oh, but Lou had such an irreverent sense of humor. When I mentioned that I had traveled to her house under a "lemony sun," she was delighted and sent me a marvelously detailed painting of a lemon with flowers on it - and guess who was sitting on top of the actual sized "lemon," - no other than Lou herself. There she was in the tiniest drawing having a grand laugh. She was an original. No project, however small, warranted anything other than Lou's best effort. Lou's wisdom came from her belief, her awareness that sight and sound and thought and movement were interconnected. They were all part of a complex rhythm that had to be in motion for that rhythm to be perfectly clear. If something was working well, the rhythm was good. If something wasn't working it was time to put back in shape the part that was out of order.

As a child, Jefferson was prompted to take off her leg brace that she wore as a result of contracting Polio while traveling with her mother who sometimes sang on the Potomac cruise ships. One day, after school, she got an axe. She took off her leg brace, and hacked that brace into pieces. Lou didn't like the teasing she got from the noise it made. That brace had destroyed her rhythm. Jefferson had climbed a tree after destroying the brace, expecting a swift reprimand from her father, but that never came and Jefferson never regretted her decision. Jefferson's keen eye, talent, and discipline were encouraged by her parents. Her father was a gifted engraver who did fine engravings on bank charters for the United States Treasury Department. Her mother was an accomplished pianist, and even her grandmother sang in concerts given in their own home. Lou became truly animated when talking about her family, "Our family home was 'alive' with music, she said. We had comfort, we were close, there was always laughter in the house…Grandfather, Grandmother, and Aunt."

Lou, too, had a fine ear for music and she taught herself to play the piano and the drums.

"Anything I do, I train myself to do," Lou often quipped but she did study Fine Arts at Hunter College and Graphic Arts at Columbia University. Her artistic impulses led to her mastery of the skills of bookbinding, cartography, drawing, and photography - and as Art Director of Friendship Press for over a quarter of a century, she did maps of virtually every area of the world, published by major publishers. Lou's originality of rhythm was sometimes controversial. In 1936 she illustrated a songbook depicting black and white children playing and singing together. This simple work incurred the wrath of Georgia's governor Eugene Talmadge and he ordered the book banned and burned. Lou went on with her work of promoting goodwill by designing the Holiday Seals for the N.A.A.C.P. She continued to work for them for another forty years. While living in Harlem during the Harlem Renaissance, Jefferson kept her cameras busy photographing many famous people, including poets Langston Hughes, Countee Cullen, Gwendolyn Bennett, Pauli Murray, her closest friend who was also a lawyer and ordained Episcopal priest; civil rights leader Dr. Martin Luther King, Jr.; tennis great Althea Gibson; Supreme Court Justice Thurgood Marshall; and music legendary artists Louis Armstrong, Duke Ellington, and Lena Horne, to name just a few.

I asked Lou once if she would tell me about the process by which she created her detailed drawings. "Doll, Jefferson said, have you been plotting all that time to dream up more work for me." A feeling of warmth bathed my heart because I knew she only used affectionate terms to the closest of her friends. She took down one of the drawings from her wall and quickly and quietly loosened it from its entrapment. She began to carefully peel off its three layers, loosely glued on the edges. The bottom drawing was done in larger strokes and shadowed areas of pencil. The second drawing was done in colored pencils and acrylic paint. And the final layer was a polished milky looking non glossy plastic sheet with even a finer detailed drawing on it. Lou´s eyes gleamed with devilment and I fell speechless. "Ah, the cat´s finally got your tongue, has it, she said." Lou, I said, I had no idea there was so much work involved. "There´s only one way to keep them from stealing your work, and that is to make it so hard, it isn´t worth their while," she retorted. Oh, how Lou chuckled as she carefully reassembled the drawing and returned it to its place on the wall.

I often think of the times when Lou would take some of her treasured drawings off the wall, pack them meticulously and send them to me in New York with a note that she was clearing out some stuff because she had more things than she had "cat food." I would quickly call my Hollywood friends to buy some of her Originals and get off a check to her. Once, when I sensed a real urgency in her voice I called Diane Dillon, a brilliant artist and illustrator who worked with her husband Leo and son Lee on many important Caldecott Award Winning Books and Diane expressed real sorrow that Jefferson was having such a struggle because she said Lou's work was treasured by every Museum in the country.

Shortly thereafter, Diane called me back and told me she had a check for $5,000.00 dollars from The Society of Illustrators for Jefferson in appreciation for her lifetime of achievement in the Arts. When Lou got the check she called me and said she was going to frame our little "fantasy check" and get back to work. I took more than a few minutes convincing Lou that the check was genuine and that she would be better off going straight to the bank than wasting real money by putting it on the wall. I heard Lou sputtering for words, and for the first time in her life, she was rendered speechless.

The fondest memory I had of Lou was an autumn day when daylight was slipping away.

We had jumped into the car and had proceeded up a winding hill to a little country roadside bar. I felt foolish because I hadn't realized that Lou was hungry as she had, for many hours, good naturedly brought out folder after folder of her meticulously catalogued work - but now she was commenting on the changing light, the shadows falling across the slat wooden floor as we found our way to our booth.

The first thing Lou did, as I was seating myself, was head for The Juke Box - which literally startled me. She took a long time pondering over her selection. Finally, the music burst forth and Lou began to dance to Michael Jackson's "Thriller." I laughed so hard my body was actually convulsing. I watched Lou joyously dance with complete abandon. She was then perhaps eighty-five, on the plus side, and seeing her working off her restless energy I could well imagine that her childhood home was indeed "alive with music" My friend, Louise E. Jefferson, was a true Renaissance Woman – Spirited, Talented, Rare.

I was always (and still am) interested in how people have risen to be role models, how they can (and should) be mobilized to help others. *When Lou was in a nursing home briefly at the end of her life, I took a few Harlem children from the Creative Find Gallery that I had founded for at risk children up to Connecticut to visit Lou so they could meet personally the woman whose Excelsior mode of working they had been encouraged to follow when they created their works of Art in our Harlem gallery.*

Always when we had big Gallery Exhibitions for the public, the children who had really worked diligently on perfecting their Artwork were privileged to hang it alongside Lou Jefferson's work and that of Gordon Parks, Adger Cowans, and Lloyd Stevens, noteworthy mainstream artists. Oftentimes, the children's works were singled out for praise and brought in big dollar profits that benefitted the children and gave the Gallery much good publicity. The children had gotten for Lou several stuffed kittens and she did not at all appreciate these puffed up fake concoctions as she had her own live cat living in her hospital room.

Lou did not like the noisy shenanigans of these frolicking young artists and she looked uneasy as she pulled her blankets up around her shoulders. I think that in her frail state she had revisited the unhappy times when her childhood classmates had made boisterous mockery of her wearing her iron leg brace as she walked to her classroom seat. I could not get out of my mind the image of Lou's marvelous illustration of children holding hands and dancing in a ring – her iconic poster that was popular for decades. Still, nothing could change the fact that I had made a grave mistake and I felt bad for Lou who was trapped in her bed and for the kids who were thrilled to be in the room with an artist whose works they had studied and, moreover, works that hung on their very own Creative Find Gallery walls.

I wanted the kids to be on the receiving end and really appreciate a wonderful encounter with one of their living heroes, but it was not meant to be. When Lou died, in her will she left all of her framed and unframed Artwork to me. When the executor of the estate - who was in Lou's hospital room when the children and I had visited – delivered the Portfolios of Lou's treasured works, most of the first and second layers of her meticulous three layered drawings had been removed from the frames, leaving a drawing but not the multi-depth magic that Lou had created. I feel sick when I think about this miserable woman's action who did not understand or care about my love and commitment to Louise E. Jefferson.

Meeting Lou Jefferson had changed the course of my life, had helped me to dream another existence, to looks through another lens. I shall always be grateful to Lou for the amazing work she did on the Lives and Art of Africans from the Continent of Africa and on African Americans.

How does one bear witness to the legacy of slavery? We can see the ways in which great activists, historians, writers, and artists were called upon to address it. In the works of Tom Feelings, especially in "The Middle Passage," we can appreciate in Tom Feeling's magnificent drawings the suffering endured on these dreadful slave ships - and in the detailed illustrations and maps of Louise Jefferson we are able to understand how diligently Jefferson worked to document so much rich history that was quickly disappearing.

Enslaved Blacks endured the most humiliating and humbling of circumstances. They were forced to labor more hours than their bodies could bear and those that did not endure were found murdered or hanging from The Lynching Trees. My great grandmother Missy's own mother, as I said, was put up on the auction block and "sold for fifty cents." Missy lived to the end of her life with her sister who my Granny called Aunt Mary, and Missy was never able to buy the humble little log cabin (shack) that she lived in with my Granny at the back of that big old "sawed off cornfield."

While Missy my great grandmother was living in a little shack at the back of the cornfield on Captain Knowles' plantation in Troy - Charlotte Forten, a Black woman born to the prominent and free abolitionists, Robert Bridges Forten and Mary Woods Forten of Philadelphia - was busy organizing herself to become the first Black school teacher in the Sea Islands in Beaufort, South Carolina during the actual fighting of the Civil War. Charlotte Forten took a steamboat to Beaufort where she promptly went to the Commissary's office to await the boat that would take her to St. Helena's Island where she would begin her teaching assignment, just six miles away. There in the office, a Colonel talked roughly about rebel attacks and yellow fever with another army officer, frequently using the word "nigger" in Ms. Forten's presence. Forten wrote in her diary that she was not alarmed. She "saw through them at once," (their efforts to discourage her.) Later, as she reflected on traveling along the lonely roads in the dark of night on the way to her final lodging - "how easy it would have been for a band of guerillas, had any chanced that way, to seize and hang us."

Charlotte Forten was a brave spirit, who chose to focus her attention on the poetic aspects of her journeys rather than the trying and dismal dark sides. Even when in danger she spoke of the loveliness of the pines and the palmettos, of the large noble trees whose great beauty was the long bearded moss with which every branch is heavily draped. She wrote about "the grand Southern sunsets, the gorgeous clouds of crimson and gold reflected in the waters below which were smooth and calm as a mirror." Her diary entries were filled with her awe and her mysterious reminisces of the Old South, of gliding along as "the rich sonorous tones of the boatmen broke upon the evening stillness...their singing was so sweet and strange and solemn - Roll Jordan Roll was grand."

Yes, Forten herself was grand; a grand inspiration to me when I chanced upon her diaries when I was fourteen. Forten was a woman who gave up the safety and privilege of being a free Negro to come to the Sea Islands to teach slaves, some who were still being recaptured by their Masters. Certainly, Forten could so easily have been harmed as she put herself in harm's way in the fight for the "Liberty of Others." In her entries, I could imagine that I was there, with her. I could easily see the "black soldiers in their blue coats and scarlet pants, the crowds of on lookers grouped in various attitudes, "wearing happy, eager, expectant looks."

I envisioned the noble trees with their shiny small green leaves and deep, curving drapes of funeral moss. Yes, I could imagine the one hundred and fifty people being baptized in the creek near the church. I could see them "looking picturesque in their white aprons, and bright dresses and handkerchiefs." I walked with them down to the water, and sang "Down In The Lonesome Valley" with them. Yes, I closed my eyes and imagined my Granny and Poppa singing "Swing Low, Sweet Chariot." I imagined that sweet, sorrowful refrain coming from Missy in her little one room shack at the back of that old sawed off cornfield in Troy and I had no trouble imagining Forten singing with the slaves, gently swaying as their music touched the chords in her heart. I had no trouble in imagining Charlotte Forten teaching the slaves and their children in that one room cabin deep into those hauntingly beautiful and dangerous woods. I can fully understand how she became attached to the children's' earnest faces, all eager to learn to read and write.

In one of her entries in her diary, she wrote, another day, one of the black soldiers came in and gave up his account of the expedition of the First South Carolina Volunteers sent up the St. Mary's River to capture Confederate supplies and cripple a vessel. I asked him what he would do if his Master and others should come back and try to re- enslave him. "I'd fight um Miss, I'd fight um till I turned to dust."

I am grateful for Charlotte Forten's teaching and mentoring and her many beautiful stories and poetry. Despite her ongoing battle with tuberculosis, she found a way to bring much beauty and hope into the world. I've always wanted to bring beauty into the world, too, to tell others how we can continue to benefit from the wise and beautiful stance of heroes and heroines like Jefferson, Feelings, Marsalis, Ben Carson and Reuben Cannon – to move beyond one's own little world to reach out to be of service to others through our work and through mentoring.

There are many great heroes and heroines, big and small. Forten, herself, was inspired by two children who were successful in escaping and she made certain others would learn about them as she carefully recorded their journey in her diary." Two young girls, one ten and one fifteen were taken away by their Master. The girls bravely stole away one night, traveling through woods and swamps and though their strength would sometimes fail and they would sink down in the swamps and think they could go no further, they had brave little hearts and struggled on until at last they reached the Ferry. The Ferry could not take them because it was too full but the passengers promised to carry word to their father. The father managed to come and fetch the girls and when they were brought to their mother she fell down "just as if she was dead - she was so overpowered with joy." Charlotte Forten wrote, "I want to see the heroic little creatures." Through Charlotte's remembrances of them in her diary, I felt that I had known them, too.

As I said previously, I first started writing in my diary when I was fourteen and unlike Anne Frank who was writing while hiding in an attic from the Nazis for nearly three years or Charlotte Forten who was writing the important and deeply personal events of living through a very ugly Civil War between the North and the South, I was writing about living through much fun and great turbulence in a family of eight children. I documented in a book of blank pages all of my thoughts about my immediate family. I included photos and the daily activities that made up the life of my family – my high spirited, fun loving, entrepreneurial father, my beautiful, temperamental strict mother and of course, my four very different brothers and three sisters.

WHEN I WAS FOURTEEN

Eight siblings we were, as you already know, just roughly a year to a year and a half apart, all born within an eleven-year period. I remember being given the assignment to write a short story about something important and I knew immediately that I wanted to write about my family. My story was definitely not going to be just a couple of pages. When my ninth grade teacher saw the story she decided to send it off and have the pages bound in black leather. I had named my story "When I Was Fourteen," and this was engraved in gold letters on the cover of the book. My mother saw the book many years later tucked away in a corner of the attic and she said she spent a full afternoon first crying about what I had written, and then laughing so hard that she thought she would be sick.

I realize now that I told some very personal stories about our private lives and the many fights my parents had behind that closed door of our modest white frame home on Euclid Avenue in Akron, Ohio. Not much of what was going on in that house remained private because of the tempestuous nature of both my parents, but certainly my Mama had not expected me to bare my soul in my school papers.

One fight that took place that spread like wildfire across town, happened in a very public Dance Hall, the East Market Gardens. It was a night when Mama's nerves were not the best and she tried really hard to keep her temper in check. She was dressing to go out and she did not want us underfoot to interfere with her laying out her beautiful evening dress, high heel shoes, and all of the fancy combs that she had placed at the side of her dressing mirror that would be soon attached to her pompadour hair-do. We peeked in the halfway opened bedroom door in our self-appointed little groups of twos and threes, whispering loudly, "it's my turn now." We giggled and gasped at our Mama's beauty as she piled her shoulder length hair in an elaborate swirled roll on top of her head and attached the sparkling combs. After layering several lipsticks and grabbing her spangled purse she made her way to the door, pretending to call out to the babysitter that it was time to ready the children for bed. Of course, this gave us a few seconds to scramble down the steps and pretend to be dutifully seated, smiling innocently, as we waited for a goodnight kiss from our Mama.

What I gathered from the events of that evening that thereafter transpired, I heard from an emotional exchange between my mother in a telephone conversation with her best friend Marion in the wee hours of the morning as I made my way down the creaky staircase from my attic bedroom that I shared with my three sisters – trying my best to place my bare feet ever so softly on the steps so I could noiselessly reach the bathroom which was just to the left of the doorway, right by Mama's room. We girls often got harshly admonished for disturbing our mother and got sent back upstairs before we ever got to use the bathroom. To this day, I find myself constantly putting off "Nature's Calling" as though I expect a reprimand from Mama. Nevertheless, that evening, when Mama called out, "Who's there?" I did not answer and sat on the steps and helped myself to Mama's private conversation.

"Oh Marion, you don't know how I regret not going with BT earlier," because I would have never run into that miserable woman." Mama went on to explain the events as they had transpired. It was a hot, sweltering night but Mama said she didn't mind because the air was charged with excitement. Mama's ride had let her out of the car a good half block before the entrance because the crowd of people swelled into a long line waiting to be admitted into the huge portico building. Standing on her tiptoes in her platform shoes Mama had looked over the crowd's heads for Slim, Johnny, or Kenny, my Daddy's helpers, the ticket sellers that would have recognized her, but seeing no one that she knew, she made it up to the front of the line past a maze of sequined and beaded dresses and fast talking men with arms out front in combat mode, trying desperately to curb the surging party goers.

There were colorful flags and posters everywhere announcing that "The Joy Boy presents Duke Ellington" and other signs about the All Star Band appearances of The Ink Spots and Billy Eckstine. Mama said that even though she was annoyed at having to be in such a throng that she was getting excited and anxious to get inside to see firsthand what all the fuss was about.

Mama told Marion that My Daddy had really done something big and that he had been right – that the era of the Big Bands was back with a vengeance. She said she just could not fathom how all of those people would ultimately make it to the dance floor, but was grateful the she had finally gotten through to two authoritative looking guards and announced that she was B.T.'s wife, and needed to be taken to her husband. Mama told Marion the men looked at each other and laughed and that one guard pointed in the direction of a buxom, coffee colored girl with hazel eyes and replied with a smirk, "You'd better check with her about that because she is the missus of B.T."

Mama brushed the man aside and headed for an elaborately draped flower table where the woman was standing. "I'm told you know where I can find B.T," Mama said. The hazel eyed beauty turned and said, "Yes, but I'm afraid he is much too busy to be bothered, but may I give him a message." "Oh yes dear, indeed you can give him a message," Mama said. Mama burst out laughing. Then, I heard Mama say to Marion, excitedly, "I just turned as though I was leaving, and with a little twist and a furious fist, I gave her my message, right in the face - and sent her and all of her complimentary flowers, flying North and South, East and West."

That was Mama. She always made her point. I learned, as this tale was told and retold over the decades, that the injured woman was taken home by My Daddy's brother, Fred, and that Mama was complimented by Mr. Ellington himself for packing a powerful punch into her beautiful evening bag. Mama danced the night away and let everyone know that she could deal with any smooth talking floozies or jokesters that came her way. But one smooth talking woman named Pauline, my Mama was not able to deal with so effortlessly. After many rumors and emotionally charged phone calls, Mama learned that Pauline was pregnant with my Daddy's child and there was nothing further that my Daddy could say to our Mama. Mama was finished and she began the process of plodding her divorce. I tried for many years to piece together how this divorce actually happened as my Daddy was well connected with Courthouse Judicial friends, and he certainly wanted no part of any divorce.

But Mama was not one to give up on anything that she had set her mind to, and as things became uncommonly quiet around our house I suspected that Mama was planning something, something big. My worst fears were realized when my siblings and I were taken into court and each asked who we wanted to live with should Mama's divorce be granted. We all watched behind that court railing as our Daddy rose to fight for custody of his beloved Egg Heads. My Daddy would not win. Strangely, Jacqueline was awarded to our father, and the remainder of the children to Mama. To this day, the decision remains a baffling one. Why would a judge break up a family in such a drastic way? That decision would alter the course of my elder sister's life.

After the divorce, Mama would send me down to Granny's house where my Daddy lived to try to coax him into giving us the necessary money she needed to make dinner and my Daddy would hold the money hostage if he was angry with Mama about something. I'd run my hand back and forth across his brow, trying desperately to soothe him. "Everything is lost," he would say as he wept. "My babies don't love me anymore." I would keep running my fingers across his brow and say, "It isn't true that we don't love you, it isn't true – we love you with all of our hearts. You are our only Daddy." But our Daddy would not be comforted.

Everything was going badly. The accountants had used the money that was intended for taxes, and our Daddy's decision to sell or consolidate or whatever he did with his little dynasty on North Howard Street was ill advised and poorly planned and nothing was working. His Lake Glen Country Club was not doing well. People were watching too much television and not coming out anymore. And the cover charge was too high and the dinners too expensive. And certainly, the liquor inspector wanted too much money to "turn his cheek" after the "last call." Perhaps, too, the people simply didn't have any money left after they had spent so much betting at the race track. It was apparent that a great nightclub didn't belong next door to a racetrack. My Daddy's plan was not working. He was dangerously close to losing everything.

Though I tried to persuade our Daddy that we absolutely loved him, he protested, "You only love me for my money." I became frustrated, "There isn't any money, not even enough for dinner for the little boys." I always referred to my three youngest brothers as "the little boys." And on and on our Daddy went with his childish lament, "so it is just the money that you came for." I cried out, "Stop acting like a baby - just because you and Mama are divorced doesn't mean that the little boys don't need dinner."

Mama married then. Yes, married another man after dozens of such encounters failed to prompt our Daddy to act in a more responsible way. The man moved in with us. One day, there he was, a new man named Jimmy. Well, none of us accepted Jimmy. It was not long before Jimmy moved out - without any of us ever meeting Jimmy's two children. I remember that he was a handsome, kind man, this Jimmy, who looked at us individually, not as a hostile group of eight children who refused to give him a chance. I don't think I ever learned Jimmy's last name. It was a strange happening, Jimmy moving into our house that in the eyes of the Brooks children, was "My Daddy's House."

Many years after I married, a young man came to my door in Philadelphia and said he had something to tell me. I looked into his face and understood that I already knew what he was going to say. He looked exactly like my brother Reggie, and I soon guessed that he was my brother - Jerry was his name - my Daddy's child that had prompted my mother to pull the plug on her marriage. Like Jimmy, Jerry was a stranger that came too suddenly into my life. I tried for My Daddy's sake to accept this brother that I had never known, but I never truly succeeded. It was not only that Jerry's mother had broken up my parent's tumultuous marriage, but I had no bonding experiences with Jerry and I never managed to successfully forge them so that they felt genuine.

For some reason, when I think of not being able to bond with my brother Jerry, I think of one of my dearest friends Dr. Meredith Gourdine, telling me after he had gone blind from diabetes that he was "all at sea" about not being able to bond with women that he could not see. He had always had an eye for beauty and he divorced his much beloved and very beautiful wife to marry a red haired woman who had captured one of the Southern State's Crowns in the Miss America Pageant. This woman was an extraordinary beauty Meredith told me and he risked all to make her his own but, unbelievably, the woman stood him up at the altar and Meredith managed to seek his wife's forgiveness and remarry the woman who had brought his children into the world.

Stranger stories have been told, I'm sure, and none more unusual than Miss America re-entering Meredith's life to stand him up at the altar for a second time. Meredith's wife was more than forgiving but in the end she had finally had enough and she divorced and married one of Meredith's best friends. Meredith tried to laugh off these events but I could not help but feel that when he went blind, that he really missed and needed the comfort of memories that are naturally there when one has shared so many experiences with a life partner.

I think that the fact that my brother Jerry and I were virtual strangers for thirty odd years greatly impacted my inability to bond with him. Meredith, though his mind was willing, was having difficulty with his heart bridging the world from the sighted to the blind in terms of embracing the unfamiliar – though he did succeed somewhat, remarrying and doing much important work with his scientific inventions. Meredith was a genius and his story is a compelling one. I feel so privileged to have known him and to have remained friends with him over the course of our lives. Meredith told me his riveting life story one day

DR. MEREDITH C. GOURDINE

Did you ever have to fight your way to school and back? That is what Dr. Meredith Gourdine had to do when he was young boy living in Harlem. He lived in a neighborhood so rough, Dr. Gourdine said that "we learned to fight and run." Imagine a tall, skinny Black kid running through the streets of Harlem, past the crumbling stoops and patched brick facades of homes that had seen too much living and too little care, past littered empty lots, past men and boys grown intolerant of even a curious glance, slipping by like a flash of lightening, moving so fast that he literally couldn't be caught. Not by anyone. But Gourdine said he became so bored running to get away from fights that he started memorizing math equations in his head just so he would have something interesting to do while he was running. He began calculating square roots in his head while he worked to increase his speed – and that gave him the focus he needed to keep up with his math classes. Dr. Gourdine also loved to laugh and have a good time with his buddy Ralph. Ralph and he would do many crazy things. One day they even stole some math books from the library. Imagine two young boys wanting to steal math books? Not beer, not cigarettes, but math books!

Gourdine was uncertain about where he would land in life because he and Ralph ran with a "pretty rough" crowd. One evening, something happened that changed Gourdine's party focus. Changed it fast. Ralph had sneaked into the movies and while trying to grope his way to a seat he fell over the balcony. The fall was not a good one. It put Ralph in a wheelchair and he no longer recognized Gourdine. His brain had ceased to communicate. Gourdine had lost his best friend. He thought about the realities of his life, of his father setting pins in a bowling alley when he could have taken the scholarship that he had won and gone on to college. For certain, Ralph had lost his chance to have an interesting and productive life but Gourdine was determined that he would not lose his.

Gourdine at the Helsinki Olympic Games

Gourdine enrolled in Brooklyn Tech High School where his math professor taught him solid Geometry by lecturing about the perfect proportions of actress Ingrid Bergman. As Gourdine grew to love physics more than math, he also pursued swimming but he settled on becoming a track star, earning the nickname "Flash" for being one of the fastest quarter milers in New York City. This focus of Flash Gourdine's on science and athletics, two very different pursuits, would lead him to win an Olympic Silver Medal for America in the broad jump track competition at the Helsinki Olympics in Finland in 1952 and later would garner him a permanent place in The Science Hall of Fame for inventing the trash conveyor belt and the paint spray gun.

When Alan Field, a writer for the Houston Chronicle, asked Dr. Gourdine how he managed to stay on his rigorous course, he said, "my father had me and my three brothers hauling garbage and mopping floors and that was motivation enough for me to stay in school." Gourdine won the prestigious Guggenheim Fellowship to study at Cal Tech, married, began his family, and received his Doctorate in Engineering Science.

Dr. Gourdine liked to have fun and with a burst of outrageous laughter he would tell the story of the many engineers who have two left hands, who don't know what a screwdriver is, of the many mathematicians who don't need to know about screwdrivers - but that he, being in engineering science, needed to understand the physics behind "all" disciplines. He would stretch out the "all" as a prelude to dramatically taking out his imaginary wrench, telling you about the various solders he might use for this or that, and then with his eyes twinkling he would say, "I have a fascination with gadgetry."

Dr. Gourdine launched Gourdine Systems, a company which at its peak had sixty full time employees studying the interaction between magnetic fields and gases that are hot enough to make electrons split from the atoms. He had over six dozen patents and worked hard to develop his products – some of which were used by NASA. He had an exhaust gas device to recover and recycle the lead so as not to harm the environment and an important airport defogging system that needed further testing - but a combination of things, including unleaded gasoline coming into the market, stopped Gourdine in his tracks.

Struggling with turbulent passions, he would leave his 26 room English Tudor home with swimming pool on his three-acre estate, close down his multimillion-dollar Company, manage the difficult task of divorcing a wife he adored, and fall hopelessly in love, as I mentioned earlier, with a red head who had captured her State and was a finalist in the Miss America Pageant. The doomed romance faltered but more urgent matters awaited Gourdine's immediate attention. Gourdine was doggedly trying to save his eyesight from the throes of diabetes. The deterioration of his vision was a shock for this fit and dynamic man.

Laser beam treatments on two continents failed to stem the rapidly encroaching disease and darkness passed into one eye and then the other. Gourdine lost feeling in his feet and it became impossible for him to read Braille since he lacked sufficient sensation at the tips of his fingers. Gourdine's luminous life had plunged into darkness and threatened to fade away altogether. But no need to feel sad because Flash Gourdine had not given up. He just required refocusing. He found new quarters, a good cane, and a healthy sense of humor. He settled down to his number one love, "inventing." Fortunately, he had the unfailing dedication of his son who moved with him to help with his experiments. Daily encouraging calls from his three daughters and now again ex-wife boosted his morale, and for good measure he adhered to a regime of calisthenics, yoga, and transcendental meditation.

Gourdine called me in New York one day and told me he missed dancing and asked what I thought he might do to replace it. Though he laughed uproariously, I knew my friend had just lost his foot and was feeling shaky - though he tried hard to mask his fear with his laughter. "Stand on your good leg and then move your arms in all of the beautiful positions that ballet dancers move them and you will get the most exquisite feelings out of doing that," I said. Gourdine knew that I had been a ballet dancer and with a big, contented sigh, he said, "I am glad I called you, I am dancing already." And I knew that he was being truthful. He had the most inventive spirit for living a joyful life. There was no space for loss or regret.

THE GOOD DOCTOR

I believe that Dr. Gourdine accepted his life and fought to the end to make the best of it and I always hoped that he truly did not have any regrets. Regrets are something particularly difficult for me to deal with. In my efforts to come to terms with my decision about the necessity of getting a divorce, I always turned over and over in my mind why I did this, why I did that. I blame me for causing my son and daughter irreversible grief as they never recovered from my husband and me divorcing.

I called my husband, Dr. Richard B. Lynch, Jr. one year long after we had parted and asked him what his regrets were, if any. There was a long pause, and finally he said, "Just ask me what you want to know." I told him I wanted to understand why he had gambled so recklessly with our lives. I wanted to know why he risked everything, literally for "gambling." He answered quickly, "Because I was stupid," he said.

I told him I wanted to remember his answers and I hurried from the phone to hook up our conversation to the tape recorder. I have not listened to that conversation again in over thirty years. It is just too painful. My husband said he got a thrill, an adrenaline rush from not knowing what the outcome of a given event would be - whether it was a tennis match that he bet $50,000 dollars on or a heavy weight boxing match where Muhammad Ali would try to win back his crown. The anticipation of not knowing which way it would go until that very last second was intoxicating. It was a feeling of euphoria that he could not duplicate in any other area of his life, he said.

This was puzzling to me and I thought of my friend Dr. Gourdine and wondered if he had felt this euphoria when he thought he had captured the heart of a Southern Miss America Pageant Contestant, thought that "a skinny black, poor kid from Harlem had gotten the much sought after golden prize." Both Dr. Gourdine and Dr. Lynch were good looking, smart, goal oriented men and both had attained much acclaim in their lives but the allure of the dark side would capture Dr. Lynch and hold him a prisoner whereas Dr. Gourdine would move forward to achieve much good despite the darkness that would envelope him. I remember uncovering one day that my husband was storing money, in large paper grocery bags in the closet, and this hiding place was intended to be his safety deposit box area. Of course this was a ridiculous thing for him to do as many housekeepers were in and out, cleaning all of the time.

Later, I heard that one of our housekeepers had purchased a home for $30,000 cash dollars.

Easy enough to guess where the money most likely came from. Nevertheless, despite strange practices like the one noted above, I did not feel that anything was horribly wrong in our little world. My husband worked very long hours at the Medical Center and played much tennis on the weekends with his attorney friend. I worked both at the Medical Center three days a week, and in New York where I was establishing myself as a documentary filmmaker. I worried about my husband's gambling naturally, and once had to scramble for money to secure our home that Dr. Lynch had lost in a poker game. And though I tried to get the Good Doctor to therapists to help with his gambling addiction I did not feel we were in any imminent danger. I could not have been more wrong.

I was in New York City, editing a film when I got a frantic call from my husband's secretary telling me to come home immediately. I was terrified during the two and a half hour ride from New York to Philadelphia because the secretary would not tell me what was wrong, just that it was an emergency. Upon arriving at our home I learned that there had been a drug bust at my husband's offices and that he and a number of others had been arrested. What brought me to my knees was the fact that thrown into the mix of drug suspects was also our fourteen-year-old daughter and her friend who were visiting the offices at the time that the undercover drug agents burst in and announced that all present were going to be arrested and taken into custody.

A maze of surreal memories come to mind. I was told that our daughter and her friend were arrested along with my husband. This nightmare, that I could barely fathom, played out in real time in my fourteen-year-old daughter's life. Just imagine the shock of finding out that your young daughter who had casually stopped by to visit her Dad at his medical office was arrested in a violent drug bust, and had ended up being taken into custody with her friend in a police van.

What happened next is still a murky memory. My daughter and her friend were somehow rescued and released to her friend's parents, one a psychiatrist and the other a psychologist, who were livid with my husband who professed complete innocence. There were many days of confusion, meetings with dozens of lawyers, and then after many more days of anticipation and actual dread, a trial date was set. After many weeks of public shame and constant newspaper articles about whether my husband was indeed framed or guilty of selling controlled substances to his patients, my husband was found innocent of all charges. I remember my husband raising his fist to the air after each "not guilty" proclamation from the jury foreman.

The jury congratulated me for my strong testimony in defense of my husband, and our little family ventured back into our muddied lives - hopeful that we would indeed survive all the gossip and controversy swirling around Dr. Lynch's Medical Practice. I totally believed that my husband was innocent and I was grateful that the jury backed me in that belief as I had never seen my husband sell anything to anyone. I was thrilled to get out of the dismal, dull garb I had been asked by my husband's attorneys to wear during the many days of testimony and was happy to once again be wearing my pretty, fashionable dresses. During the trial, box upon box of medical records had been examined and found to accurately reflect that my husband had not prescribed an unusual amount of amphetamines, and the record of visits recorded of patients that had come to see him was so great that there was huge doubt as to when Dr. Lynch could have had time to see the many people he was supposed to have sold drugs to. People were forced to abandon malicious innuendos and gradually the buzz quieted down and everything went back to normal. The notoriety of the trial had not diminished the number of patients though – and in fact, we had more than ever. It was not easy being The Doctor, or The Doctor's Wife during those heady times.

I have spent far too much on these sad events that had happened to me and not the joyous ones but it would not be real if I did not tell you that there were two more awful trials that The Good Doctor went through. The second one, which was pretty much the same as the first – accusing him of selling illegal drugs to his patients – he won. I did not, at my husband's request, attend that trial as he felt I had gotten too much attention when I testified for him the first time. He did not like that a few jury members had complimented me after the trial for being the persuading factor for them determining that my husband was innocent. One juror had said, "We knew that a woman like that would not have stood behind a man selling drugs." Well, that woman did not testify and Dr. Lynch won again.

The papers ran many articles. One in the Philadelphia Journal in 1978 was particularly sensational and ran the headline with his photo, "Convicted Osteopath Slurs Undercover Narc." The female journalist said, "An osteopath convicted of pushing drugs appeared to have no remorse at his sentencing yesterday." My husband's retort to the judge had been, "It is just unbelievable that you would believe that man, who is nothing but a house nigger, over me," It all boiled down to an undercover police officer who had reportedly made several visits to Dr. Lynch's office and received large quantities of amphetamines, and is reported to have received $750 for them. Dr. Lynch was arrested and tried and sentenced to three to six years in prison on four counts of delivery of a controlled substance. Dr. Lynch's attorney, the former District Attorney Emmett Fitzpatrick appealed and Dr. Lynch never went to prison. I don't remember whether my husband lost his license at that trial or the one thereafter.

I concentrated on getting a divorce after the last trial but I couldn't let go of the fact that I had dreamed one day of my husband entering politics and becoming the President of the United States. He was such a beloved and gifted doctor and he was an amazing history buff who knew just about everything that had happened politically in all the countries of the world over the centuries. He understood clearly why the events had happened and could present formidable arguments for the opposing sides. It was hard to think of this husband of mine, who visited the orphanages regularly and treated the orphans free of charge, who never turned down a patient who could not pay, or failed to bring a smile to a lonely, elderly patient's face - as a criminal whose photo would rest forever in a mug shot book.

Many years later, I found dozens and dozens of bottles of amphetamines hidden in all of the furniture that I had in storage from our big thirty room house that we had shared together and I was forced to confront head on what my husband had done. I tried to flush down the toilet those tainted pills but all I achieved was a stopped up toilet. Finally, after nights of torment, I threw the pills into big bags and put them in a dumpster. My husband went back to school, and got his medical license restored and though he practiced again and was on the board of many hospitals, he never fully regained the Star Status he once had.

I never regained my status either. The friends that I thought I had stopped calling and the many invitations I had once enjoyed just disappeared. My women friends seemed concerned that soon I would be looking for a husband, and it might be theirs. Money was becoming scarce. I found it necessary to sell our thirty room Germantown house in Philly for internal revenue taxes owed, and then I felt the crunch for meeting my expenses on my beloved 74th Street Madison Avenue apartment in New York City. I had bought an apartment that Cole Porter had lived in at one time, Dorothy Parker at another time, and even Dame Margot Fonteyn, the great ballerina, who I later met and who incredulously wanted me to come to London with her because she thought I had the grace to be a Prima Ballerina. I loved my apartment with all my heart and I felt so lucky that other wonderful artists had lived in the space that I was so fortunate to occupy.

I contacted Adrienne Vittadini and asked her if she would buy it. She readily agreed and just a few days before the deal went through I found out through my attorneys that I could attain a Bridge Loan on the Condo I owned on Rittenhouse Square in Philadelphia to secure my Manhattan home. I felt tremendous relief and called Adrienne to tell her the good news. She was not happy. She said a "deal was a deal." Rather than lose face with a friend, I went through with my deal to sell my apartment, a decision I have regretted every minute of my life.

A NIGHT TO REMEMBER WHILE I PONDERED WHERE TO LIVE

I was never good at being sad for long. I always managed to fit in a vacation here and there or some interesting project to ground me. I felt fortunate throughout my apartment woes to have been working on a book of photography, "With Glory I So Humbly Stand," that I did on the rural country people of Jamaica that was shot in a fantastically beautiful area called Roaring River near the ancient caves. I fell in love with Westmoreland County, deep in the interior of Jamaica – with the nearby villages having endearing names like Lucy, Big Bridge, and Little London. The people were poor but majestic and to this day Roaring River remains one of the purest places I have ever photographed or visited. When the book came out I got fabulous reviews from the Jamaican Press, and I enjoyed some interesting book parties in a variety of cities. Then, I was asked to show my large photographs from the book (which were 30 x 40 mounted sepias) along with famed photographers Gordon Parks and James Van der Zee in a major Exhibition. The show also featured noted artists, painters, and sculptors.

I was excited about this Exhibition because Van der Zee and Parks were two of my favorite photographers. I worked hard making sure that my photographs were in perfect shape for hanging and I stopped by the exhibition venue the night before the opening to see how everything was going. I was invited into the office of the President and I noticed stack upon stack of handsome stamped envelopes atop his desk. I said, "You must be really busy, looks like you are preparing for another big event after ours." He laughed and said, "No, your event has just about engaged every employee we have," and he picked up one of the envelopes and his face turned scarlet red. It turned out that the hundreds and hundreds of invitations to the prestigious opening that I was soon to be a part of had never been sent out. They were right on the President's desk. He was profoundly embarrassed and said the event would have to be canceled. "Oh No," I gasped. Excitedly, I convinced the President that if he would allow the Company's limousine drivers to drive a dozen actors that I knew around town that we could hand deliver the invites.

I explained that I would get Gordon Parks to write a compelling note that we would print out on fine paper that could be hand signed by Parks and we could attach a personal note to each invite as we were driven in the limousines to our various destinations in the City. The actors could get out and walk block to block and meet up again with the driver. There would be no need to cancel. This man looked at me in amazement, laughed nervously, and said that if Mr. Parks was willing to do it, he surely could allow us to use his limousine drivers for the evening.

Wow. I sighed in relief but I also felt a bit panicky. I knew my work was cut out for me. I got on the phone, lined up my actors, raced over to Park's apartment, secured his witty note asking people to be his personal guest, had the note printed out, got it back to Parks for his personal artistic signature, and by the time Parks was finished signing the several hundred copies, three limos had shown up with the actors in tow and we were off in different directions to deliver our unusual mail. Parks checked in with me throughout the evening and said his phone was ringing off the hook with people saying that their doorman had just hand delivered his invite and they wanted to know if they could bring a friend or two. We worked for hours, stopping to grab sandwiches, and to take on more volunteers.

By the time I got home that evening I had dozens of messages and I talked throughout the night, draining myself so that when it was necessary to dress for the event I was profoundly fatigued and convinced myself that a beautiful hand beaded vintage dress that I was intending to wear, looked better turned around backwards. I was worried that the neckline was just too revealing for a serious photographer. When I arrived at the exhibition the crowd was large and festive, despite the pouring rain. My photographs were hung right between two masters, Parks and Van der Zee, and so excited was I that I failed to just stop there and remain by the photographs, not realizing that everyone would come to where Parks and Van der Zee were stationed. Instead, I spent my time roaming around the room talking to various people, foolishly missing the important action taking place where the photographs were located. In my efforts to enjoy myself, I literally missed a historic event in my life. Later, Gordon Parks and I stole away in one of the company limousines, headed for a much needed seat and a warm meal. I was so disappointed in myself that I had failed to take in the memorable moments that I would have preferred to have gone home alone with a McDonald's hamburger, even though I thoroughly dislike fast food. In my pursuit of not wanting to miss anything, I had missed everything that was important.

In some weeks I found a charming two-bedroom apartment in a stately doorman building on 79th street on the Upper Westside of Manhattan and sold my Condo in Philadelphia to help keep my children in College. I put an ad on Craigslist and started the long process of finding a roommate, a task that would become a permanent fixture in my life and one that I wish I had never undertaken. People that you don't know can present plentiful problems and in hindsight it was a poor decision on my part and I greatly would regret my loss of privacy and sense of freedom. I was racing forward with my life without taking the time to really watch that I had moved carefully from one gear to the other, making sure that all the parts were sound and in the proper working order.

I decided to co-produce a ground breaking Acting Seminar in New York and asked my friends Famed Producer Reuben Cannon and Director Bill Duke to fly to NYC to give a marathon weekend of one on one acting critiques to fifty chosen professional actors on how to audition and land a plum film role in Hollywood. I spent twelve thousand dollars that I could ill afford to spend on plane fares, hotel bills, and production costs and the seminar was a resounding success. The woman that I had Co-Produced the Seminar with did not put my name one time on the program, not one time, and I had to accept that her name would take credit for my creation and my hard work. This woman worked really hard on this ground breaking Seminar for sure, and it was held in her own Artist Space, but her name appeared no less than a dozen times on the coveted program, without mentioning me once even. In my eagerness to move forward with my career I had failed to take care of business. I was terribly hurt that a dear friend that I loved (and still love) would allow this to happen but I had to face the fact that you do not get what you deserve in business but what you negotiate.

Nevertheless, I did receive the satisfaction that Cannon refused the following season to return to give the seminar again unless I was on board. I had, by this time, determined that it would be ill advised to work with a producer who cared only about her own credits, but I remained cordial to this woman who I had loved dearly, and who has always been most generous and kind to my son. I was pleased, though, that I had done the Seminar because during its short duration I was able to bond and work with singer Abbey Lincoln. Abbey recited an original Bill Duke poem, The Young Country, and gave such a riveting performance that the audience looked toward the exit doors for an escape route because Abbey convinced all that she was in danger and needed to get away. She played the role so well that it was impossible to believe that Abbey was not in danger.

JAZZ GREAT ABBEY LINCOLN

Abbey Lincoln was both virtue and venom. She was a contradiction of personas so unique that one never quite understood her aura or her mystery. She was childlike, kind hearted, vulnerable, passionate, and tearful. She was fiery, contrary, impossible, jealous, and unpredictable. She was vibrant and intense. She was genius. She was an angel and a devil. The two spirits walked hand in hand. The one thing the spirits always shared, though, was artistry. Her coupling of words, her phrasing could bring you to tears, whether you appreciated it in song or experienced it in one of her meltdowns in person. You felt the machete that she held in her hand that had ripped through the wind or the comfort of velvet that had enveloped your weary soul when she hugged you and told you "give it up to Heaven." Abbey would always say that when things got rough, "Leave it to Heaven."

Abbey would often cry, and it would be heartbreaking to see her cry because you knew you couldn't fix what was wrong. You couldn't fix what was wrong because more often than not, Abbey didn't know herself what was wrong. I asked her about one of these crying spells one evening and she said, "You sound like my brother, David. He said to me one day…this was back in Kalamazoo when we lived on the farm…and David said, Abbey, why are you crying? I looked at him, and said, David, I d-o-n-t know." I looked hard at Abbey's face, looked at her in amazement as I could see the devilment in her eyes as she elongated the words, "I don't know," and we both broke into a fit of laughter.

One New Year's Eve she asked me if I was going to hang out on 79th Street and I smiled and said, "I am going to hang out alone, in my pretty apartment and be grateful that I have that to hang out in." I invited her down and was surprised when she showed up close to midnight. We had a drink, talked a little and Abbey headed off to sleep in my little guest room. She spent the day with me and seemed content to be away from all of the things that made up her life. When Abbey was not writing songs or preparing for a recording date she would sit for days on end painting very skilled, genuinely unique, oil paintings. The paintings adorned every wall in her house and the portrait she did of her producer Jean Phillipe Allard sat for months on her easel before she reluctantly put it in the hands of a framer to enclose with wood the essence of what she had so perfectly captured in Jean Philippe's portrait.

Abbey adored Jean Philippe and his family and always remained grateful for the great career boost he gave to her when he took over as her manager. When Jean Phillipe was in town, his priorities were Abbey's and she was truly excited, almost childlike, when she was scheduled to have an appointment with him. He would send her two dozen long stem red roses before his arrival and Abbey looked after these flowers tenderly. Abbey would show Jean Philippe the strange, mystical looking African Dolls that she had created out of heavy African black or brown cotton cloth, all hand sewn and Abbey would recite the dolls' names to Jean Phillipe and he would treat these mysterious creatures with great respect. There was no disputing that Abbey's songs, her paintings, and her dolls were very much a part of her, part of that magical space she inhabited with them and it was best if you did not touch what was most precious to Abbey, her work. Abbey and I often went to lunch, and once, I remember, several other women joined us at a little Japanese restaurant near my home. They were talking about varied things and Abbey became annoyed when one woman dwelled for a long time on the issue of her menstrual cramps. Abbey brought her fist down on the table and declared, "I am Abbey Lincoln and no one talks about B.S. when they are lunching with me." Well, the woman was furious and got up and excused herself from the table. We sat in silence for a bit and I think none was more surprised than Abbey that the woman had actually gone. No one tried to analyze what had happened. Abbey was complicated. You accepted that fact when you entered into a friendship with her and usually in Abbey's company, nothing was ever boring.

One evening I was called to come to her home because she was not feeling well. More often than not, it would be the fact that she just did not really like being alone, yet she was adamant about not wanting anyone to stay with her. This particular night I felt it was something more but she convinced me that it was nothing and that if I would just spend the night in the guest room she would be fine. Abbey was asleep when I prepared to leave the next morning so I left a note and told her to call me if she needed me again.

I got a call that she was in the hospital and I went up to St. Luke's to see her. She was sitting up in bed, complaining that she looked like an orphaned child, without a robe or slippers to call her own. I told Abbey that I had another appointment but that I would be back later to check on her. I went straight away to Macy's and purchased a dramatic full skirted chenille robe embroidered with flowers and found fluffy white slippers to compliment it and went straight back to the hospital to give them to Abbey. Abbey was overwhelmed with the gift, cried a great many tears. Fortunately, my instincts were right – Abbey just needed to know that she indeed was worth going that extra mile for. Had I gone back to Abbey's home and picked up one of her own robes, it would not have worked at all. Abbey wanted attention, got it, and now she was convinced that it was all right to go home. The doctors evidently told Abbey she had Lupus, but she was not buying it. She said to me, "They can give that diagnosis to their own 'bleeping' Mama. It is not something that I am going to own." Whatever it was that was ailing Abbey, it was clear that it was something she had decided would not interrupt her singing career which was going strong, heading upwards. Abbey was invited everywhere, playing Town Hall, The Blue Note, Lincoln Center, and she was frequently booked out of the country.

Once, I went to Abbey's house to go to her concert with her. Her limousine was right outside the door waiting to take her to this much anticipated concert and Abbey would not get into the car. She sat calmly on her bed while Jimmy, her Manager who handled all the details of her concerts, made frantic phone calls. Abbey could not be convinced to give the concert. She said while sipping her drink, "Let them eat cake." There was no point in arguing with Abbey when she had her mind made up to take a course of action. The concert was canceled and Abbey sat listening to album after album of her own music. Life returned to normal. Abbey enjoyed a full schedule of appearances, and received utter devotion from both her Managers, Jean Phillipe in Paris, and Jimmy Lewis in NYC.

I was busy trying to live my life, and haunted by what was not right, in my life and in my best friend, Abbey's life. I wanted so to fix what was not working in Abbey's life and though I pretended to put on a brave front for Abbey, I was always worried about her, and to be honest, I was really worried for myself too. Abbey had played at the Blue Note and she had stopped her brilliant pianist Marc Cary suddenly over something she did not like that Marc was playing and though nothing was ever trivial musically to Abbey, the incident had diminished Marc in front of the audience. And I knew that Abbey was unhappy with her action, too. Abbey loved her musicians, all of them, and respected them. I knew that Abbey was sitting on a keg of gun powder that could explode at any moment and for that matter, so was I. We were two friends that loved each other dearly but rarely dealt with our own personal demons.

I acted like all was fine with my gifted composer son, RB, in terms of what was happening in his life. RB pretended to have it together with his music and with his life, and nothing could have been further from the truth. I was haunted by RB's accounts of how he missed his dog. My son RB was writing beautiful music but it was not saving him and he was stuck with terrifying memories of being responsible for his dog's death. The dog was sixteen, and RB had practiced the piano a little too long one day and delayed getting the dog to the Vet. When they did go finally, the dog, Dayan, died an hour later at the Vet's office. The Veterinarian told my son his dog could not have survived - that he was very old in dog years for an Irish Setter- and that RB was fortunate to have had his dog for so long. But my son was not comforted. And Abbey was not comforted either that her life was what it was. Abbey was a famous, revered singer, but that was not enough. Abbey missed her mother. My son missed his dog, and nothing, it seemed, could make either my dear friend or my son content. I kept having this dream about being stuck in asbestos. I still have that dream sometimes.

This is my dream. The walls are very white, thick, and in places look like clouds, clusters of cottony areas that could break open at any moment and lead me out to the sea. I would rather that my hand would be holding a fancy umbrella to protect me from the sun. I don't want the crude pick I am using to hammer away at the asbestos which reveals itself in puffs of white smoke when I chip into the wall and actually get out the cottage cheese looking stuff. I think these poisonous clumps will ruin me and my lungs, forever. I am struggling in this asbestos dream for three nights now, hacking away at the curved walls trying to get to the oval doorways that lead to the great columns beyond.

I imagine that the columns must be beautiful but I fear I will never see them because my hammering has been so intense that this asbestos choked room is now filled with an eerie haze of white- white smoke - as though I am looking through a heavy veil. It is a real veil though, of tears and muck and regret, and I must keep at the hammering, or my vision will dim and I will never see how to get out of my body that I once thought of as my temple. Abbey always talked about her body being a temple and her knowing what was right for her temple. But my temple is definitely ruined with this asbestos that is clogging my veins, making my feet lead, rendering my heart steel, making my thoughts bitter so that they cannot leap with joy and life anymore. I keep listening for Dayan. I can't hear the sound of his bark. I can't hear my son calling Dayan's name in his dreams. And, I can't hear Abbey's voice singing, "Bird Alone." This song that Abbey sings so beautifully always soothes me. But now I cannot remember the words. I am lost.

My Temple is intent on withering and dying. I can feel it in my tooth. I must get the tooth out, away from me. It is diseased and it is bad. I know how badness can stalk you and you can't push it out. It shows up one day like an ugly grin and little by little the grin grows and turns into a grimace and before long you can no longer recognize your own face. Ugliness has taken root and your goodness begins to disappear. Yes, my thoughts scream at me, assure me that I must finally accept the truth – that these peacock men have come to defile, not fortify me, have come to take what I own, not share with me what they own. I am terribly frightened. I know I must hack away and get their asbestos spirits out of my skin, out of these cell like walls that enclose me. "Please, I plead to the forces in the Universe, I want out of this room that presents itself three nights now. I have only this little wrecking pick – tell me what it is that I must do to free myself."

Go slowly, my dream says. Go slowly. Excise them, the poisons, one and all, but go slowly because you must take care to say what you always wanted to say to them. Do not let them die before you tell them how they clogged your veins, squashed your spirit, how they made you lose your grace. Your grace was the one good steady trait that stayed with you the whole of your life - until now. Now, especially now, I must claim the task of getting back my grace. But first, I must rid myself of the poison. I think hard. I know that a few written words will not accomplish the task of helping me to reclaim my grace - but maybe - an abbreviated verbal Shout Out will do the trick. Here goes: "Hey that was mine. You took my grace and it doesn't belong in your life.

You betrayed me, dishonored me and I want that part of me that you took, back. So take this asbestos that I dug from the muck you left in my soul and in my heart and put it back where it belongs – in you. It is your job to dig it out, work through it, not mine. Come and get your "Crap." Give me the grace of an apology and move away from my life. Let me move on from the pain of your sad ass remembrances. You celebrated, demented person that you are. I don't want your memory in my heart. Why would you just want to be an asbestos memory?"

I hammer and pick, cough and choke, and shout out the names of all my real and imagined enemies. Some are long ago would be paramours - and God only remembers the mal formed souls that came to rob me of my beauty and spirit. To you, all of you ugly ones, I say, "I am finally chipping out the bad memories my acquaintance with you caused me. It took me a life time of recurring regrets, but

I am getting over those regrets now, those sad memories. Good Bye. Good Bye."

I think of the recipients of my fatal attractions that had such devouring egos. I am quite amazed that their spouses bothered as long as they did. Really, I have no cherished memories of those stupid times we spent together, times where I was told the lies that they were separated from their wives, and awaiting their divorce. Mostly, I remember always waiting, waiting, and being very hungry, waiting for a "Peacock" who would take me to dinner but who always arrived with ruffled feathers and had no time for dinner, comfort, or anything else. A Peacock that needed to be soothed in three minutes. I want to tell them that if they get a go around again in this life, they should try nesting in a park where the floozies hang out. They will surely be sent to dine with the pigeons.

There was a Doctor, a prominent Plastic Surgeon that I loved dearly for a few months, years after my divorce, and I thought that God had given me again what I longed for most - a chance for an interesting and honest life partner. I couldn't have been more wrong. He convinced me he had separated from his wife and was waiting for his divorce to be finalized. I moved out to California to be near him. I waited for days at a time, between his surgeries, for him to honor our dinner appointments. Always, he would call very late with the excuse of a medical emergency. Patiently, I endured these painful calls and I began work on drawing caricatures of people in my much amplified spare time. I called my little caricature people "Ediekins"- meaning my kin folk or kindred spirits. I wrote stories to accompany their detailed illustrated personas. I gave them names, and documented what they did in life. I created Dandy Dan - the gentleman charmer and Bologna Maroni, the friend who always invites you to dine but when you call to take him up on it, has always just stepped out to lunch. I had sixteen characters, and often in my correspondence to friends back on the East Coast, I would doodle these little characters in the margins of my letters.

Gordon Parks called me one day and told me that if I seriously decided to pursue another career that I should consider putting my little Ediekins characters into some form of real Art. I did just that when I got back from California and enrolled in school, for a number of years actually. I took Jewelry Design at F.I.T., in New York City. I had the great fortune to study under one of the world's Jewelry Masters, Gennady Osmerkin, who designed and made some of the most exquisite works of Art for Van Cleef & Arpels, Samuel Winston in New York City, The Louvre in Paris, and The Metropolitan Art Museum in New York. I introduced Gennady to Abbey Lincoln and we three would meet for drinks and have fun times talking about the fun and perils of striving to live an artistic life. Gennady would marvel at my determination to execute complicated designs despite my limited training, but what we three had in common was our "Excelsior Motto." If you were going to do something, it always had to be your best effort. Excelsior had to be the reigning factor.

Eventually, I embarked upon a successful adjunct career in the production of fine jewelry but that odyssey had to go onto the back burner until I got through my California experience. I did not want to make the same mistake that I had made with my husband of putting my life on hold while I attended to all of my partner's needs. Soon, I tired of the late dinner appointments that never materialized. One night, I got on a plane to return to New York. Just like in the movies, the Doctor convinced me to get off the plane. He said he did not want to lose me. His resolve lasted all of one week, and I was back to the routine of waiting for dinner dates that did not happen. I forced myself to accept reality and I managed to get back to NYC.

My mother became very worried about me as I lost my normal enthusiasm for life. Of one thing I was certain, I was finished with Doctors - and I was definitely not interested in the dating scene. Mama wrote to my celebrity California Doctor friend and surprisingly, he wrote back. Somewhere, I have that letter where he explained to Mama that there was real feeling on our parts for each other but that it had not worked out. I never understood the letter. What was there to work out? He had made it clear to me that he had time for only himself. Shortly thereafter, he married again, someone a good two decades younger than himself, someone that I could never be, a White woman. I have always hated racism but one thing that a great many professional Black women had to accept before the

Internet Explosion, was that professional Black men were intrigued with women who were simply, *White*. Thank Heaven The world is slowly realizing that good people are simply good people – whatever color their skin happens to be.

I threw myself into my jewelry making, drawing and carving around the clock with the ingenious help of Lee Dillion, one of the most gifted sculptors I have ever known. A CEO of a big advertising company in Manhattan generously gave a gift of $20,000 to me for the production of my little Ediekins characters that Gordon Parks had encouraged me to produce for the fine jewelry market. I thought much success was sure to come. Wempe's on Fifth Avenue gave me a window display of my colorful, whimsical gold characters and just a few blocks away, the high end fashionable store, Henri Bendel, featured my line. I was always running out of money trying to meet the demands of production as the stores did not pay in advance of the required deliveries to stock their glittering show cases.

The CEO who became a dear friend and partner would advance me money for which I was very grateful – and to this day I remain grateful for the help he rendered to me during a rocky period in my life - but he always seemed to coax me out of a piece or two from my prized collectibles and antiques that were the treasures in my apartment. He always said, "I shouldn't be taking your things but they give me such pleasure as you are such a unique talent." I became more and more depressed about the dwindling assets in my apartment - a rare Angola African mask collection, an English sideboard, Dorothy Parker's actual writing desk, an ornate carved chair from Spain and so on - but this man I trusted. He had a complicated life and it took me awhile to understand that my life would become complicated as a result of my interactions with him. His company featured my photography and that of Gordon Parks and James Van der Zee in a much publicized exhibition along with other well-known Artists and it was a productive period of my life. I was much too busy to fret about the loss of my beautiful possessions in my apartment so engrossed I was in the design and production of my jewelry. I used Zaven, a remarkably gifted jeweler from Turkey, to help me in the technical assembly of my 18 carat gold caricatures, carved intricately on both sides.

I stored my jewelry in a safe deposit box in a bank on Park Avenue and unbelievably there was a robbery one night, where the door of the bank was pried off with drills and the contents of most of the bank's safety deposit boxes were stolen, including all of the jewelry in mine. It was devastating to learn that the bank was not responsible for the contents of customer's boxes. I did not have any outside insurance. It was a sobering loss and it greatly affected my ability to fill my orders. Tiffany's offered to take me on – they would generously give me their invitees list for my introduction into their prestigious enclave with one important stipulation - that I pay for the party and a full page Ad in The New York Times. Well, if I could afford to do that, I wouldn't have needed Tiffany's. Needless to say, I didn't take them up on their offer. Shortly after that, one of the biggest costume jewelry makers in the world, Alexis Kirk, called to offer me $5,000 for my necklace designs that were in Bendel's on Fifth Avenue. I said no. He increased the offer to $10,000. I still said no. Three weeks later Bendel's withdrew my designs from their store and replaced them with Alexis Kirk's goods, all exact copies of my designs, but executed in much cheaper metals at a fraction of my costs.

When I was unsuccessful in defending myself in court with a copyright suit that I brought against Karl Lagerfeld of Chanel - I knew that I was out of the jewelry business. It wasn't that I lost the suit against Lagerfeld, it was just that I did not have the money to give to the Law Firm I had hired to continue the fight. I have to give credit to the first Costumer, Kirk, who at least, offered me something for the efforts of my hard work. I learned that one cannot fight with the likes of those that have billions of dollars who can send a dozen lawyers to Court to fight their case and can easily afford to throw away a few hundred thousand dollars on a law suit.

I took off to repair my battered spirit to one of my favorite beaches in the world, the aquamarine waters and white sand beaches of St. Martins in the Netherlands Antilles. I stayed at an exquisite, off the beaten path establishment that catered to European families that favored nude bathing. Though I never abandoned my bathing suit, I was happy relaxing and reading seaside - far from any intrusive eyes. One day, a brilliant looking blond man came over and asked me to lunch. I said yes, providing that he agreed to wrap a towel around his waist. We both learned that we had each put our spouses through medical school and that our houses bore the same numerical number on the address, 5401. After determining that he was really divorced we began to date though we lived far apart, he in Michigan and me in New York. I was invited to spend some days at his lakeside cottage and just hours after being there, while we lunched – he was a true epicurean and had fixed a masterful meal – the phone began ringing incessantly. Then, there were numerous knocks at the door, and all went unanswered. It didn't take long to figure out that he had no intention of providing any explanation and I demanded that he take me to the airport so I could return home. He was terribly embarrassed, but he obliged me.

We remained friends but I ceased dating him. Over the next eight years I received many postcards and letters from him telling me of his world travels and offering me a chance to join him. I never took him up on his offers and one day he showed up at my door telling me that he missed me terribly, loved me, and wanted me to travel with him to Poland to see his grandfather's ancestral home that had been used to house hundreds of soldiers during the Second World War. My friend told me an account of being placed under house arrest in his grandfather's two hundred room mansion along with other family members who were caught up in the war unexpectedly while they were visiting Poland. After many decades, the government determined the mansion should be returned to its rightful owners. With most of the family members long since dead, the home had been given to Sas, my friend, and he wanted to turn it into a bed and breakfast with my help. To entice me, he said he had built a lovely cabin for us in the mountains of Warsaw where we could relax while renovations of the mansion were underway. My head was spinning. I then learned the grandfather belonged to a Royal family and my friend was a Count. Not ever having been a history buff and having little interest in Royal families, I laughed and told Sas that I didn't see myself as a Black Countess.

Sas declared that marriage was something he had not thought about but he was determined not to lose me again. We should go to Brazil first to visit my son, he declared, and in time life would work out what the next step would be for us to take. But first, he needed to go to Michigan to get some tests done as he had for some weeks been nursing a stomach ache – nothing to worry about he assured me. I agreed to accompany him to Michigan. While we traveled there I thought of the dozen languages that Sas spoke fluently, of his ability to play difficult classical pieces on the piano, and surmised that his Royal confinement had probably afforded him the opportunity for such pursuits. Imagine spending a good many years with countless soldiers as well as governesses living side by side in a lavish abode. I was amused to see his childhood photographs of the extravagant lace trimmed sleeping gowns he wore. Sas was a PhD engineer and certainly the rigors of that training would not have given him the time to pursue the many eclectic and privileged things that he so enjoyed.

When we arrived in Michigan Sas learned, after lengthy tests, that he had Stage Four Stomach Cancer and that he would never see the outside of the Hospital again. He introduced me to his former wife, insisted that his son transport me to and from the hospital each day and encouraged me to spend time with his daughter who was just ready to enter Medical School where his son was already enrolled. Sas talked about me signing him out of the hospital and encouraged me to learn the operation of all the machines he was hooked up to. He talked non- stop about us taking a world cruise. I looked head on into the face of a man who realized that he had no way to stop the disease that was ravaging his body but he was determined to talk out his dreams.

It was a brutally hard time. I stayed in Sas' little cottage and advised him to throw out the hundreds and hundreds of photographs that he had accumulated of him posing with nude women across the globe. "Why are you judging me at such a tough time in my life," he said. I just could not believe that all of the men I seemed destined to have major interactions with were such womanizers; first my Daddy, then my husband, and sadly, Sas, too. Exasperated, I replied "Because that is not the kind of legacy that you want to leave your daughter, especially since you were absent from her life from the age of twelve onwards." Sas was deeply disappointed in me that I did not see that he had lived a rich and full life. I refused to search for the photo of the beautiful cabin he had built for us in the mountains of Poland. I boxed up a van full of what I had considered ridiculous porn photographs and, I did not want to waste my time looking for a photo of a cabin he had built from another of Sas' lost dreams. I felt very sorry for my friend, but I thanked my lucky stars that I was not having my regrets from a lonely mountain cabin in Poland. Three weeks later, my friend was dead. And, for certain, there would be no chance of my becoming a Black Countess. Anyway, I had wanted to be a Ballerina, not a Countess.

And here I sit, wondering why am I even bothering to put pen to paper the memory of such events. The truth is, and we all know this, events matter. Everything that happens to us in life matters. We just have to determine how we will let it matter. I found it so taxing to recall my California experience that I took to my bed and fell into a deep sleep. I dreamed, at least for the fourth or fifth time in my life, that I was in this huge, tall, oval shaped barn like structure. The structure did not have a roof but it had a narrow waist tall bannister balcony that had multiple doorways that could be opened. I traveled along the balcony and opened the same doorway that I always opened in this dream. It led me to a pathway of crudely made stone steps that traversed all of the way up a hill. When I reached the top of the hill - I was home. My house was oval shaped, over-looking tall corn fields, and everywhere the blue sky poured through the plentiful windows.

Can this be Missy's house; I wonder? Is this the place my grandmother dreamed of that lay beyond those blackened sawed off corn fields that she ran through in Alabama when she was a child? This beautiful house, did it rise from the dreams of my dear grandmother's mother, Missy? Was the little shack my grandmother shared with her mother Missy and her old Aunty Mary transformed into this house that I keep returning to in my dreams? Can the dreams of my ancestors be the same ones I am living?

This time, in this breathtaking, oval shaped hillside house, I step through the window and go to the room that houses the gold leaf trimmed piano/organ that belongs to my son, RB. The piano has been moved from its normal place to the room my brother is staying in. I am not happy about this. This is not my brother's house, but mine. And, it is not the first time my brother has taken my family's possessions and claimed them as his own. I hear Missy's voice telling my grandmother Josie to find a place where all of the family grave markers can rest together. I wonder, am I being told through the mystery of my dreams that what I own will always be mine, even if it is lost or claimed by someone else? Did not Abbey Lincoln tell me a hundred times that "You cannot lose what belongs to you."

Am I to forgive my brother and his son for stealing my things that were in my mother's house when our mother died? Does what I own belong to all of my ancestors, too? Is this why I keep revisiting this hillside house that I can only get access to by first opening the door from the oval shaped barn that I enter from my dream? Were our ancestors lives so fractured by the divisiveness of slavery that we, their children, can never hope to have peaceful and noble lives? My grandfather, Poppa, lost each of his children to tragedies. There was only My Daddy, The Joy Boy, remaining to restore Poppa's dreams.

The Joy Boy prospered but failed. But The Joy Boy left eight children - four died tragically like Poppa's children - Jacqueline, Michael, Gail, Reggie but there are four of us left. I wonder, do we, the remaining four have what it takes to make Poppa proud? Would Poppa want The Joy Boy's Daughter's story to be published. I have held the story of a great grandmother being sold on the auction block for fifty cents close to my heart all of my life. I have wept that Missy, my beautiful grandmother's mother, saved scraps of lace her entire young life but never had enough lace to fashion a lovely dress for herself, or for that matter, never had even a decent home to live in. I got to wear gorgeous clothes on the runways of the world. Does that make up for my blood relative never having had a suitable garment in her life? I have owned three beautiful homes and I have lost them all.

Am I destined to have the life I am having? Or was it personal folly that caused the circumstances of my present life? Can't I be the strong one that changes the destiny of our family? I don't want to believe that it all boils down to fate. I can't help but ponder these things because as resourceful and smart as Poppa and Granny were, they could not change what happened to their family. I have a grandson - MISSING. Poppa has got to be crying about that. Can't I find my grandson, restore him to his formidable self, and say to the world "it can be done, just look at what I managed to do." Is the secret to surviving with Grace being able to say and know that you treated other human beings in a just and human way because they, like you, are vulnerable human beings? And, being human is sometimes a very sobering experience.

AN UNEXPECTED REUNION

I landed in Phoenix, found myself navigating through a maze of people and cumbersome thoughts and finally located my seat on the tiniest aircraft I had been in for a good many years. My seatmate was overly talkative explaining loudly that he was on his way to Santa Barbara to witness the birth of his firstborn grandchild but the child had been given up for adoption because his daughter didn't want to raise a kid. I tried to hang on to the dramatic soundbites of his story, "that his daughter was a slut, that he couldn't raise his grandchild child because he was bi-polar, that the least he could do was to give the child a kiss and a real goodbye"

The story depressed me, made me want to scream for him to "Please, Shut Up." But I sat there and tried to be civil for I needed to think that I, too, could be civil when I would soon be reunited with my daughter who had called and asked me to come to Santa Barbara because she was ill and needed me. Needed me after refusing to see me for seventeen years. I blocked out the incessant ranting by silently saying a prayer for my troubled seatmate and repeating over and over in my mind that "my daughter will be happy to see me, that all will turn out fine."

I endured a bumpy landing and was relieved to see that the soon to be grandfather had already retrieved his bag and was pushing ahead of others in the crowded aisle. I found my way out of the nearly empty terminal and saw few cars waiting to pick up arriving passengers. I looked for any sign of my daughter but saw absolutely no one, or for that matter, did not see any taxis. Anxiously, I took a seat on a nearby bench. Coming across the cross walk I saw a familiar lop sided gait which I recognized as my daughter's. Seconds later my daughter and I were embracing each other, and I looked into a pair of very sad eyes. My daughter's eyes were swollen and blackened underneath as though she had endured days of crying without any sleep.

We crisscrossed through the lanes in the parking lot and climbed into her car where she informed me that we were going to spend the night at a hotel because she did not feel strong enough to make it home. I could not convince her otherwise and we drove to a supermarket to purchase bottled water, cheese, crackers and a bunch of grapes. After securing our meager food supplies, we checked into the room my daughter had secured at one of those hotels that make a swift change of sheets daily and call to remind you that you are five minutes late per your check out time.

On the third day of watching my daughter sleep and take her "meds" in a darkened room with the draperies pulled tightly – I reached the end of my endurance for this solitary penal like existence and opened the drapes to let a ray of sunshine in. My daughter was horrified by the light and announced that we were going to spend another night and then we would go home. I told her that I was going to breakfast and that in an hour, I would return to the room for my bag and would be leaving the hotel, with or without her. I was starved for food, and was more than ready to face whatever demons we had to face when we got to that Illusive place my daughter called home.

I had a mediocre, over-priced breakfast in a gaudy and dusty breakfast room with fake flowers. The waiter did not have change and I was forced to leave a tip that was far too generous for the service. I asked to have the croissant I had not eaten wrapped to go and I returned to retrieve my daughter. She hungrily munched on the croissant and argued for more time to gather her nerves. I took my bag and stood by the door. When I opened the door to leave, my daughter jumped out of the bed and scurried into the shower. She kept calling my name to make sure I was still in the room and with energy I did not know she had, she secured her belongings and we proceeded to the reception desk for checkout.

We stopped at a local eatery for coffee and better food fare and finally found our way to my daughter's apartment complex, a twenty-minute drive across a highway that was parallel to the ocean. After minutes of sitting in the parking lot where my girl dreaded the fateful meeting with her landlord, my daughter and I finally climbed the steps to a second floor balcony and knocked at the manager's door. A very friendly woman opened the door and embraced my daughter, said she had been worried about her, and welcomed her home. The manager said nothing about any trouble, and handed my daughter her key. I never learned the source of trouble my daughter had referred to about why she was fearful of returning home. With great unease about so many unanswered questions, I began the odyssey of watching my daughter return to her bed to sleep and take her meds.

I tended the house as much as I was permitted to as my daughter was territorial about her stacks of unopened mail and piles of unpacked moving boxes. Finally, my daughter reached the stage where I was asked to join her in her many hours of movie watching, and one day she even reached for my hand as we lay side by side watching TV. My heart was more than ready to heal the wounds we both felt the other had caused. We began talking about the experiences she had gone through during the period of our estrangement and I learned that the man who she had declared she hated had actually been invited back to her home and had lived with her and their child for four years.

What actually shook me up the most was my daughter's admission that her son had suffered a shock when he was ten years old that had forever altered his life – and that neither he nor she could talk about the event. I was terribly upset to be given such mysterious news for surely whatever it was played a role in triggering my grandson's episodes of running away from home.

I remain in the dark about the root causes of my grandson's distress as this dear boy is still missing - over three years now. My grandson was such a joyous toddler. He loved meeting people and made each individual feel that they were indeed very important to him. I always felt that he was destined for great things, that he was a born diplomat. On train or plane trips he would walk up and down the aisles, greeting each individual as though they were friends he had not seen for a long while. It was heartwarming to witness how he interfaced with people. I would not have been the least surprised if he ended up being the President of the United States. He loved all of the goings on around him. He used to say, "Grand-mom, come quick, Pavarotti is singing on TV." What three-year-old is as interested in an opera star as he is in his playtime?

When I would sit carving wax figures to turn them into gold and silver jewelry brooches, my little grandson was a huge fan. He would look at them with such understanding and affection. I have always believed that people can save themselves from much emotional turmoil by tapping into the Arts. As I said earlier, I founded a non-profit Arts organization in Harlem, Creative, Find, Inc. and taught *at risk children* from fractured backgrounds how to enhance their self-esteem by practicing the Arts. Kids whose fathers were in prison, or mothers were crack addicts or alcoholics learned to make handmade meditation chairs and paintings and to document these experiences in their journals. In fact, they truly learned the art of saving themselves from troubling experiences. I took these techniques to the homeless street children in Rio de Janeiro to help them find some brief moments of solace from the arduous task of begging for food so they could stay alive.

Little did I realize then that the government of Brazil shoots their homeless kids at night because it is easier than finding ways to help or save them.

Life was hard, is hard for so many people. I want so to save my daughter from her worries, to find and save my grandson from his flights of escape, but time is running out. Being away from home makes me miss the daily entries that I make on my computer of what I hoped would be a book about my life. These hard fought for efforts of mine to save myself from all of the troubles I am trying to puzzle through come with heaps of angst. I admit to being very weary.

My daughter begins going to Bible Study at her Church. She encourages me to attend with her, and finally I agree to spend my last two weeks going to the classes with my daughter. I do not enjoy the classes. They are very structured, with much recitation from the bible. I grew up Baptist, and switched over to Episcopal as an adult. I remember the stories of my priest leaving his wife and children and running off with a seventeen-year-old. And, there was always that uproar in the news about the Catholic priests molesting young boys.

So many crimes have been committed in the name of Christianity. I do believe, though that it is critical to be open to all of the religions in the world and to strive to be the best person that you can be for the betterment of the world community. I sit quietly in the bible classes, determined to make it through to the end.

We count down the hours. My daughter and I are mother and daughter again. We vow to be there for one another. The next day I will head back to Atlanta, secure the cheapest possible ticket, and start my long journey to Brazil to try to help save my son from his schizophrenia which had grown worse. My cheap flight requires the acceptance of a five-hour layover in Toronto, a seat in the middle row with no leg room, and the news upon my arrival that my luggage has been lost. I haggle with more than a few taxi drivers for a reasonable fare to the little village of Muriqui where my son lives in a Chalet, a good two-hour drive away. My driver speeds down the highway, swerves dangerously from lane to lane, brakes so suddenly that my teeth rattle. I am terrified but my grinning driver makes it clear to me that I am getting what I deserve for such a cheap fare. I am tempted to offer more money so I can arrive alive, but I fear that such an offer will only escalate the demands for more money. Amazingly, my taxi trip ends successfully and I take a deep breath, and try to prepare for another trying saga which I can already foresee. The appearance of many broken steps on the staircase leading to the veranda of my son's Chalet is not a comforting sight. I revert to my combat mode, and recall Abbey's words, "Leave It to Heaven." I am weary. I can do no more.

I climb the wobbly steps to the Chalet, trying my best to stretch my swollen ankles the distance that used to hold two full steps, which lay broken on the ground. I knock at the door, and knock, and knock some more. The door opens slowly and my son looks at me with vacant eyes and says, "I think you should leave." With a heart that plummets with every word, I say feebly "I've have no place to go and I am going to stay here for a bit." I move into the darkened room and turn on the lights and look upon the dirtiest and untidiest place I had seen in all of my life. I have paid generously, weekly, for a cleaning person who clearly has not cleaned in six months. My son calls me Wally and berates me for not greeting his son. Startled, I looked about, and then I sit down, eyeing my son cautiously. My son yells that I am sitting on Wally. "Are you crazy," he says. Jumping to my feet, I realize that my son is comforting an imaginary person, named Wally. Not only will I have to deal with being called Wally myself, but I will have to contend with RB, my son, talking incessantly with his imaginary son, Wally.

I feel faint, and very afraid. I unzip my carry-on bag and hand my son a pair of sneakers and two new shirts. RB always enjoyed trying on the new sneakers I brought with me from the States, and fortunately for me, he tries on the new sneakers, talking animatedly with Wally the entire time. I know that somehow I will have to gather the courage to help my son, again, and to put all of the broken puzzle back into place, but for the moment I just zone out and go to that place that I sometimes retreat to – my encounters with the homeless youth of Brazil that have taught me more than a thing or two about surviving tough and confusing times.

I recall one particularly sad and forlorn day I that I began talking to the homeless kids that lived on my street in Leme, a neighborhood in Rio de Janeiro. I was on my way home from visiting my son in the psychiatric hospital where he had been a patient for a few months. My heart was heavy and I was only too glad to leave the awful scene of seeing grown men walking woodenly around a hospital courtyard, circling over and over around that cemented compound – some muttering, others having given up and just sitting on the ground staring vacantly at some unknown object or distant memory. I had watched my son traversing that same compound and I wanted to yank him home, to make him stop the incessant walking – to force him to let go of the voices and the confusion in his mind. I left in tears, my plea of "Son, please, just come home, we will work this out. The voices are just your own thoughts and you are smart enough to let all of that garbage in your mind go and move on." My plea fell on deft ears. My son couldn't or wasn't ready to let the voices go and move on.

Walking home I passed cluster after cluster of homeless young people sleeping or sitting on the street and I decided to stop and talk to a group of them just before I turned down my pretty tree lined street where I lived in an attractive doorman building. I learned the kid's names -Thiago, Wallace, Alexander, Eduardo, Andrea, Maryanna. I listened to their family stories; a mother who had lost her husband and had to take in washing but couldn't afford to feed all of her children so some were forced to beg on the street; a father who had been murdered which led the fatherless youngster to a life of forging from trash baskets and sleeping on the sidewalk; a mother who had remarried whose new husband did not want to raise a pre-teen who was not his natural child. I marveled at how tragic and compelling their stories were. I thought, "These kids just needed someone to validate and appreciate their loss, someone to mentor them until they were strong again." Their stories were sad, sure, but solvable I thought. I decided to be their friend, to teach them how to paint and sculpt and to sell their Art artifacts on the street so they would not have to beg.

It wasn't long before I realized that I had gotten myself into a formidable project that would require all of the energy and resources that I could muster up. Our Art classes were held right on the street with little more than some clay, a bucket of water to wet the clay and clean the paint brushes, and a good dose of fortitude to withstand the impolite stares of neighborhood folk and business owners that were not too happy that the homeless kids were making efforts to thrive on their well swept and manicured streets.

When the Art actually started to be bought by kindhearted individuals, the police began scooping up the kids Artwork and throwing it in the back of a government van claiming the kids had no Vendors License and therefore were selling Artwork illegally. Later, I would see the police selling the children's Artwork on the boardwalk to the tourists.

I would take the kids to lunch and urge them to not to give up, promising that somehow, someway we would prevail. I would remind myself that at first the restaurant owners had refused to allow me to bring a half dozen homeless kids to lunch but had finally relented, and that in time I would solve the current crises and figure out how I could come up with the needed funds to buy new Art materials. Of one thing I knew for certain, that I would not give up. Just as I would continue to help my son, I would help the homeless Leme youth that wanted a chance for a better life. I decided that I would do my best to continue my education so I could advance myself and help my son and the Rio homeless youth all at the same time. I would immediately undertake the task of trying to get into a Master's program in the United States that would allow me to work both online when it was necessary to be in Rio near my son and the kids and when courses required that I be on site at the actual campus, I would fly back to the States and live in a rented room near the campus. How I was going to do all of that I didn't know. I just knew that I had a plan and I had to execute it.

BACK TO SCHOOL

I stood facing my mailbox afraid to open it to see if the letter I wanted most to receive would be there rather than the one I most dreaded. I needed to believe that I wasn't crazy, that actually the University I had applied to would agree that admitting a sixty-five- year-old woman would mean that they had the foresight to choose someone who not only deserved a chance to finish their education but that they had chosen someone who would distinguish the University – someone that would be innovative and work hard to empower them self and the world community. I prayed, "Please God give me this chance to save my son and to save myself so that we both may find our way back to safety and creativity."

RB, my son had just gotten horribly ill again and I had run out of monies and ideas of where to work, where to find the help and financial resources needed to keep us afloat. My social security monies were a pittance as my husband had illegally, with the help of his accountant friend, altered several decades of our returns so that the bulk of the monies earned had showed up to benefit him, not me, even though we filed our returns jointly for over twenty years. I would have to go to Court and my husband might go to jail if I presented the damaging evidence. I had all I could do to try to keep our boy well, and I had no interest in pursuing anything on the dark side. I hoped never to see the inside of a courtroom again. I was scared. I had lost more than a few jobs while I juggled film production work while racing off from my job to an emergency room in the US or in Brazil because the tragic voices my son sometimes succumbed to had taken over his thinking processes again. I had to get back to school to get my Masters, and then surely I would find a secure job – but most importantly, I would at least have the money

I would be borrowing from the Government coming in during the school semesters. I was in dire need of a temporary solution until I could figure out what step to take next. If ever I need a little miracle, I needed it to present itself in my mailbox.

There were several important looking letters in the box and I quickly took the one that could bring Grace into my life, the one that could be my miracle. I opened it with firm hands but a fluttering heart. I dropped to my knees, right in that mail alcove of my beautiful doorman building. I wept so hard I could hardly finish reading the letter. I cried, loud and hard. Yes, I did really cry. I was "in." I had been accepted at The New School in NYC, a famous media school, and I would be given a partial scholarship in addition to my regular state and federal government loans. My life would go on. I would not go down in shame, in defeat, not yet. I would have another chance, and so would my son through my efforts. There was much work to be done. I arose and went back to my apartment where I kneeled again and prayed for the strength and courage to do everything in my power to be a determined and diligent student who would strive for excellence, be clear about my goals, and stay humble and grateful to all who had helped me on my path to receiving my good news. I remained so long in prayer I could barely move my knees to stand.

I could not have imagined how utterly confusing it would be to arrive at the school in the midst of so many hundreds of young people from every country across the globe – who all had to go through the dizzying process of attending orientation, meeting counselors, choosing subjects, and filling out heaps of papers about every aspect of one's work, social, and personal life. I soon found that two persons, one my instructor and the other a counselor, who singled me out for praise because of my one lucky Academy nomination when I was directing my first documentary film while being an under graduate in George Stoney's film classes at New York University – did not really like me. I learned to stay as far away from these two, a woman and a man, as I could because it became clear to me that their snide comments about my desire to create a forum for my storytelling within the framework of my classwork clearly indicated that they considered me an arrogant woman who thought that my life was especially interesting to others, which obviously to them was not. I was striving to create a Heroes and Heroines Website and I took every opportunity to incorporate relevant contemporary stories into required classwork submissions and discussions. I would always find a way to tie in little known historical or social facts into classroom discussions because I felt they were critical to what was being deliberately or unknowingly left out.

I was not trying to be a rabble rouser, but I felt an obligation to speak up about social and civil rights issues that I felt had long been ignored. I was not returning to school to relearn the things that I had been taught when I was in high school. I had had enough of being fed limited and often untruthful information. The woman, of whom I speak, would keep me waiting for weeks for an appointment and then change it at the last moment, and then say when we finally met that she was sorry but she had nothing useful to tell me. The male professor always grilled me about petty issues when it was clear that little fault could be found with my final work submissions in our classroom presentations. The students were enthusiastic and gave me much praise. The Professor would make derisive remarks about my hairdo or fashionable attire and try to get me to analyze, for instance, the difference between an apple and an orange rather than my choice, why a black man was four times more likely to end up in prison than a white man. I could not wait to get away from that classroom.

Some nights, my brain would be so fatigued from the opposition I faced, I thought of going to him and giving him Hell, but I kept silent and resolved to being wiser in choosing my subjects. I was fortunate to have an ally, the Director of International Affairs, Professor Michael Cohen and finding two Professors that I truly treasured, Peter Lucas, and Richard Wolff. I learned a lot in Professor Boyle's, Professor Carpignano's, Professor Berkman's, Professor Crow's, and Professor Royal Brown's classes and I counted on the encouragement of Leslie King in Financial Management and gifted staffers, Janelle McKenzie, Nancy Wei, and Anita Christian. If I had not known what I wanted to accomplish, and fought really hard to stay on course, I would have lost my way at The New School. A dear friend, a gifted jazz singer Ellen Starr, allowed me to stay for a time in her pleasant West Side apt. I managed to graduate with my Masters in Media and then continue straight on to receive my Masters in International Affairs. Though I really thought I wanted to go on and pursue my PhD at a noteworthy school, I fortunately realized I was already doing what I truly want to do, helping at-risk Children, writing my Heroes and Heroines stories, and keeping my son on track.

I was so hungry most of the time I was in school, I think I would really like to experience a lot of fine dining in my favorite restaurants in Paris, Florence, Mexico, and Mykonos. Going back to school is not for the faint of heart. I even had my original films stolen by a woman who was helping me with editing issues and to this day she refuses to give them back to me. She was from an Eastern bloc country and had a fatal attraction to who she thought I was or was not - not so unlike my experience with the man and woman I refer to above who were supposed to be guiding lights to help me navigate my courses through school. And then, one day after I had moved to yet another apt. to be nearer to school, I came home to my rented room and found my roommate nude, masturbating on the couch. He looked nonchalantly at me and continued with his task. Shocked, I packed my bags and left without saying anything further to him. I was confused and disappointed as I had thought of him as a friend. I decided that he was probably so fed up with my struggle to stay in school and to stay an A student that he probably just staged that act, knowing that it would drive me away. I am pleased I persevered and have my advanced schooling under my belt though I wish I had taken another course of action as I never felt that I was challenged academically. I understand why one of the most gifted editor students, Jason, that I met at The New School did not stay to graduate. He helped me edit the film I did about my son's schizophrenia when I was virtually penniless. I owe Jason Bennett his editor's fee and much, much gratitude.

MAMA CALLS TO SAY GOODBYE

Mama was not surprised that I had gone back to school but she was disappointed that I did not spend more energy looking for a rich husband. Like so many people, she just could not fathom how I could have walked out on my "rich life" and why I did not have an urgent need to get it back. I always seemed unable to make her understand that I had not married a rich man but had, instead, helped an ordinary man become a doctor through much personal angst and sacrifice. My Mama liked my husband and in her eyes, there was little that I should not be willing to forgive him for, because he was nevertheless, "a doctor." Mama liked the presents I had been able to send her over the years as she shared my penchant for beautiful things but surely she had noticed that the presents were no longer exceptional or plentiful. Mama was living in the woods in upstate Pennsylvania in a house that my eldest brother had built and one that she had not allowed my brother to get rid of when he and his wife divorced. Mama kept up the mortgage payments and maintained the upkeep of the house and she adored living in my brother's house. She prided herself in her growing fascination with the animals that lived on her terrain, bears, deer, chipmunks, woodchucks, and even an occasional mountain lion. One day when she had been plucking weeds in the snow she had become overheated and had discarded her fur coat at the base of a tree trunk. When she finished her weeding, she casually leaned down to pick up her coat and the coat stood up. It was a mountain lion who had been resting by her side the entire time she had been weeding. Mama said the lion accompanied her all the way back to her house, and try as she might, she had not been able to control her knees that were shaking violently. Mama loved all

175

the animals but that mountain lion was more friendly than she had bargained for.

Mama would call and let me listen to the thumping sounds of three baby bears rolling down her rooftop that they used as a sliding board. No one could convince Mama that she entertained a dangerous passion for helping the wildlife. Encouraged by my youngest brother, Tony, Mama prospered in her wooded home and with her devotion to the care of her personal dogs (who were spoiled and more than a little mad as Mama would not get rid of a dog, even if it bit her) – Mama was content with her life. My children had raised three Irish Setters but one had turned mean and I had found a farm for him to spend his remaining days. Mama would have none of that kind of talk and she made me give her the dog, build a fence and dog run for it and pay $500 a month for its upkeep. I did this for many years and finally refused to have a mean dog cause me such financial strain and I bowed out of taking care of the dog. Mama continued, though, and was proud of the bite marks she had survived from this bad tempered animal. She loved and fed her wild animal friends and once when she sweetly started talking as I was reading on her Veranda, I thought, "How odd for Mama to be talking to me in such a strange fashion (as her manner was never sugar coated but curt and to the point) and I looked behind me to see who on earth she could be talking to and I stared right into the face of a big black bear. I never left a door open in Mama's house after that or ever again thought of reading on her generous and pleasant veranda. Mama was happy living out her life with her many four legged friends and with the help of my brother Tony and a grandson, Senor, who always had her by the hand, Mama was able to transform her wooded retreat into a fetching sanctuary for many glorious plants and flowers.

But Mama was beginning to grow old, and she resented it. I learned that though she had told me and my siblings that she was eighty-one - in fact, Mama was actually ninety-two. She had kept her age a secret from us her entire life. Mama wanted her adult children to come and visit, but as she had throughout our childhood, she wanted everyone in bed by eight o'clock. It was just not easy to visit Mama or to take part in her care when she needed "in home nursing."

I left school for a number of weeks to relieve Tony, who abandoned his Master's studies for the semester to assist our mother. Mama was so difficult (nothing I could do was right) and one day after I made a special meal that Mama wanted but took straight to the toilet to throw down the drain without even tasting a morsel, I knew I did not have the resolve it took to withstand Mama's erratic moods and I left in tears and returned to Brazil. As Mama became more fragile, tempers flared in the family as to what medical course to follow in Mama's care despite the fact that Mama had made it clear that she wanted every means possible to be put in force to save her life. When Mama ended up in the hospital after much debating about whether she should go or not, Mama began failing and it seemed that indeed she was in for the fight of her life.

It was a troubling time as I was thousands miles away and my youngest brother Tony and my eldest brother had opposing views as how to proceed with her urgent care. Finally, Mama had decided that the eldest brother should be in charge and from what I understood, Tony, my youngest brother, left the hospital, distraught that Mama had become so ill and that he was helpless to change the course of her treatment as all authority had been taken from him. I received a long distance call from my eldest brother that Mama wanted to talk to me. I could hear nothing but garbled sounds as my Mama tried in vain to communicate with me. She was simply too ill to make anything other than garbled, choking sounds. When the call ended after a few awful minutes, I realized that I had heard the last living sounds our mother would ever make. I was in the midst of school term papers and I just could not accept that Mama could be dead. I sat numb and lifeless for hours on end, my mind a barren wasteland of memories. I couldn't breathe. I couldn't think. And, I couldn't imagine not having Mama's presence in my life. I tried to weave a tribute to her in several of my assignments, but I was at a loss to make sense of what I just could not accept, that our Mama, a force of iron will and fierce determination had lost her fight to live.

I thought of who, of her remaining living children, Booker, Reggie, Tony Beverly, might give her eulogy, and then I tried writing one but kept recalling that Mama had told me personally that she did not want me, especially me, to write one for her. I paused to think things through more carefully. I had always written and given the eulogies in our family and I needed to understand why Mama had definitely not wanted me writing a eulogy for her. Finally, after failing miserably at coming up with anything that could help me to understand what our Mama would want in terms of our goodbyes to her, I realized that Mama just did not want to ever be thought of as dead and the best tribute I could ever make to Mama would be to continue to work with the homeless children I helped in Rio. Mama was proud and touched by the work I did with these tragic and beautiful children and I knew that the best way to remember Mama was to remember these forgotten youth.

LEANDRO, A HOMELESS BOY THAT CAN NEVER BE FORGOTTEN

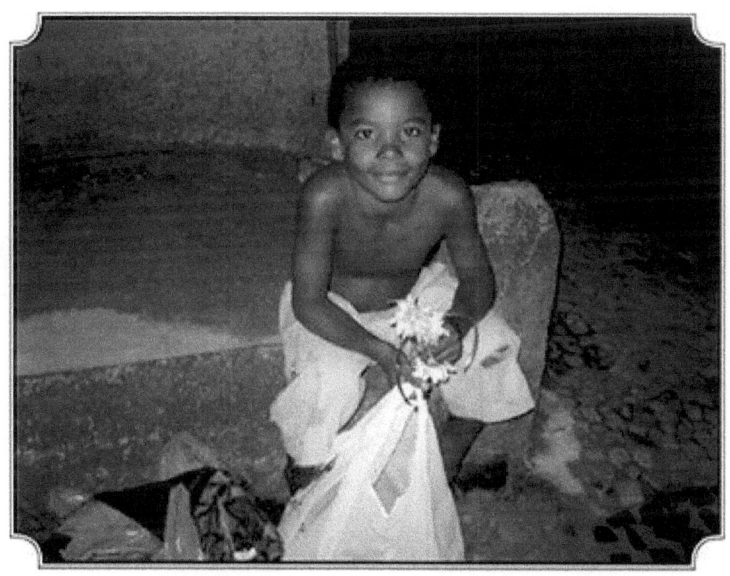

All is well on first glance on this balmy night in Rio de Janeiro. A young, shirtless, barefoot boy sits on a stoop at midnight holding blossoms in his hand. The boy's eyes are gentle and seem misted with drops of rain that are just beginning to fall. "Boa Noite, Criança," I say. The boy bids me "Boa Noite," asking if I am going home. Yes, I say, and so should you. The boy's face radiates with sweetness and mystery. He tells me that he got separated from his mother who sells water on the beach and he does not know his address and they do not have a telephone.

A neighbor joins us and pulls me aside to tell me that – though the boy looks sweet – these homeless children in Brazil are dangerous, that they grow up around drugs in Favelas and learn to kill in order to survive. The neighbor says Leandro must be given a bath so that people will treat him more kindly and he takes him to his home, within sight of the stoop. Leandro emerges wearing the neighbor's daughter's pink slippers, and a festive tee shirt. The neighbor gives Leandro a sheet to wrap around himself while sleeping on the street. When the neighbor leaves I take Leandro to my home. The doorman smiles at Leandro wearing his pink slippers and we proceed into the elevator where Leandro pushes all of the buttons. On the ride up I think of Joel Rufino dos Santos words in the book, "Lost Arguments" written about the many human rights abuses committed against the Brazilian Homeless Children. Santos says: "The poor appear to be disqualified as human beings and because they have nothing, they threaten those who do."

Leandro's eyes light up upon entering the apartment. He loves a chair that the Harlem kids living in homeless shelters in New York City had hand crafted out of wood. The chair is an animal with its head cast toward heaven – howling to the forces beyond that control the Universe. Several sandwiches later, Leandro is asleep in the guest room. Morning finds Leandro rested and in no hurry to find his mother as he shyly and, very carefully, arranges my collection of candles and sits again in the Meditation Chair.

Maxine Green in her Lectures on Aesthetic Education says, "There is no human being, who cannot be energized and enlarged when provided opportunities to sing, to say, inscribe, to render, to show – to bring through his or her devising, something new into the world." We finally head out to the beach and walk its miles long length. Leandro stops along the way and insists upon posing in front of an amazing hand crafted Sand Castle.

Edie with Leandro who ran away from his Favela home to be near green grass, flowers, and the ocean. Edie allowed him to spend the night after she found him crying on the stoop near her beachfront home.

Leandro and I stop off while we are on the Copacabana Beach to visit my friend Sophia who lives right near the Copacabana boardwalk. Sophia is recovering from a broken leg she got as a result of being hit by a motorcycle while crossing the street from the beach area to her apartment. Leandro is thrilled to visit Sophia's home and he gently touches her leg, telling her "I will come and visit you every day, and soon we will walk on the beach together."

Leandro tells me that where he lives the air is thick with smoke from dope, thick with crime and thick with ugliness of every kind. There are shattered bottles, spent bullets, blood, filthy trash, and drunken bodies on the black dirt field that serves as the play yard for Leandro and his friends.

Leandro wants to sun himself in a real beach chair of his own and he asks a woman putting bleach streaks in her hair to dab his hair a bit. We all laugh as Leandro's hair is patted lightly with the cream and for a good hour Leandro is in dreamland as he naps and becomes a blond.

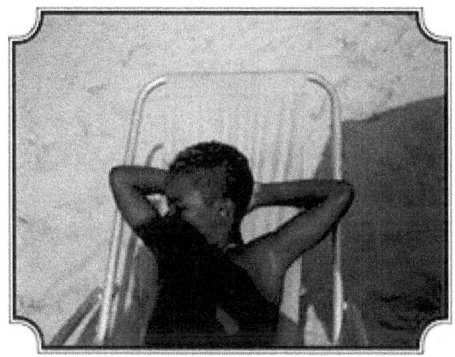

I awake Leandro and tell him that we cannot put off finding his mother any longer. Leandro grasps my hand tightly and we walk to the Copacabana Police Station. The Captain tells us that where Leandro lives is too dangerous to go into at night. Leandro will be taken to a shelter and they will try to find his mother in the morning. Leandro bolts from the station and the police give chase. A weeping Leandro is brought back to the station and he suddenly remembers his phone number. At two o'clock in the morning a very beautiful woman comes into the station carrying a baby that is eight months old and a three-year old toddler is clinging to her skirt. She has ridden on several buses for two hours to fetch Leandro. Leandro's mother smothers Leandro with kisses and tells us that he often runs away to places that have blue water, green grass, trees and flowers. She says that in Benfica, Leandro's jaw is always clenched, ready for some disaster. In the abandoned warehouse where they live, the disasters often come with a Capital D. Leandro's father is a fisherman and must rely on his wife's work of selling water on the beach to feed the family when he simply has no fish to bring home. As dawn is breaking Leandro's family boards one of those speeding buses that stop so suddenly your teeth are jarred. Waving goodbye, I pray that I will see this little miracle boy again who imagines a different kind of life for himself and who has the courage to go and find it. Leandro makes his little escapes when his spirit can no longer handle the degradation around him, but he loves his family and always returns home. Twice he knocks at my door in the beachfront community of

Leme where I am helping other homeless children and I let him stay a night or two. Then, strangely, I hear from Leandro no more.

Four years have now passed by and I am teaching Art in another Rio neighborhood, Vila Isabel. I go daily to a modest home where an amazing force of life, Marcia, looks after a group of children with a small staff. Marcia is a woman who herself was a homeless child on the mean streets of Rio for fifteen straight years. She cooks and administers heaps of love to the two dozen troubled and orphan boys who are given the opportunity to live in the orphanage for six or eight months while they attend school. A tall, barefoot boy walks into my class and sits next to me, shoulder to shoulder for a full three hours. My heart flutters and I ask myself, "Who is this arresting boy who is as drawn to me, as I am to him?"

Days after he quietly slips out of the Art class I realize the boy is Leandro, the brave little boy who risks all to have a moment of peacefulness and natural beauty in his life. I have a pair of sneakers and a warm sweater waiting for him and pray that "My miracle boy" will show up again.

Leandro has traveled such a long, long time, with little time to rest – and somehow he knows he will be all right to weather the storms that come his way. I wrote Lyrics to a beautiful song my son composed – "With candles that flicker brightly and return with a much stronger flame," Leandro simply never gives up. It is so dangerous what Leandro does – escaping for a few days to rebuild his spirit. The homeless children in Brazil are hunted down at night and killed by the police, killed before they even have a chance to grow up because someone does not want them begging from the tourists.

No one will say who the someone is or who the "someone's" are. It is an old problem Brazilians say, an old problem that needs much studying and political reform. But in the meantime, while the Human Rights Agencies fight their hard battle to keep as many children as possible alive, many thousands of street children are murdered each year by police and private death squads so that Brazil may maintain its sunny, picture perfect image. Every time Leandro runs away to find solace, he is in danger of finding much pain – in danger, truly, of losing his life. Leandro's life is a life of long roads and many stops, with little time to rest, because always, his new journeys begin. My heart is always with Leandro and my presents are still waiting. I shall be so happy to buy Leandro a larger pair of sneakers, and for now I am grateful that I had the strength and will to bring my own dear son a new pair of sneakers and I hope that, like Leandro, my son will thrive and conquer the many battles he must face on a daily basis. It is hard to accept that my son who was always gifted, quirky, and talented could be stricken with an illness that would conquer him. It is so hard to believe that he graduated from college with four distinguished degrees, had the gumption to approach a famous singer and get his favorite compositions recorded and published in ninety countries by the much revered jazz great Abbey Lincoln, teach himself to speak and write French and Portuguese fluently, write a term paper that celebrated Scholar and Professor Daniel Ellsberg singled out for praise, hold his own on the tennis courts with professionals, do so many amazing things and then boom– this gifted person is stopped short by voices in his head that control his every thought.

My son's grandfather, his Dad's father, was equally a gifted soul who was a virtuoso Front Page Journalist and violin and piano player. He had played in Harlem with the big bands before the depression. Every year for a month at a time he would stop working, put his weekly Poet of the Piano Radio Show on hold, and remain at home with the excuse that he was ill with heart disease. Once, during the first year of my marriage, I went to pay my regards – the house was filled with flowers, baskets of fruit, and hundreds of cards from his fellow journalists at the town's biggest newspaper – and I found him ranting and raving at the top of the staircase, completely nude. It didn't take me long to figure out that heart disease was the excuse, but a yearly alcoholic binge was the reason. Fortunately for this gifted and celebrated man, no one ever found out. Ironically, he died on his job of a heart attack at the age of fifty- seven.

My son's grandfather was a kind man, who wanted with all of his heart to have a grandson before he died. I met him before I met my husband at an Ohio State football game. I was seated in the bleachers and he came over and told me how beautiful he thought I was. I was startled for sure, but what was more unsettling was the fact that he said he was sure that his son would definitely want to marry me if he saw me. He promised to bring his son to the next game and I put the incident out of my head, believing that the man had probably had too much to drink. True to his word, this man showed up with a gorgeous son at the next game. The son, as it turned out, was in his Captain's Air Force Uniform, a striking sky blue suit, and he caught the eye of every woman within a hundred yards of where I sat. The son was more handsome than a movie star and though I was embarrassed, I was certainly impressed.

The son, it turned out, was a pilot. He was finishing up his Master Studies at the University before applying to medical school. We began meeting in the Classical Music Library where I pretended to study. One day, my mysterious pilot asked why I never turned the pages of the book I was engrossed in and the game was over.

I told him the truth, that I was a freshman and unaccustomed to studying with another. I was hardly a match for someone who was almost ten years older than me, and honestly I was nervous because I knew that I was not allowed in the Graduate Study Building. At first my pilot said he certainly wasn't a cradle robber and seemed truly shocked to find out that I was only seventeen. He had thought I was in Graduate School like himself and he assured me that our meetings must cease. Having grown up around many sophisticated people at my Daddy's nightclubs and used to interfacing with all age groups I simply shrugged and said I understood, but I was crushed. I assumed that I would not see my pilot friend anymore and was most surprised when he showed up at my Aunt's house to say that he would like to meet my parents. I told him that was good because I was going to return to my hometown to study as I simply did not have the funds to continue at Ohio State. My Mama was thrilled to meet my handsome pilot friend and tried her best to laugh off the fact that her dog, Hoppy, had literally deposited a slab of meat at the doorway of my brother's bedroom that she was showing off and Hoppy refused to let us exit. The pilot was certainly not scared of a growling, common dog and he proceeded to pass by. There was a horrific growl and bared teeth and I witnessed my courageous pilot jump frantically upon my brother's desk. No one exited that room for hours, not until Hoppy had eaten every morsel of his meat.

The wedding of this handsome pilot who hoped to be a doctor to the young woman who wanted to be a ballerina seemed to be a foregone conclusion by the pilot's father who had literally picked me out for his son at a football game. I thought I was in love though I knew little about love, never having been allowed to date. I was distressed by the fact that I heard that my soon to be husband had been engaged to a popular night club singer who was sure to become famous. I heard that the engagement was broken off, or rather that the father had demanded that the engagement be broken off. I didn't know what to believe – only that I was caught up in a whirlwind of activity and that my wedding dress was picked out and finally bought. My family had little money as my father had lost his nightclub and restaurant in town and was still paying off his tax bill to the government for his posh country nightclub that had been closed down.

My three sisters were to be my bridesmaids and I heard rumors that I was pregnant. I was definitely not pregnant and, in fact, I by this time held down a secretarial job with the Democratic National Committee of Ohio. I was happy to get out of my living situation for I feared of being molested by a disgustingly creepy second cousin whom I was sharing a home with, along with his wife and child. He would barge into my room with flimsy excuses and one day, after I had returned home from the funeral services for my mother's brother, he broke into my room with a male friend of his. I barely had time to race to the window where I threatened to jump out. I was soon to be married and I feared that I would not make it to my wedding day with my dignity intact. I felt most unsafe.

The wedding day approached. All parties seemed happy but I was terribly confused. I knew that I had strong feelings for my husband to be, but honestly I still felt like a teen that was just beginning to sort out who I was. I knew nothing about what it takes to make a marriage successful.

I confided my fears to my Mama just as the wedding party was assembling at the entrance of the Church. I had a terrible foreboding that I was making a mistake. My Mama slapped me hard across my face and told me that I had cost her untold misery of trying to fashion together a beautiful wedding with little money and that if I never did another thing in my life, I would hold my head high and proceed to the altar. "You are going to walk down that aisle and wed that beautiful young man," she said. And so, I walked and gave my vows and tried to look happy. My husband paid little attention to me and seemed not to notice how distressed I was when a drunken uncle spilled red wine all over my velvet wedding gown after giving me a crude and unnecessary toast. If that were the only thing that had gone wrong, the wedding would have been a success. But the truth is, my groom did not come home our honeymoon night. He spent the evening partying with old girlfriends and I lay on my bed sobbing real tears of despair. I, though, convinced myself that I came from sturdy stock, as my Aunt Ruby's husband Reid always told me and I vowed to make my marriage work.

As we settled into our daily routine, my husband would pat my forehead at night and wish me a good night's sleep. Romance was not an ingredient in our daily ritual and I think we were both surprised when I learned that I was pregnant. Our son was born just nine months and seven days after our marriage and I was delighted that all of the skeptics had to put aside the rumors that I was pregnant before I wed.

There wasn't a week that went by when my husband's father did not insist that we bring our baby to his house so he could hold him in his arms at the piano, gently cradling him in his right arm while playing beautiful jazz and classical renditions with his left hand while he chanted over and over, "*you are going to be a composer one day.*" Our son had little chance of escaping his destiny of becoming a composer as his grand-father, by sheer force of will, chanted into the baby's ear, hour after hour, "*you are going to be a composer, a famous composer.*" And though, our son could have hardly understood a word of his grandfather's mutterings as he played, RB was told over and over that his Dad, Dick, had sat on the knees of Jelly Roll Morton while he played his unforgettable tunes. My husband's father only lived for a year and a half after our son was born but he instilled a love of music into our son RB that borders on being a compulsive obsession. Clearly, the hours that his grandfather played to him while rocking him in his arms at the piano helped cement RB's fatal attraction to music.

RB begged to have guitar lessons when he was only four years old. He listened to the radio non-stop and was always informing his Dad when some noteworthy musician was playing, Charlie Parker, or Bud Powell, Bill Evans or Andre Segovia. It was impossible not to be aware of how much our son loved music – all forms of music- piano, guitar, flute, and saxophone. There was just not any instrument that he was not fascinated with. When he was six, we bought him an inexpensive guitar and his little fingers moved over the strings with an amazing familiarity. We found a noted guitar teacher, Anna Kotsarenko, who had studied with Segovia and RB had his first guitar recital at the tender age of seven. By the time he was ten RB was so proficient that Anna convinced Segovia that RB must study with him. Kotsarenko and Segovia decided that RB should be shipped off to Spain to study with Segovia, the master himself. Well, I couldn't imagine my son living in Spain away from his family so we encouraged his interest in the piano. It became apparent that the piano would be our son's main interest in life, though RB often berated himself for not taking it seriously until he was fourteen years old.

It has been a lot of years since my son was fourteen, and as I sit weaving the events of his life through the fabric of my life I realize that I hold in my hands important clues as to why things unfolded the way that they did in my son's life and in my daughter's life. I tried to make the cloth strong so the threads of the tapestry would bear up under the weight of wear and tear. But now I must face the task of scrutinizing that fabric that I helped to create and I am forced to realize that much restoration is needed. Honestly, it is heart rendering to admit that perhaps the decisions that I made in directing my children's choices were not perhaps the wisest decisions that a parent should make. I was away in New York a lot with my film work and my children were too often under the super-vision of their father who was busy with his medical practice so he delegated a great deal of responsibility to housekeepers who I have come to realize couldn't have cared less what the children were thinking.

I spent plentiful time with the kids on the weekends and we did many interesting things together but I realize now there is a reason why mothers are encouraged to stay home with their children as long as they can. I loved the Arts and encouraged both my daughter and son in like pursuits. I ask myself over and over if I should have stressed so ardently: *Follow your heart. Make sure that when you wake up, you are doing something you love.* In this stressful world in which we all must try to flourish, wouldn't it have been wiser to have encouraged my children to: *Find something you are good at that will carry you through, and find spare time to do what you love.*

I guess I am wondering and worrying about how much I am responsible for the way my children's lives turned out. My son, though, never loved anything but music. And though my daughter earned six figures as a very successful pop music promoter, she sacrificed her personal life, never having the time to pursue a stable relation-ship with a life partner.

I do so want to restore my family and I have no sure way to do it, but I know I must move forward and find a way to renew my faith, to re-ignite my spirit. Earlier I told you that I wrote my own handwritten book when I was fourteen and in it I revealed just about all of the family secrets that I could tell, secrets that would later cause my mother both chagrin and amusement. Though the book has long ago been put away I am still surprised that its rediscovery made such an impression upon me. The wallop of those heart felt feelings that I had dredged up so long ago make me want to reflect on those life lessons I learned that I can still profit from.

I wrote in that black leather handwritten book as a fourteen-year old, It's not really so bad anymore because now when there is trouble, I have more courage and I am better prepared to face it. I know that many people have a lot more to worry about than I do.

That was certainly true then and it remains true today. Things are so much more difficult for so many people than they are for me. But life, for me, remains troublesome. I shall celebrate the good in my life and find ways to be of help to others. I must move on.

Perhaps we all do the best that we can, but I don't think so. Maybe we don't do well because the choices we have are not so apparent. We have to be more diligent in seeking out better choices. In this increasing dangerous and nuclear world of 2016, we should look at the millions of once secure, even privileged people, who have had to flee their homelands because of deadly warfare, because of *Isis* threats. What is there to learn from such experiences? Oftentimes, the only choice is to be brave and to move on. I have learned that every voice, every life matters. I realize just how fragile life is. I felt so encouraged recently when one of the young girls I helped in Harlem in my Creative Find classes that I taught for so many years called to tell me that she missed me and loved me. I have not seen Kayon for a good ten years but she looked me up on the internet and wanted me to know that she had never forgotten me. What a wonderful, graceful thing for her to do, to reach out to extend to me the Grace of knowing that I mattered to her, that my presence and teachings had given meaning to her life. I was humbled and grateful that she, Kayon, had persisted in her quest to find me. This young person, now twenty-six, soothed my tired spirit.

I hope always to strive to live with Grace, but I do admit to having some regrets about certain events in my life that ended without Grace. I was always fortunate to have many friends, really interesting people that I delighted in talking to and visiting with on occasions, occasions that I considered very special even if they were just everyday events. Jan, my best friend when I was fourteen, and a lifelong friend for another half century after that, got Alzheimer's the last few years of her life. She was a beautiful blond German girl who had taken a lot of flak in our prejudiced high school because she hung out with me, a Black girl. Jan called me toward the end of her life and asked me what the number eight looked like. I said, *"Jan, you can't be serious,"* and I laughed like a fool, admonishing her to ignore what the doctors had told her about her having Alzheimer's and assuring her that she knew what the number eight looked like. There was an uncomfortably long pause and finally I said, *"why eight is nothing but two circles piled on top of one another."*

"Oh yes, Jan said hesitantly, that's right, now I remember."

Though Jan tried to laugh it off, her once joyous laughter sounded flat, wounded actually. I knew in my heart that she would never trust me with another confession of something she had forgotten because of her Alzheimer's. How I regret that I did not treat Jan's forgetfulness with more Grace. She deserved that, she had earned that. Jan had always been there for me. I regret that I was not there for her when she needed me most.

A ONCE BELOVED DAUGHTER RETURNS HOME TO BE WITH HER MOTHER

The planet is in chaos with wild fires and droughts out West. Isis threats and bombings are an almost daily threat in all parts of the world. Innocent lives are claimed in Paris, France; North Africa; Belgium; the Middle East; and San Bernardino, California. Hillary Clinton, Donald Trump & Bernie Sanders fight a brutal battle to win the Presidential Bid for The White House.

"Mommy, can I come home to live with you?" I could not believe that I was actually hearing those words in the realness of the day I was engaged in. I was just surveying the damage from the huge water break underneath my apartment building that was allowing water to seep into the walls behind my pretty white couch, seep along the baseboards of my hall closet and stream water from top to bottom of the actual walls, walls and hangers that housed my antique evening dresses from London and Paris, treasures from my long ago Fashion Days. The water seeped deep into my manuscript boxes that housed my writings and my films, my music discs and my cameras. My treasured original miniature paintings by Lou Jefferson, Stephen Ettinger, and Mildred Simonson were not spared either.

"I will call you back this evening, I said. I have got to put a finger into the dike like that little Boy who saved Holland in Dr. Boli's Fables. I've got to go now or your mother's once sturdy stone home will float away."

But I wasn't able to save anything. As fast as I moved things from one spot to another, a fresh stream of water would appear, and the walls started to buckle, and then the mold started to appear. Before long, everything in my apartment was beginning to be covered with mold, even the mattresses and dust ruffles around the bed frames

Just like my life that had slowly begun to erode away - from my lying husband to my tragically ill son - to my "can't be bothered daughter," to my sweet but "you can't see him grandson," I was still experiencing the ruination of a family that had intended to be a dynasty but had turned into notorious characters that had whispered snippets of gossip forever buzzing around them.

"Oh no," I thought, "life can't go on, not the way it is. If I could save Wendy's brother RB, then I can save Wendy, too"

I couldn't imagine what would propel my petulant, arrogant, irresponsible but successful daughter to ever want to come home – and home to a mother she had ostracized for seventeen years. What had propelled this Marketing Director for one of the biggest and most successful Entertainments Firms on the planet, Al Hayman Productions, Inc., to jump ship, and come home? Wouldn't Wendy miss the world of putting on concerts and huge events for Mariah Carey, LL Cool J, Beyonce, Eddie Murphy, and a long list of stars too numerous to mention.

When I got my daughter on the phone she declared that she was lost without her son (for now she had given up reporting that Cary did not want to see me) and she was admitting that he had run away, run away some four years ago. I thought of the only email I had ever gotten from Cary written just recently - in April - done completely in Chinese characters, a unique way of not letting his Mom know anything about him but letting me know he was alive. I had to put it on Google Translation to see what it said. It was "and is" a haunting email because Cary wrote in Chinese - his birthdate, 3/20/92. That's all the email said but it included a gaunt photo (that mysteriously disappeared after I opened the link on the internet.) Yes, disappeared, a gaunt, barely recognizable photo of the young man, my grandson, that I still love with all my heart and soul though I have not seen him for well over a dozen years. The photo was a three quarter head shot where the eyes staring out were vacant and had a far-away presence to them but those eyes were sadly those of Cary, my grandson. I told my daughter about the photo and she did not seem disturbed that I had heard from Cary in this mysterious way. Perhaps Cary just wanted me to glimpse him for an instant, the instant that he remembered that once he had a Grammies he loved and that Grammies had loved him back. I got rid of my roommate, temporarily shut down my Bed and Breakfast Business, and prayed to all of the Angels in the Universe to come close and stay by my side. I said to my daughter, "Yes, come. We will work out our problems. We will find your son, go to Brazil and see your brother, RB, and we will be a real family again."

My daughter had always been an exuberant and witty person with extreme highs and dark lows. She was a talented, original artist, and she could make you weak with laughter when she imitated people with heavy accents, whether British, French, Irish or Australian. And her Brooklyn accent was hilarious. Everyone laughed with her. She loved to socialize and wear unusual clothing but abused my beautiful model's designer samples with cigarette burns that would appear on items I hadn't loaned out, and I had never smoked a cigarette in my life. Antiques I loved would end up sold, and new cars that were gifts from her Dad would be found later in a cornfield, traded for a beat up camera. I just did not want to go through those same inane types of things again. Had my wild child grown up or was I in for another serious dose of grief? I finally got my nerves together, and my daughter arrived.

I am overcome with emotion to be able to hold my beautiful girl in my arms again. But I do not trust my daughter's motives for returning to my shaky, humble home. She does not seem to want to tell me anything. And what I want to know more than anything is what happened to my beloved Grandson's life. Why did he go missing? Why does she not hear from her son? I desperately want answers. As I said earlier, In April, I got this cryptic Email from my grandson in Chinese. And I know I am repeating what I already said, but I took the Chinese characters and put them into Google and translated them into English. It was the birthdate Chinese characters of my beloved little boy's birthday - March 20, 1992. I believe Cary wanted to come and see me. No address, no phone number, no message. But I believe that Cary wanted to see his Grammies. On April 30, 2016, I sent an E Ticket to the return address on the Email I had received from my Grandson in Chinese. I sent an E Ticket for a flight from San Francisco to Atlanta. But, my grandson was a "No Show" on the intended flight. My heart is broken. I have heard no more from him. And though my daughter now says she truly regrets ever having written many dishonest emails to me saying that her son was with her and that he wished no contact with me, I am not enlightened one bit about what really happened to Cary, my grandson, or for that matter to my daughter Wendy, during the surely tragic years that led up to my grandson running away from his Mom. "Luck is a star, money is a plaything, and time is the storyteller," as Carl Sandburg, the great poet, said. I just have to wait until facts are revealed over time.

Cary Alexander Lynch. I was not permitted to see this beloved child, my grandson, during this period of his life and I wonder if he was thinking of me at this moment. He had said to me once, "Grammies, when you see the number 7, think of me Cal Boy, because when I think of the number 7, I always think of your golden smile."

LEAVING THE DARKNESS BEHIND

There are milestones in each person's life where something happens that forever changes the way things are or will be again. For me, my sorrow and regret have been so frequent that I have reached that point where I know I must chart a new course for myself. I believe I am ready to take on that arduous task. In writing this small book I know I have gained important insight about the darkness I have traveled through. I am changed, and I hope it is for the better. I am glad that the many stories I have held onto are finally on the loose and perhaps giving pause for thought to others who, like me, struggle to make sense of what was and to find ways to move on to what can be. There is a dream deep within me. You might say it is the melody of the unsung child. Though I am no longer that little child, I am that big child in an adult body who is finally ready to sing. Harriet Tubman said it so much better than I can - "Every great dream begins with a dreamer. Always remember that you have within you the strength, patience, and passion to reach for the stars to change the world."

I just heard that Muhammad Ali had died. It struck me down for a moment. I felt weak, and really sick inside. I remembered that Ali was someone who had changed the world. Though he bragged relentlessly about himself and his greatness, in his heart he knew he had the potential to do great things and he pushed himself to accomplish innumerable worthwhile goals. He made the world aware that Black was indeed beautiful and he refused to go fight in Vietnam when Blacks were being mistreated in the United States of America. And, Ali did not believe in killing people in whatever country they were in.

But the bigger picture of Ali's life revealed that Muhammad Ali was a ***man who tried to unite all mankind through faith and love,*** words that he first said himself just before he lost his life. As we know, Ali did in fact change the world. I met him in the seventies through my husband Dr. Lynch. The three of us had breakfast together one morning at the Marriott Hotel, one of my husband's favorite breakfast spots in Philadelphia. Ali ordered eight pieces of toast with his meal and he folded each piece of toast over once lengthwise, and then he folded it over once more and put it in his mouth. I remember wondering if only fighters did that. Dr. Lynch and Ali boasted of how big their swimming pools were going to be and other fairly humorous topics. Ali said little to me, and I wondered if that was because women in the Muslim world were expected to remain in the background in the accompaniment of their spouses and if that was expected of me, too. I know that we never built a swimming pool. Ali had a life of frequent global travel, so if swimming was one of his passions I am certain he got to do plenty of it. Ali enjoyed being a showman, entertaining people every place that he went. Dr. Lynch had a similar personality. He was always reaching out to community members in an upbeat, joyful, flippant kind of way. Muhammad Ali made people laugh and I am certain that news of his death made thousands of people worldwide, cry.

I shall return to the world I love best, the Arts, where I hope to bring some magic. In my son's paper about the Creation of the Atom Bomb he talks about the way society is structured, and the critical need for it to be rethought. So much of our reasoning centers around getting more money so we can have more things, do more things. Critical decisions are morally compromised because of the desire for money. There is so much greed in today's world, so much excess, so much trashy nonsense. We all know when we are thinking or doing something wrong but we proceed with our flawed ways. The world can do better. We are not doing much real good with all of our toys and our advanced technology, for half of the world's population is not living a decent life. Too much of the world lives in poverty and degradation. We each can reach out to community members to target corporations that bring detriment rather than substance to our lives and urge them to work with us, to change their ways, and to implement procedures whereby they help our communities rather than harm them.

I have met and lunched with fabulous people that have done great things for so many others, and they are exciting to be around. Tahir Amin and Priti Radhakrishnan, New York Law Degree award winning attorneys who are husband and wife and founders of I-MAK, have made big wins against pharmaceutical companies seeking to scam poor patients on life saving drugs, resulting in access of critical medications to millions of people worldwide who are suffering from malaria, tuberculosis, and HIV. I met them in a Portuguese class and the professor later told me that he did not appreciate my mispronounced phrases or the irrelevant questions I sometimes asked. Tahir and Priti and I had lunch later and laughed about my attempts to bring humor to a regimented learning process. Priti and Tahir are easy going and warm hearted individuals and committed professionals who have made a huge difference in the world.

Every day people who have no lofty ideals can do amazing things as well by voting for what they stand for with their dollars. They can just stop buying the junk that is offered every minute of every day. Meeting with community members and pressing big corporations to give back, rather than take away from the communities they so often pretend to serve is a must priority for everyone concerned with the present state of affairs in the world.

Our world is dying because of the obscene greed and the nuclear technology that has seeped into every corner of our lives. I believe that *Nuclear Power has to be rethought.* The encouraging news is that reasonable affordable equipment and processes could be put into place to protect critical components in the electric power grid and its nuclear reactors all over the world thereby averting the worst case scenario, as happened at both Chernobyl and Fukushima. *Mankind has proven not to be responsible with Nuclear Use and we must all strive to safely eliminate its use for the sake of not only our lives now but to safeguard the lives of our grandchildren and future generations.*

Our spirits need rejuvenation. We need to stop the noise everywhere. We are all starving for silence and real thinking time. Just look into a baby's eyes and see the real wonder there, the purity of the soul. Deep down, we were all once like that. Each of us can strive to find that beauty within us. We can carry it into our work, and into our communities, and into the world as we travel around it. We can unite in friendship, and hope, and yes, love.

We truly can mentor one another and have meaningful, creative lives. I have my thinking cap on now and in the time I have remaining, I want to have a new beginning. Not only do I want a genuine relationship with my grandson that I pray I will be reunited with, but I want to have peaceful, enjoyable interactions with good people in every country on this planet. I want us all to live in peace and work for peace. I don't plan to spend much time sleeping.

"This is a photo that I took of my precious grandson, Cary Alexander Lynch, who I always called Cal Boy. Not only is this my favorite picture of him but I want to give it to Cal Boy personally when he comes home. He has been gone much too long. His Grammies misses him so very much."

This is the paper written by my son RB

THE CREATION OF THE ATOMIC BOMB

Outstanding work. You have put very expressive powers of intellect and judgment to work on a profoundly important subject. I hope and expect you will continue to use your talents as well.

This deserves publication. I don't know a better paper on the subject. It's very gratifying to have a paper of this quality come out of this session. Good luck. Dan

RB LYNCH, Sophomore Undergraduate
45 Seminar Professor Dan Ellsberg

On August 6th, 1945, a U.S. airplane dropped a single bomb on the Japanese city of Hiroshima of some 300,000 people. The subsequent explosion, equal to about 15 kilo-tons of TNT, killed 70,000 Japanese civilians and began an ominous era for all humanity – the era of nuclear weapons.

Since Hiroshima, and the subsequent bombing of Nagasaki, there has been much controversy over both the moral justness of this first use of nuclear weapons, and the circumstances surrounding the momentous decision to use them. Yet, much of the argument over the actual decision to drop the bomb overlooks one important fact: since the very beginning of the Manhattan project in 1941, policy makers had always assumed they were building a weapon to be used. For those policy makers who were in a position of power to decide the matter, the decision to drop the bomb was never an issue: they had always assumed it would be used, and had justified early on any objections to the use of the bomb on moral grounds.

The issue, then, is not why the bomb was dropped, but how did policy makers come to assume the bomb would be used and why they never questioned this assumption. This shift in emphasis brings up a new set of pertinent questions to the foreground which hitherto have often been ignored in the debate: Why did policy makers continue development of the bomb even though it became obvious that the bomb would not be needed to end the war? Did the assumption that the bomb would be used emerge from the decision to build the bomb? If so, is the event which provided the impetus for this decision morally justifiable enough to excuse the creation of such a monstrosity? Must we conclude, as Dwight McDonald, that atomic bombs are the natural products of the kind of society we have created, and the mentality of the modern nation state?

Indeed, this latter question is of central importance, because it points to the very structure of society, the assumptions governing the modern state, and the leaders who wield its power as the primary and inevitable cause of genocidal weapons, which someday could bring the end to us all.

The debate over the Hiroshima episode remains valuable in that the most accurate interpretations of it expose the underlying diplomatic power conscious motives of policy makers and demonstrates to what extreme leaders of the modern state are willing to go to prove a point. Whether one agrees with the latter statement or not though is not important for the purposes of this discussion. What no one can deny, however, is that the bomb was dropped for the express purpose of killing a large number of defenseless civilians, and that, in order to be dropped, it first had to be built, and later developed and refined for some reason closely related to that purpose. The real beginning of disaster for the 100,000 people who were killed by the bomb and for the rest of us who must now live under the specter of nuclear annihilation occurred well before Hiroshima. It can be traced back to the development of conventional warfare during World War II, the assumptions giving rise to the phenomenon of total war, the insensitivity of our leaders to the massive destruction of cities and death of large numbers of civilians, the depersonalization of modern warfare, and the very structure of society which enables leaders to create such monstrosities as the atomic bomb without the knowledge of the people they represent; all of these factors presaged the impending disaster.

In these respects, the Hiroshima episode follows logically from the decision to build the bomb, and the legacy of World War II. The combination of these elements enabled the creation of the ultimate weapon and the ultimate disasters for humanity.

The German Threat and the Decision to Build the Bomb

In 1939, Professor Otto Hahn, a German radiochemist, published a new discovery in Berlin scientific journals. His revolutionary theory proposed that a reaction initiated by neutrons might generate more neutrons, and in the process might release large quantities of energy. Later in that same year, Lise Meitner described for the first time the process of nuclear fission. Physicists all over the world realized the ominous consequences of this great new discovery: atom energy could be used to build a super bomb. It was however those German scientists who were sympathetic to Hitler's new Reich who first began looking into the military uses of atomic energy. They reluctantly convinced the German War Office that further research was needed in this area. Although atomic energy research was given low priority, "by the time war broke out, Germany alone – of all the world powers – had a military office exclusively devoted to the study of the military applications of atomic energy." But the rise of fascism and anti- Semitism had driven away many important scientists from Germany, of which almost all of whom were Jewish. Alarmed by the possible dangers of German nuclear research, these Jewish emigres were largely responsible for alerting the British and American governments to the German nuclear threat.

"Of the five scientists who provided the necessary stimulus for the American project in 1939, Szilard, Wigner, Teller, Weisskopf, and Fermi, all were foreign born, and all except Fermi were Jews."

Even before the German program was officially sanctioned, Fermi went to the state department in Washington to warn officials of the German nuclear threat. Fermi then discussed the issue with Szilard, Wigner and an economist who had access to the President. Together, the group drafted a letter warning the President of the dangers of German nuclear research and had it signed by Albert Einstein. In response, the President established an Advisory Committee on Uranium in November, but no large funds were provided for the following six months, and soon interest began to wane. In the spring of 1940, Albert Einstein addressed a second letter to the President urgently warning him of the growing dangers in Germany. At about the same time, the former director of the Kaiser-Wilhelm Institute, Dr. Debye, reached America. It was Debye that provided the real scare regarding the nuclear program in Germany, although his disclosures were greatly exaggerated by the American Press.

In general, however, British and American scientists were unaccustomed to applying science to military needs. Although the Uranium Committee now could request large sums of money, it refused to do so. Its concern for secrecy and cautious research precluded any urgent effort on the problem. Consequently, the bomb project in America moved slowly. The project took a fateful turn in September of 1041 when, the only American experimental physicist who had experience in dealing with problems on a large scale became convinced of the German nuclear threat and the need for the quick development of the bomb. Ernest Lawrence pursued the project with the utmost urgency: "the outcome of the war," he said, "depended on whether Germany or America got the bomb first."

Convinced that the U.S. was better industrially capable of building the bomb in a shorter period of time, and that the German threat was real according to intelligence reports, the British government offered to divulge the extent of its nuclear research to the Americans. If the bomb was to be built, the U.S. would have to do it. Lawrence, the nation's must forceful and influential physicist, took the helm of the bomb project as the importance of the Uranium Committee diminished. Lawrence enlisted the help of theoretical physicist Robert Oppenheimer who was only too glad to be of service to his country. Both Lawrence and Oppenheimer became increasingly convinced of their duty to the United States to develop the bomb and protect the free world from the Nazi threat.

Once the bomb was needed in their eyes all that mattered was success. For all of the scientists involved early on in the project, both British and American, there was indeed no moral dilemma associated with their efforts. The British scientists were deeply committed to the war effort and the defeat of Germany. The American scientists had become convinced the British war effort was in the national interest of the U.S. and therefore, in their interest as well. Most importantly, the refugees from Europe, who were the most committed of all to the struggle against Germany, provided compelling reasons for ignoring moral considerations early in the bomb project. They brought home the reality of the Nazi war effort. In addition, intelligence reports inside Germany seemed to indicate a real possibility that Germany could make the bomb.

Oppenheimer later became head of the Los Alamos Nuclear Research Laboratory in New Mexico. The choice of Oppenheimer as director in retrospect seems to have been a momentous one. Few men had his ease for handling people, or his intellectual capacity for organizing seemingly unrelated parts in a coherent manner. Oppenheimer diffused a sort of pain-dispelling glamour. It helped them (the physicists) forget that their calculations were less for the advancement of physics than for the mass incarnation of human flesh.

Under the leadership of Oppenheimer, the project proceeded smoothly, in spite of the demands made upon the physicists by their military overseers. However, there was one incident of note which temporarily halted the project. Upon explosion, it was calculated that the bomb causes an atmospheric ignition of the entire planet. For the first time, the scientists questioned the purpose of their work, for each realized it would be better to live under Nazi rule than bring an end to humanity. After the mistake had been found in the initial calculations, Oppenheimer computed a three in a million chance of such an occurrence, which all agreed was a low enough risk to be worth taking. It is interesting to note that the incident caused none of the scientists to reevaluate the moral justness of their endeavors, once the possibility of atmospheric ignition had been ruled out.

Oppenheimer and his fellow physicists worked with increasing diligence. Their orders were to convert the uranium materials into a workable, deliverable bomb as soon as possible. Toward the end of 1944, the German nuclear threat had been dispelled by intelligence reports but Oppenheimer was not affected. He had begun to regard the bomb as a goal in itself. The explosion of this bomb would in his opinion, "shake mankind free from parochialism and war." To keep his faith in the project he would refer to the following poem: Batter my heart, three personed God...o'erthrow me and bend your force to break, blow, burn, and me new.

That the development of the bomb had become a goal in itself is best illustrated by the long expected German surrender, as it had little effect on the Mesa. "Everyone worked harder." Whether scientific curiosity had become the primary motivation or the Oppenheimer desire for a "new force" to freedom is unclear. What is certain is that exterior events mattered less to the Mesa scientists; all that mattered now was the completion of the project. The bomb was to be tested in mid-July and everything was set into motion in preparation for that test.

In the meantime, the scientists at the Chicago laboratory had essentially completed their work, and now had the time to ponder the moral implications of the project. Controversy over the use of the bomb against Japan developed. Some of the scientists who had participated in the project mainly out of fear that the Germans were building the weapon were unwilling to sanction the use of the bomb against Japan now that Germany had surrendered. Moreover, these scientists could now clearly foresee the possibility of a nuclear arms race, if the U.S. decided to drop the bomb on Japan. Szilard led the first organized opposition against the use of the bomb. He tried to make his views known to FDR, and later to Truman but was unsuccessful. The Franck report, led by Chairman James Franck, was a later effort by Chicago's scientists in opposition to the use of the bomb. The report cited many negative repercussions the dropping of the bomb would have on world affairs. But the opposition which developed in the scientific community to the potential use of the bomb, had little impact on policymakers. Truman and his advisors virtually ignored the Franck Committee Report, and for that matter, all objections in the scientific community.

"In the last analysis, what the scientists said would worry the politicians less than what they refused to do, and none showed readiness to boycott a policy they opposed." Either because they felt the issue was not important enough to risk their careers, or because they felt obliged to submit themselves to the authority of the politicians who had more experience on these matters. Scientists were not willing to take their opposition to the logical extreme. For the politicians, it did not matter what the scientists thought, as long as they were willing to obey orders and continue the project.

Initial Conceptions: The Bomb and Policymakers:

Until now, we have focused mainly on the role that the scientific community played in the decision to build the bomb and its subsequent development. Though, as we have shown, they provided the necessary stimulus for getting the project underway, once the decision to build the bomb had been made, their role was not determining. Policy makers would now take it upon themselves to formulate what they considered the "appropriate" use of the bomb; scientists were from this point on relegated to the status of mere laborers, who had no other purpose than to complete their work as quickly as possible.

We have already stated that policymakers had always assumed that the bomb would be used well before 1945; the Hiroshima episode in this sense followed logically from that assumption. The question then is when was this assumption first conceived? Did it originate as early as the very beginning of the atomic project? Were there other considerations relating to the bomb at the time? There is a great deal of evidence which bears directly on this matter. It seems that the key policymakers in Britain and the United States were not naïve to the potential wartime and diplomatic advantages this revolutionary weapon afforded them. As early as 1941, even before the project was fully organized, Stimson, Roosevelt, and other members of the 'top policy group' conceived of the development of the atomic bomb as an essential part of the total war effort." In fact, it would be misleading to describe their initial conceptions of the weapon as "not naïve" and "not unaware." This characterization would be too lenient; they immediately grasped the political significance of the weapon and its potential wartime value. Though the suggestion to build the bomb was initially made by scientists who feared that Germany might develop the weapon first, those with political responsibility for prosecuting the war accepted the circumstances of the bomb's creation as sufficient justification for its use against any enemy.

Policymakers not only accepted the circumstances of the bomb's creation as a justification for the creation of the bomb itself (for that alone was a fateful decision) but also as a justification for its use against any enemy!

This "moral leap" by policymakers is of crucial importance. They conceived the bomb as essentially in the same moral category as any other military weapon, and therefore, appropriate in the field of battle. Policymakers made an immediate and deliberate connection between the bomb's creation and the bomb as a usable military weapon. They perceived no moral distinction whatsoever between the bomb's status as a deterrent to the German threat and the bomb's status as a usable military option. The importance of this conceptual leap with regard to the bomb cannot be emphasized enough, for here lies the origins of the assumption that the bomb would be used. That policymakers could regard the bomb so quickly as a usable military weapon calls into question the very moral justness of the decision to build the bomb and the circumstances which surrounded that decision.

We know now that the German nuclear program was well advanced in the early years of the war, at least more advanced than any other major power. We may wonder though in retrospect, how credible did the German nuclear threat have to be in order for policymakers to justify the decision to build the bomb, and by their logical extension, its status as a usable military weapon. We many speculate that once policymakers became convinced the creation of the bomb was a feasible project requiring only the will and the commitment to do so, almost any circumstance would have justified its creation from their point of view. The German threat not only did not have to be credible, it could be non-existent. But this is problematical, however, because the German threat was credible early in the war, or at least could be justified as such. There is, however, a great deal of evidence which points to the military and diplomatic value policymakers assigned to the bomb early on in the project.

'If such an explosive were made,' Vannevar Bush, director of the Office of Scientific Research and Development, told Roosevelt in July 1941, 'it would be thousands of times more powerful than existing explosives, and its use might be determining.' Roosevelt assumed nothing less. Even before the atomic energy project was fully organized he assigned it the highest priority. He wanted the program 'pushed not only in regard to development, but also with due regard to time. This is very much of the essence' he told Bush in March 1942. 'We both felt painfully the dangers of doing nothing,' Churchill recalled.

What exactly were the dangers of doing nothing remains unclear. We may speculate that these "dangers" had less to do with the German threat than policymakers would later publically admit. Secretary of War, Henry L. Stimson, offers us more clues to the real concerns of policymakers with respect to the bomb early in the war. "In 1941 and 1942," he said, "they (the Germans) were believed to be ahead of us, and it was vital that they should not be the first to bring atomic weapons into the field of battle." On the surface, this comment just seems to reiterate that the allies were fearful of the German threat. But why was it "vital that the Germans should not be the first to bring atomic weapons into the field of battle"? Is this to say that it was vital for the U.S. to do it first? Undoubtedly yes. Furthermore, if the bomb was created just for the deterrent effect why was it necessary for the U.S. to actually use them first? Simson's comment implies more important underlying motivations. By the end of the war, these motivations crystallize into concerns for purely diplomatic matters.

Viewing the bomb as a potential instrument of diplomacy, they were not moved to formulate a concrete plan for carrying out this exchange before the bomb was used. The bomb had 'this unique peculiarity' Stimson noted…'success is 99% assured, yet only by the first actual war trial of the weapon can the actual certainty be fixed.'

Even though Nazi Germany had surrendered, the use of the bomb had become axiomatic to the point where all diplomatic discussion hinged on the military use of the bomb. Needless to say, that the bomb would be used, if dictated by military necessity, was a forgone conclusion. Most importantly, dropping the bomb on large number of civilians posed no moral problems for policymakers who had long ago become insensitive to the mass destruction of cities and the mass- killing of civilians.

Allied forces had already initiated such massive attacks on the German cities of Hamburg and Dresden. In a single raid on Tokyo, 125,000 civilians were killed. Any moral problem associated with the massive destruction of civilians was compromised in these raids well before Hiroshima. The proposed use of the bomb was considered on the same moral plane as the conventional raids, "only its technique was novel – nothing more."

Policymakers in 1941 could foresee the possible use of the bomb as an integral part of total war even to the point where they claimed to have the right to use the bomb against any enemy. However, at this point in time the war had not yet become "total." If by some miracle, they had gotten the bomb in 1941, it is doubtful whether they would have used it right away against a city with no warning or no moral compunctions whatsoever as they did four years later. The phenomenon of total war and the ethic of city destruction as the surest way to win wars had not yet fully developed. "Something" happened in those years which erased the sole moral objection against the use of the bomb in the minds of the policymakers. In 1945, the bomb not only was considered a usable military weapon, it was considered acceptable for the express purpose of killing large numbers of non-combatants; this was the primary difference with the 1940-41 policy; this was the legacy of World War II. Why was the decision to use the bomb never an issue? More correctly put the question should read why was the decision to use the bomb for the sole purpose of killing civilians never an issue? The difference was that between 1942 and 1945, city bombing was an officially sanctioned target while in 1940-41 it was not. The central question is when did "civilian morale" become for our leaders a legitimate military target. This alone was the great barrier that prevented the doctrine of total war from exhibiting its full effects. Once passed, the atomic bomb would become the inevitable technological fulfillment of the new self-righteous ethic of mass destruction and mass murder. It was the British who began the revolutionary practice of city bombing as a matter of policy. The Americans followed suit as allied bombing campaigns developed into one cohesive and powerful destruction force. It was a fateful decision. War would never be the same again.

Evolution in Thinking: The Road to Total War

The transformation which British wartime policy underwent in the years 1940 to 1942 was to have tremendous important bearing upon the assumptions governing modern warfare. At the end of this transformation, not only was a new precedent of terror and destruction established, but the massive destruction of cities and civilians became accepted as a morally legitimate military procedure of modern warfare. F.M. Sallagar gives a detailed account of the evolution which was to have profound effects on all of humanity.

Early in 1940, Germany had already attacked Poland, and was now preparing to launch an attack against Western Europe. British leaders were as yet unsure of the kind of war Hitler wanted to fight but they publically claimed that they hoped the cities would be spared. Germany attacked relentlessly, however, and it appeared as if "no holds would be barred" when reports of 30,000 civilian deaths came in after the German attack on Rotterdam. The British felt they had to respond to what they "considered" an act of blatant terrorism; for the first time they officially sanctioned the bombing of industrial targets, and thereby the killing of some civilian workers as a by-product. Although not fully recognized at the time, this was a fateful decision because it started the spiraling escalation to total war. The British response to the Rotterdam attack, though, was not due solely to the motivation of revenge – a feeling that they had to retaliate in like and in kind to what they perceived as indiscriminate German bombing.

There were many other significant factors involved in the decision which were to play a greater determining role in the years to come. First of all, British leaders had put primary importance on strategic and military considerations from the very beginning of the war, well before Rotterdam. Although they did not give the military free reign to do what they wanted, British leaders were very susceptible to pressure from the military. The early bombing directives issued to the military were fairly limited in their scope and designation of targets; it was still understood that cities were to be largely avoided. But military commanders were adept at pointing out the operational limitations of these early directives. Characteristically, they preferred a more flexible and widely dispersed target system which would essentially enable the crews to choose the most vulnerable targets. In this way, the crews could take advantage of favorable weather conditions, vary their attacks, and create an increased "moral effect" by the alarm and disturbance created over a wider area.

Military commanders realized that Bomber Command was better suited for area bombing, and hence a waste, in their opinion, not to use it for its intended purpose. Secondly, British leaders were desperately trying to convince the United States to join the war effort against Germany. They felt that the only way to elicit American support was to prove their worth to the U.S. in some way. Lastly, policymakers decided very early on, that the "full power of the British armed forces" would have to be implemented in the case Britain was confronted with decisive military defeat. They long expected an attempted knock-out blow by the German Luftwaffe to be ordered by Hitler. An air attack of this sort would more than sufficiently satisfy this third condition.

Little did British leaders know that their three concerns would soon stand the test of action. First the fall of France in six short weeks, and then the German Terror attack on London in September, 1941 were the two events that triggered a major change in the already evolving British war policy. The three primary concerns which had always been integral elements in the British policy framework now took on added significance. They were put to the test by the German War machine.

As the bomber raids on London grew in intensity there was an increasing cry for retaliation from the masses. British leaders, Churchill most of all, felt they had to respond - which is to say, they felt they had to retaliate to the German attacks "appropriately." But the only possible means open to them at the time was inaccurate area bombing which was best suited for cities and not precision military targets. Thus if they were to strike back at all it would have to be by bombing cities and killing large numbers of civilians.

Clearly, it was at this point, that British leaders most keenly felt the pressures to act decisively. They surmised that the U.S. would be watching their actions closely. If they failed to fight back now, then the U.S. might not think it worthwhile to join the war effort against Germany. At the same time, they were feeling the pressure of the demands from the military for more flexibility in target choices. Military commanders were correct in asserting that Bomber Command was having very little success in hitting precision military targets. The German war machine seemed to be little affected by the British efforts. Only at night could Bomber Command safely bomb German military targets without suffering unacceptable losses, but night bombing (without radar, the military realized, was extremely inaccurate. Only over cities could night area bombing have any tangible effects at all - mostly "moral effects" upon the civilian population.

British leaders succumbed to the pressures, although reluctantly, as there were some who insisted that the targets be morally legitimate in some sense of the word. A new bombing directive was issued which pleased both those leaders who wanted unremitted revenge, and those with moral scruples disapproving outright city bombing. However, the directive was tantamount to outright city bombing, failing to take into account operational limitations. Based on the information supplied by the Bomber Crew pilots, British leaders believed that Bomber Command could hit precision military targets.

They also believed that civilian deaths were acceptable as long as they were not expressly intended. Sallagar summarizes:

In short, the rationale behind the bombing offensive was still based on the fiction that it was possible to single out specific objectives in a city at night, and that there was a difference between inflicting civilian casualties as a by-product and doing so as an end product of strategic bombing.

Espousing the above rational was the British leader's way of reconciling their moral scruples with a desire for retaliation; only those military commanders with enough experience to be skeptical of the accounts relayed by Bomber Crew pilots knew exactly how inaccurate night bombing was. They knew the real effects of the bombing offensive; their decision to use this strategy had been made solely upon operational considerations. It was simply easier to bomb cities than well defended military targets.

"Operational considerations, not moral sentiments or strategic objectives, governed what was actually done as the strategic bombing offensive developed."

The choice to officially approve area bombing was made in the spring of 1942 in spite of photographic evidence attesting to its inaccuracy. But it did not matter at that point, British leaders had now totally accepted the rational of military necessity – operational considerations were now first priority matters. Their decision to bomb civilian populations explicitly illustrated for the first time that they were consciously willing to subordinate moral consideration to operational considerations. But this fateful decision had no immediate effects on the battlefield.

A mere formality, it simply ratified a procedure which had already been adopted by the military a year and a half earlier because of operational limitations. The military essentially had already made the decision for the policymakers. How could this have been allowed to happen? How could the rational of military necessity have been allowed to prevail? Since the very beginning of the war policymakers had always assumed that war was strictly a military matter and this assumption was never questioned. Did any of them take the trouble early on to make sure that Bomber Command was as accurate as it was presumed to be? Were any of the pilots reports systematically verified for accuracy? No, policymakers would leave those matters up to the military. From the very beginning, military necessity imposed great restrictions upon moral considerations. Gradually as British leaders came to accept the military point of view, moral considerations became increasingly compromised – they were viewed more and more as irrelevant, or not applicable to the situation at hand." In this light, we can view British policy rather as a gradual and deliberate evolution in thinking not dependent on specific events of German atrocities. Moreover, this evolution would have occurred even without any specific acts of German terrorism, or what could be considered indiscriminate bombing raids upon defenseless civilians. The rational of military necessity – even if it called for the massive destruction of civilian populations – would prevail in the end. Here lies the beginning of disaster.

That policymakers were willing to call city bombing something other than it was should not mislead us. The reasons they gave for attacking cities such as to "break civilian morale, undermine the war will of the German High Command, disrupt the German transport system, deny the German war machine vital resources," should be seen for what they are – euphemisms for mass murder.

So far as civilian casualties were concerned it made little difference whether a city was attacked to eliminate it as a transport center or as part of the general area offensive.

Once the turning point was made in 1942, and civilian populations became the primary objective of the allied air offensive, the rational of military necessity was carried to its "logical" extreme. Now the doctrines of total military victory and unconditional surrender were to govern the end of the war to its final conclusions. Questions which were normally difficult to find rational answers for, now became academic. Why did allies continue to indiscriminately bomb cities during the last six months of the war when all operational limitations had been overcome, and they could choose freely bombing targets that guided their moral preference? Answer: Because this was the surest and most convincing path to victory. This method left no doubts as to the identity of the winner, and the identity of the loser.

Now that the allies were on the offensive, and capable of showing their might, they would crush the Germans morally and physically. The mass destruction of cities and civilians assured total victory and unconditional victory (not "surrender" because the allies wanted victory only on their own terms, surrender could come only after "victory.")

Policymakers came to believe that the massive destruction of large numbers of the enemy population was not only the surest way to victory but a necessary way. The total destruction of Dresden, Hamburg, Cologne, Tokyo, just to name a few, were necessary to fulfill the ethics of total victory, and unconditional surrender – necessary to display American might and to give victory the touch of finality. Allied leaders became insensitive to the mass destruction of cities and the mass murder of civilians because they felt it was not other than absolutely necessary for their purposes. It is no wonder then that the bomb fitted perfectly into their plans.

The Bomb: The Product of Society and the Modern State

So far we have examined in detail three major factors which contributed to 1) the decision to build the atomic bomb, 2) the assumption that the bomb would be used which arose out of that decision, and 3) the swift completion of the project before the end of W.W. II, in other words, the three factors which enabled its creation – the role of the scientific community, the initial conceptions of policymakers and the evolution in thinking which became the legacy of World War II. We see clearly how each factor contributed in the process so that the bomb was transformed from a mere theoretical probability into a colossal reality – the explanation seems complete. The transformation appears logical given all of the elements. But still we are left aghast; we are not satisfied by any superficial causal explanations. We look back at Hiroshima, and naively ask the same question repeatedly; How could it happen?

We are reminded of the causes – the legacy of W.W.II, the assumptions of policymakers, the German threat – but still, we feel unsatisfied. Our questions then become more penetrating: How could have scientists consciously devoted years of their lives for such an evil end? How could have our leaders thought in such power oriented terms? Why were moral considerations involving matters of life and death of innocent people given such little attention? Why did the scientists continue work on the bomb although they knew the German threat had been dispelled by intelligence reports? Why didn't they refuse to continue work on this instrument of mass murder when it became plainly obvious the bomb would not be needed to deter the Germans or end the war? In short, how could real human beings have done all of those things with a good conscious?

Dwight McDonald offers us the answer: We must see these actions in the context of modern industrialized society and the mentality of the modern nation state. From this point of view, we can more readily understand the actions of the individual as he works within societal and institutional structures. In this context, it is easy to see how atomic bombs became the natural product of the kind of society we have created. Here lies the origin of disaster; society as we understand it must be changed if we are to survive the creation of genocidal weapons.

The social organization of modern society depends on the concept of the Organic State, and our acceptance of its basic propositions.

The state becomes an extension of the identity of the individual. We are presumed to owe our very existence to the achievement of the state. For the state to operate efficiently, though, our leaders tell us that we must respect authority and the authoritarian structure of modern society. If the state is to act in our best interests, it must act as a "single entity." Only through unquestioning respect for authority and strict obedience, can the state preserve the social order required for Progress and Achievement. The philosophy of the Organic State pervades every aspect of our lives – the very structure of society in the modern world. It is our leaders who know it the best, but they have just adopted it for their own purposes from the principles governing modern society: For the Organic State is by no means only an ideological slogan devised by those in authority; it also corresponds to the real arrangement of things in the modern world. The principles on which our mass-industry economy is built – centralization of authority, division of labor (or specialization of function) rigid organization from the top down into which each worker fits at his appointed hierarchical level…

The logic of the social order requires an authoritarian structure, and it is precisely those men who make it to the top of that structure who are most adept at pointing out our need for it. The mechanics of the system in modern society not only enable the development of such monstrosities as the bomb, but also the rise of our leaders – those men who have competed most successfully according to the "rules" of the system, and thus in the process, have become most capable of dropping atomic bombs on other human beings "in the name of humanity."

The theory of the organic state is useful for our leaders not only for maintaining obedience in our own society, but also for regarding entire other nations as singular evil entities which must be destroyed. Not only are the leaders of the enemy nation responsible, but the entire population as well. If everyone is "responsible" for the enemy war effort, it then becomes permissible to drop atomic bombs to destroy their cities, and destroy their people. The other side is regarded as collectively responsible and therefore collectively evil. The fallacy of this line of reasoning comes directly from the theory's major assertion.

From the "Organic State" conception, it follows that no individual citizen or group of citizens may think or act otherwise than in accordance with the policies laid down by those in control of the state apparatus.

In other words, you can't have it both ways. You cannot both demand unquestioning obedience and hold people responsible for it. But there are those, namely our leaders, who would say "but didn't the German people elect Hitler? Didn't they fight for him? Are they not his accomplices?" This line of reasoning, however, ignores one very important fact: "Everyone acts politically according to the relationship of two factors - a) his own values and b) the risk of expressing those values."

There were undoubtedly German people in the Reich who opposed Hitler's murderous policies, but we must consider the risk they ran expressing that opposition. Only the hero will sacrifice his life for what he believes; unfortunately, most people are not heroes.

The theory of collective responsibility as proposed by leaders of the Nation State bears directly on allied bombing policy during World War II. We may view it as the theory behind the rationales of total military victory and unconditional surrender which governed allied policy during the end of the war. It not only prevented allied policymakers from reassessing their strategic bombing policy in terms of morality, but also from reassessing it in terms of economics, and usefulness.

…the totalitarian powers thought in military terms and realized that from the purely military point of view strategic bombing is not worthwhile. If this be true …then our murderous bombing policy must be set alongside Roosevelt's Unconditional Surrender policy which prolonged the war by many months since it offered no inducement to any group of Germans to try to overthrow Hitler and come to terms with the allies. The theory behind both policies was that the whole German people, without exception, must be punished as the guilty accomplices of Hitler.

The totalitarian powers realized during the war what the allies did not until well after the war – that strategic bombing was simply not economical. It also had very little real effect on the Nazi war machine, or the fighting ability of German soldiers who continued the battle while their cities were destroyed behind them. In many respects, strategic bombing actually encouraged resistance.

It is doubtful if it broke down morale; on the contrary, most evidence suggests the Germans reacted as the people of London did to the great Nazi air-raids: they hated the enemy all the more and felt all the more that their only hope lay in supporting their own leaders. Even if it did damage morale, there was little the Germans could have done about it.

But none of the shortcomings of strategic bombing are applicable to the atomic bomb. The atomic bomb was very economical; it could not encourage resistance because no one would survive the attack to be able to resist afterwards; it had very real effects because it could be used on both military targets and large cities. Policymakers did indeed realize the "revolutionary" nature of the new weapon they were building. We can assume that they were not naïve to these considerations before the end of the war.

The questions posed at the beginning of this section become easier to answer seen in the context McDonald presents. Scientists were playing their part in the social order of the Organic State when they first warned policymakers of the dangers of the bomb. They were doing their duty, serving their country in its time of need. Not that they didn't perceive the disastrous potential their work might bring, but they felt that their duty to their country – their part in the war effort against Nazi Germany – was more important than any abstract humanitarian considerations.

Initially, many scientists could and did hope that some principle would emerge which would prove that atomic bombs were inherently impossible. The hope faded gradually...Yet they all accepted the 'assignment' and produced The Bomb. Why? Because they thought of themselves as specialists, technicians, and not complete men.

The only time during the process in which they thought of themselves as "complete men" was when their efforts directly threatened suicide through the process of atmospheric ignition. When this possibility was all but dispelled mathematically, they became specialists once again. But when the German nuclear threat was no longer credible, why did they continue the project? How could they then justify their work on this mechanism of mass extermination? Because the bomb had already become a goal in itself. Scientists viewed the device as a decisive, albeit dangerous step of "Progress." Admittedly the bomb was a dangerous weapon, but at least "we" – the United States – the good guys would have it first. Our leaders would be careful not to use the weapon unnecessarily – only as a measure to end the war, and to save lives. With it, the United States would keep the peace, and end all conflict – the U.S. would save the world. The bomb would be the instrument to end all wars, once and for all. Such was their logic.

Yet even those scientists who could see beyond this naïve approach, who could see that it would start a nuclear arms race which could end in disaster for all of humanity, they were willing to subdue their personal moral values to the will of the leaders of the nation state. After all, though they disagreed, these scientists were willing to admit their leaders might be right. After all, politicians knew more about moral and political issues than they did. These thoughts in mind, the scientists judged that the issue was not worth fighting for, at least, not worth risking their careers for. In the end, they would obey; after all, "they were only specialists; they could not be responsible for societies' evils." Such was their logic. Their basic attitude on the subject is best summed up by Robert Oppenheimer's comment when he first heard of moral opposition to the intended purpose of the bomb. "The matter is being dealt with at a higher level."

We must also agree with McDonald when he says that "the bomb will change the strength of our leaders but not their aims." If there is anything this account has related concerning the motivations of policymakers since the initial conception of the bomb project, and the years during World War II, it is that their aims were relatively constant. They evolved in degree, but not in kind. Their aims were essentially the same throughout the war. What McDonald has shown us is that their aims will always remain the same if society remains as it is: an impersonal automatic authoritarian social order. Only certain kinds of men who are able to compete successfully according to the rules of the "political game" will become our leaders. In the process, these men will acquire certain values, certain ways of thinking which will enable them to do things that ordinary men cannot. They will be able to order the creation of atomic bombs in complete secrecy "for our own benefit" and for "the good of humanity." They will be able to order massive strategic bombing attacks against defenseless civilians, and of course, they will be able to bring the end of the human race "if necessary."

It is clear now that atomic bombs are indeed a natural product of the rigid mechanized society we have created, and the assumption of our leaders who wield its power. Because modern warfare is so depersonalized, normal, commonplace citizens are able to kill mass numbers of people without actually realizing what they are doing – which is to say, without seeing and feeling the actual horror they are creating. On an order from the President, a button is pushed and an entire population is destroyed, but we are barely aware of the consequences.

The atomic bomb was essentially conceived as a weapon of superiority, and instrument of power, American power, an instrument which would give the U.S. the final say in world affairs. Yes, the German threat was very compelling early in the war, but it was a meaningless circumstance for policymakers; its elimination would not entail the termination of the project – policymakers had never intended it to. Once policymakers became convinced the way to win wars and maintain superiority involved the massive destruction of cities and civilians, the atomic bomb became an inevitable reality only requiring the technological know-how to build it. If the bomb had not been developed during World War II it would have been developed later on. What this account has attempted to show is that the will to build the bomb was always there from the very beginning of the war, perhaps even before.

All the great decisions during the war – the decision to bomb cities as a matter of official policy, the decision to build the bomb, the decision to complete construction as quickly as possible, the decision to continue the project, and the decision to drop the bomb on Hiroshima – all of them, all were morally compromised before they were reached. For this we must blame the principles on which modern society, culture and civilization are organized, and our leaders who embody the perversity of their authoritarian logic.

In a repressive civilization, death itself becomes an instrument of repression. Whether death is feared as constant threat, or glorified as supreme sacrifice or accepted as fate, the education for consent to death introduces an element of surrender into life from the beginning - surrender and submission.

The atomic bomb is one such instrument of repression.

MEMORIES

Miniature painting that Lou Jefferson sent Edie of the
18 Carat Gold "Dandy Dan Brooch" Edie made for her.
Edie told her that she had traveled under a Lemony Sun
to bring the brooch to her in Litchfield, Connecticut.

Composer RB Lynch with Helô Pinheiro, "The Girl From Ipanema"

Edie's Daughter Wendy Lynch and grandson, Cary Alexander Lynch

Marcia and the orphan boys at the orphanage in Rio. I taught Marcia and all of the boys how to make decorative throw pillows for their beds. Marcia is a true Angel and she cooks and cares for dozens and dozens of homeless and orphaned children each and every day of her life. Marcia has the most giving spirit and she is truly a person that gives back to the world community year after year. That is quite an accomplishment considering that Marcia lived as a homeless child on the mean streets of Rio de Janeiro for fifteen years. Marcia is a force of nature, as beautiful a human being as there ever was.

Beverly Jean Brooks, Edie's Sister

Edie Lynch, as a young child. She gave up her dolls for ballet shoes, and then finally cameras and pen and paper.

Gail Diane Brooks Young, Edie's sister, as a child.

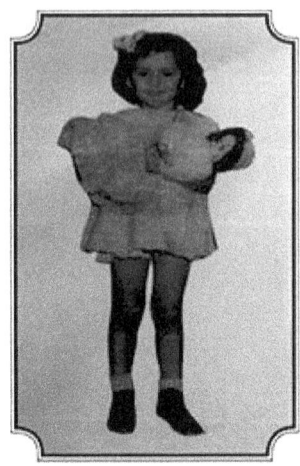

Edie Lynch and Gordon Parks at the Black Achievement in the Arts Exhibition In New York City sponsored by The Equitable Life Assurance Society. The photographs of Edie's from her book, With Glory I So Humbly Stand, were featured along with the well-known collection of Gordon Parks' photographs from his many year as a staff photographer for Life Magazine.

Edie's mother, Delores Cardel Conley Brooks, a great beauty who had eight children by The Joy Boy, Edie's daddy.

Jacqueline Sonja Brooks Stovall, Edie's beloved sister. Edie called her Annie Babe. She was Akron, Ohio's first Black Homecoming Queen, and was later killed in a tragic car accident at the age of 39, leaving a daughter Kim and a son, Stony.

This is my beloved grandfather who I called Poppa. He married the love of his life, my Granny Josie and together they had twelve children, eight of whom survived to adulthood. My daddy, The Joy Boy was the only one of Poppa's children to have children and The Joy Boy had eight, which he called his Eggheads.

RB Lynch with his Irish Setter, Dayan. Whether at school at Stanford in sunny California, or at the Berklee School of Music in Boston in a frigid winter, RB could always be seen walking or running his dog in the parks he loved.

Wendy Lynch drew her brother RB Lynch at the piano when she was eight years old.

Edie and daughter Wendy at Blue Mountain Camp in Pennsylvania. "Although I was often away with work related duties necessary to keep the family going, I never missed parents' visiting days at camp or a school play." Edie is happy that she shared so many important memories with her children in the USA and in many countries around the world where they traveled to learn about other cultures and customs that so enrich a young person's life.

Edie's wedding day. Her husband was a pilot in the Air Force when the two first married but with Edie's support, he was accepted into medical school and became a distinguished doctor. Later, he would lose his medical license and his family, but to his credit he did regain his medical license to practice medicine.

Dr. Lynch, enjoying his life and his medical practice

Andy The Ambler, one of Edie's gold Caricatures, who travels around searching for Edie's beloved Cary.

*New Yorkers are forever a satirized breed – The Yuppie, The Snob,
The Wheeler Dealer and The Bohemian – to name a few.
Now these cherished stereotypes are immortalized in wonderfully
playful 18k gold figurines known as Ediekins. Edie Lynch, creator of
this fun notion in jewelry, through her adventurous and well-traveled
life in the Arts (film production, publishing, theater, and fashion)
noticed a universal obsession with the New York lifestyle. Thus, she
invented Ediekins, a jewelry line sweetly depicting some of the most
famous Manhattan personas. Surely you've encountered "Madame Dee
la Dee" as she haughtily struts down Fifth Avenue, heading for a big
charity lunch at The Plaza. Or, maybe you've just concluded a business
meeting with "Bologna Maroni," a real mover and shaker, who has
promised to introduce you to 500 of his closest friends. Whether
Ediekins bear semblance to your co-worker, yourself, or a dimension of
yourself, they are sure to tickle your heart in a very intimate way. Pin
one on your sweetheart this Valentine's Day. Produced by Edie Lynch.*

Edie Lynch captured the stereotypes of New York City people when she created her playful sculpted collection of 18 Carat Gold and Diamond Brooches that she calls "Ediekins." First featured in Wempe Jewelers and in the Henri Bendel Designer Boutique on Fifth Avenue in New York City, Edie's whimsical finely carved jewelled people echo the varied and colorful lifestyles of New Yorkers.

MADAME DEE La DEE

Jacqueline (Annie Babe) who grew up to be the Homecoming Queen

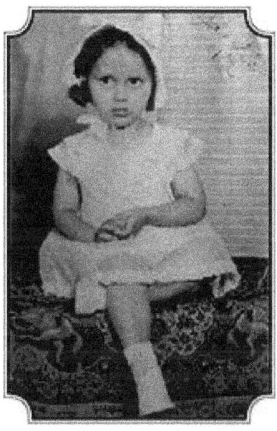

Delores Brooks (Mama) with all eight of her children.

Edie with the boys at Amar Orphanage in Rio de Janeiro. Edie frequently invites Marcia and the boys down to her chalet in the little village of Muriqui, Brazil for a day of art and fun at the natural springs swimming pool. Georgie, the little boy next to Edie, is a remarkably accomplished dancer. He also is a gifted drummer.

235

Cary Alexander Lynch with his dog, Taylor

Edie Lynch sculpted Willy Wand, a gold caricature of a person Edie thought her son RB would be like, an individual playing a vacuum cleaner on the street, so distracted was RB Lynch always with his beautiful music.

*Jazz great Abbey Lincoln teaching Cary
Alexander Lynch how to play the piano.*

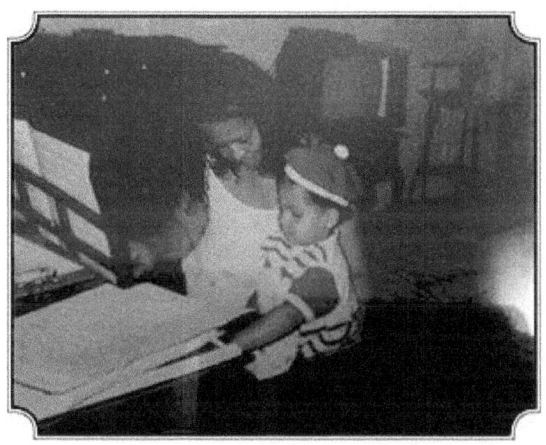

*Edie's Parents, The Joy Boy and Delores, with famed
composer and pianist, Duke Ellington.
Photo courtesy of the New Pittsburgh Courier.*

*Jazz Great Abbey Lincoln whimsically wearing Edie's hat
and scarf and holding Ediekins gold jewelry caricatures
in her hands while she playfully sings a tune.*

Edie walks the runway during the famed Ebony Fashion Fair Tour in 1965. The tour traveled by bus to every state in the USA excepting Alaska.

Edie (her mother called her Annette) wearing extravagant couturier Paris creations on the Ebony Fashion Fair runway.

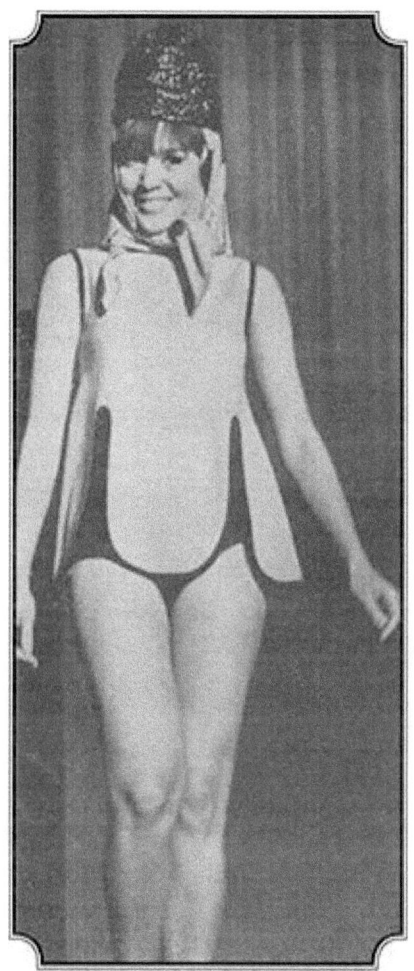

Aunt Sadie, with the white hair, The Joy Boy's sister, paid for Edie's ballet lessons during Edie's formative years and is responsible for Edie's enduring love of ballet. Here, Aunt Sadie and her husband Mercer Bratcher (who The Joy Boy's children called Uncle Boo) enjoy a moment with President and Mrs. Jimmy Carter. Uncle Boo was an important leader and activist in Akron, Ohio civic matters.

Dick Lynch, RB & Wendy Lynch's grandfather, was a pianist with the famous Harlem Renaissance bands before the Depression crippled America - and then he returned to Ohio to become a distinguished journalist.

Mr. Arpad Fekete, a dear friend of Edie's. Though he lost his entire family, excepting one sister Ecka, in the Holocaust during World War II, Mr. Fekete never lost his compassion and kindness for all of mankind. His irreverent humor hid the big secret that he actually possessed a very noble soul.

RB Lynch's Irish Setter "Dayan," a majestic dog that changed the course o of composer RB Lynch's life

Asia Tillery shows off her unique handmade meditation chair, completely crafted by Asia, herself. She went with the Creative Find children to the lumber store to have her design cut out of plywood. Then, the five pieces of wood were nailed together by Asia, and the chair was sanded, painted, and glazed by her before

Asia proudly took it home to meditate in it and pass it down to members of her family one day. For many generations, from one to another, the chair is destined to attest to a family member's value.

In Creative Find, all of the students - Sterling, Daryl, Julian, Shaquille, Timmy, Mwanza, Kayon, Shakia, Quentin, Candace, Tamilla, Daphyne, Chloe, Daphera, Christina, Ashina, Brittany, Lakeisha, Marquitta, and so many other dear children that attended the weekly classes and field trips – learned the importance of tapping into their own magic to sustain themselves during difficult times and to appreciate the healing aspects of practicing the Arts.

Sas belonged to a royal family in Poland. Though he used his own name (I named him Sas), few knew about his privileged background as he never talked about it. During World War II his grandfather's palatial home that Sas was visiting came under siege by armed forces and Sas was put under house arrest with other

242

family members for many years. Sas was very inventive and used that time to become proficient in a dozen languages and to play the piano, beautifully. He was an engineer in the Detroit area and built his own home and boat. He traveled around the world on big steamers where he would often prefer to be one of crew. He loved sailing, skiing, cooking, and building and fixing things, so many things. But what he loved most of all was having a good time. There were few countries on the globe that he did not know up close and personal. He told me that there was a town named after his family, but he told me so many things that never took root in my mind because he was always on the go, off to a new adventure. In so many ways he was the storybook gentleman charmer

Participants in Edie's Documentary Video, WELL MADE WOMAN, about women starting over minus husbands and money and rising to the top of their professions. The New York City screening was attended by an overflow crowd of savvy professionals who laughed and cried about the reminisces of the above women, Sarabeth Levine, Barbara Lapcek, Edie Lynch (Producer), Arden Shelton, and not shown, Cobi Narita Ash.

Edie's Highlights

EDIE LYNCH

Pretty girl Fan with composer RB lynch

Edie Lynch with her grandson Cary

Edie Lynch with her beloved grandson Cary (Cal Boy)

Louise E. Jefferson original painting

Abbey Lincoln original painting of herself with her mother

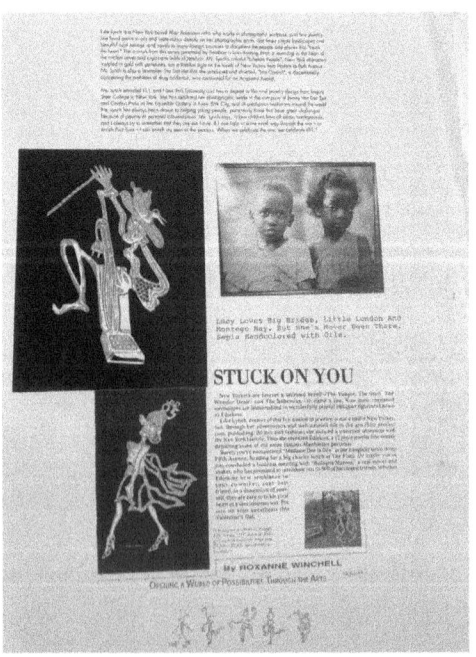

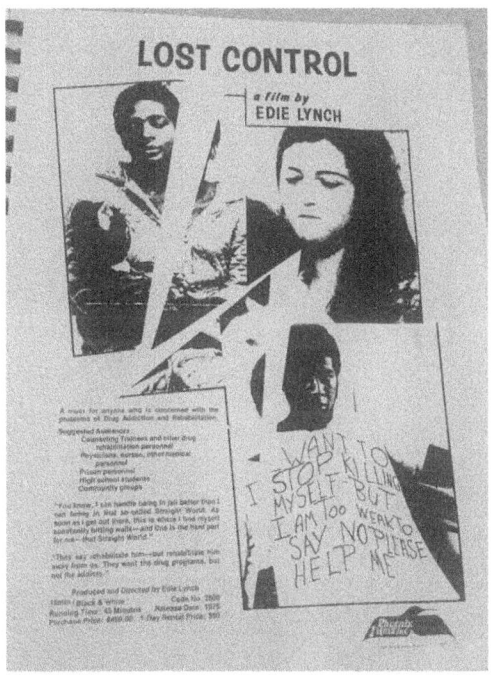

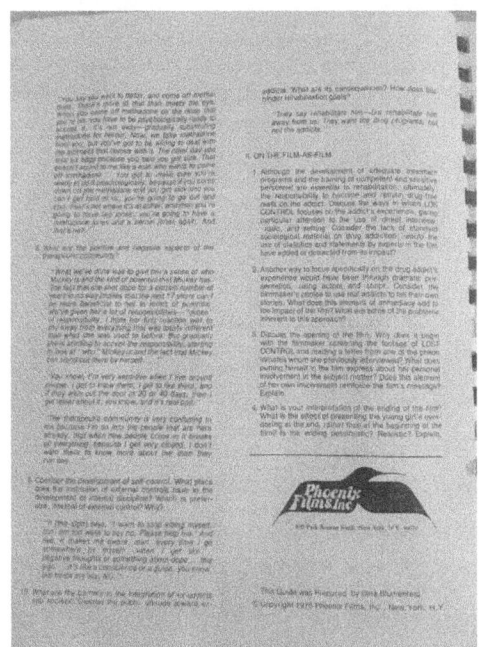

Viola Wright- a faithful friend who gave tireless help through Edie's long recovery from a broken leg and fractured telvis bones and hips injury

Gennady Osmerkin- Beloved friend and genius jeweler
who taught Edie her gold smithing skills

Itala - For giving immense help to Edie during challenging times

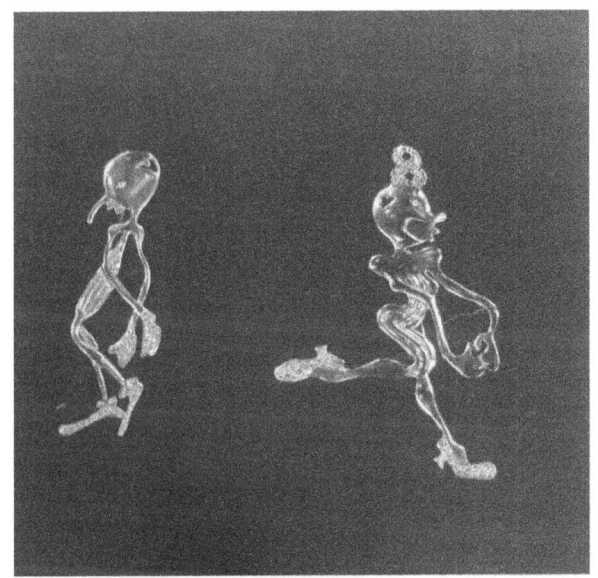

Edie's 18k gold jewelry- Dandy Dan and Sonia J

Edie's personal drawing from her diary

Edie's sterling silver and ruby brooch- Bow Buzzard

Sonia J, my precious doll that I travel with wherever I go. Seeing
Sonia's pure & innocent face keeps my memory alive of Jacqueline
my beloved sister who shares the same sweetness as Sonia J -
pictured with Mr. Squiggly, my daughter Wendy's Teddy Bear.

Thanks to Jeri Thomas for her generous support & help.

Luana and brother Luis my Brazillian art students

Dear friend Ingrid with her son Alex

MY UPDATE CONCERN AND HOPE FOR THE FUTURE

Today I am faced with the task of thinking back over the last decade of my life since my book The Joy Boy's Daughter was published in 2016 and I am seriously struggling to determine what meaning I have managed to grasp and hold close to my heart that is worthy enough to share with others who perhaps like me strive to move forward in this chaotic and dangerous world with strength, grace, and purpose. I miss my mama. I miss my daddy. And, I miss my Poppa and Granny who instilled in me the notion that I was somebody that would bring something special to others, to that bigger world I was so eager to be a part of. I was always consumed about the children that suffered in global crisis - in the wars that never seemed to end. Anne Frank's yearnings and tragic end was real to me. I wanted to bring beauty into my every living moment. When I put lilacs at the side of the dinner plates for my siblings to enjoy I so wanted to bring sweetness and joy. My brothers and sisters simply laughed at me and called me Miss Sidity. My mother said my nose would turn red when I was creating my many piles of artistic junk to beautify our crowded and turbulent household. Mama threatened to put me out on the back porch where the birds would come and peck off my nose, thinking it was a cherry. Mama's meanness & indifference about my artistic impulses and obsessions did not dim my enthusiasm, nor did I hold it against Mama. She had eight souls to look after and I knew Mama was just exhausted trying to find a place to store my clay sculptures, drawings, unfinished writings - and yes, hook rugs and ballet tutus. I dreamed hard on that worn wooden porch about my future and knew that one day I would find my way to meaningful work. My dreams would not die softly.

Peace and prosperity has not enveloped the world in 2025 in the first months of President Trump's administration despite his campaign promises that predicted a new era of wealth and security.

In fact The Donald, as Trump's late first wife Ivana called him, has set into motion strict global tariffs that have careened global markets into an almost panic that threatens to greatly alter any notion of a sane or peaceful economy for any individual person or worldwide institution. Immigration chaos and abuse persists and US citizens, along with foreign migrants, are being deported without hearings. It is a fragile and scary time worldwide for all societies. Awful school shootings in the US are a constant problem. We all must remain alert but we have to choose neighborly kindness as a means of coping in a world that seems alien to basic human decency. The Gaza War has reduced the Gaza Strip to sheer piles of giant rubble provoking worldwide protests. Deliberately set wildfires in the US have wiped out whole towns and catastrophic tornadoes have reaped havoc on communities struggling to cope. Floods and powerful tropical cyclones have killed thousands in foreign lands leaving people frightened and devastated. In the US thousands are being laid off from jobs and hundreds of Government Agencies are being downsized. Books are being banned from libraries and once revered statues of beloved Black leaders are being vandalized or torn down. Troubling changes and questionable appointed officials are altering our democracy.

To whom do we turn to in order to cope?

I always had my dear high school friend to whom I could pour out my feelings and reveal my longings and dreams. While in my freshman year at college though, we were not in touch. I was in another town, working two jobs, and determined to keep up with my studies. My beloved friend I later learned had fallen in love, gotten pregnant, and given up the child, a boy, for adoption. The events in my friend's life shocked me. She would reveal nothing more than the relationship with her Jewish boyfriend was doomed from the beginning because of her German heritage. The boyfriend's parents frowned on their son's love alliance and made it clear that their acceptance would never happen. They never learned about the pregnancy. When I urged my friend to find out the whereabouts of her son she said that chapter of her life was closed and she had no thoughts of reopening it. She told me that the doomed affair had another twist - that her fateful partner had died in a terrible accident and that his parents had come to her with regrets of their decision to disown her. They said perhaps they could have had a grandchild to ease their pain and help them to remember their son. My friend never told them they did in fact have a grandson. She reiterated that some doors must remain closed. Unbelievably the adopted son had been looking for his Mom for many years and reached out to me after finding me on an online site talking about my love of my high school friend after she had passed away from Alzheimer's. My high school friend had a gloriously gay laugh and I missed it dearly. Persistence allowed my friend's son to find his Mom and he was able to hold her hand before she passed on to her Eternal Life. He said she would not talk about her life or his adoption and that he longed to hear stories about his Mom's life. I told him many stories about what a caring friend she was and that I had urged her to find him, albeit without success.

Doors will forever open and close and each of us must grapple with the consequences of those formidable openings and closures. I am always grateful for the young poet Mattie Stepanek and Tina Turner the great singer and cultural icon for their amazing kindness and humility and wisdom that they left us with. I face this new decade with a deep hope for a rekindling of "Kindness" in every life - for each man and woman and child in the universe to have a decent and joyful life.

EDIE LYNCH

Edie Lynch, award winning documentary film director, model, jeweler and photographer tells the remarkable and tumultuous true story of her family, and her life, spanning six generations. From the plantation fields of Troy Alabama during the Civil War where her beloved grandmother Josie was born to Missy, a beautiful and ambitious slave/mistress, to the little town up North where her Daddy would establish a glittering star-studded Big Band Cosmopolitan Club, Edie's family would carve out a remarkable niche for themselves. Edie's Daddy, known as The Joy Boy was one of the country's leading Black club owners. Duke Ellington, Count Basie, Benny Goodman, Lena Horne and Nat King Cole packed the Joy Boy's club and rocked to the tunes of the times. Edie recounts these memories of her childhood and goes on to discover that the very things she found troubling in her beloved Daddy were the things she was drawn to in her husband, a doctor (who in his prime, possessing more than most men would ever need) would walk away from his family, lost in his own maze of corruption, deceit, gambling and drugs. To put her husband through medical school, and to care for their children, Edie worked as Pennsylvania's first Black model. Edie holds two Master

Degrees from The New School, in International Affairs and Media Studies. She was the founder of Creative Find, Inc., a 501 (c) 3 non-profit that helped at risk children in Harlem for many years. Edie also composes music and her Ediekins Music profits help the street children in Brazil who are murdered by the police at night, simply because they are poor and homeless. Edie has a published book of photography, With Glory I So Humbly Stand, online and envisions a world where one day, in her life time, there will be no Isis threats or warfare amongst competing nations. She plans to continue to stand shoulder to shoulder with others, human to human, to strive for Peace. You may also visit: www.ediekins.com

Endnotes

[1]   Think Big, Dr. Ben Carson

www.ingramcontent.com/pod-product-compliance
Lightning Source LLC
Chambersburg PA
CBHW051136120626
46547CB00012B/825